CHANGING TRENDS IN FASHION

PATTERNS OF THE
TWENTIETH CENTURY
1900~1970

Anne V. Tyrrell

B.T. BATSFORD LTD.   LONDON

Acknowledgments

I would like to express my thanks to the following for their guidance and assistance in the preparation of this book: The British Museum Newspaper Library, Colindale, London; Miss Diana Condell and staff of the Imperial War Museum, London; The Costume and Fashion Research Centre, Bath; The Gallery of English Costume, Platt Hall, Manchester; The Hayward Gallery, London; Mrs Dorothy Hedges; Miss Anita Horrocks and staff of the County Museum of Hereford and Worcester, Hartlebury; The Victoria & Albert Museum, London.

I should also like to thank International Thomson Publishing Ltd, who have permitted the adaptation of sketches and pattern details from *Tailor and Cutter* magazine, once the world's foremost authority on bespoke tailoring, and which is now incorporated into *Men's Wear*, the UK's only weekly publication for the men's clothing trade.

It is impossible to acknowledge all the personal contributions from which this book has benefited. I am greatly indebted to those who have given or lent photographs, fashion journals, and clothes.

In addition, I would like to add my warm thanks to my mother, who so carefully typed the manuscript; to my father for his diligence in checking the text and illustrations; and to my husband for his constant support and hard work in lettering and presentation of the patterns. This book owes a great deal to their interest, guidance and criticism. I acknowledge their valuable contribution with sincere thanks.

To David

ISBN 0 7134 5147 5

Typeset by Tek-Art Ltd, Kent
and printed in Great Britain by
R J Acford
Chichester, Sussex
for the publishers
B.T. Batsford Ltd
4 Fitzhardinge Street
London W1H 0AH

Contents

Introduction

The drawings on the following pages illustrate the main fashion trends for each year under study. They have been compiled from selected garments, patterns, photographs and fashion articles in contemporary newspapers and magazines.

The aim of the book is to provide the reader with a clear picture of the changing trends in fashion during the twentieth century, and an in-depth study of the evolution of pattern cutting. A major feature is a selection of scaled patterns, presented in chronological order, which will prove invaluable to the theatrical costume designer, cutter, student of fashion and actor alike. The patterns given are representative of each period, and care has been taken to follow pattern construction techniques appropriate to the time.

In any book of this type selection is necessary, and many interesting details have to be omitted. However, an extensive bibliography and sources of additional information are supplied which, it is hoped, may lead the reader to further research.

The costumes chosen are those which are felt to be most important or most characteristic of the time, and they have been categorized for the sake of clarity and convenience. Costumes are mostly those of the upper middle classes, but the very essence of fashion during the twentieth century is its more democratic nature and therefore, as during the fifties, teenage fashion is included. No fashion study can ignore the influence which youth begins to exert on major fashion trends.

Fashion is a strange phenomenon and one which reflects and adds to a total 'spirit of the time', and an attempt has been made to capture this spirit in the illustrations of each period. Each era begins with a detailed introduction which examines the contrasts, distinctions and similarities which exist in twentieth century fashions in relation to social, economic and technological changes within society.

The twentieth century witnesses the birth of 'fashion', as we are familiar with the term today. Technological developments in mass-production, introduction of new fibres, improved methods of transport and distribution, the expansion of the mass media with greater circulation of newspapers and magazines – providing as they did greater advertising opportunities – all interacted, as fashion became a universal, powerful, commercial interest. The availability of cheaper fabrics gave added momentum to the progress of ready-to-wear and inevitably to department and chain stores. It is the period of the 'retail revolution', in which road transport and rationalization of outlets made possible the concentration of distribution in a few large centres, and spread the concept of multiple chain stores selling the products of large, wholesale organizations. The rise of the boutique in the 1960s also served to increase the availability of fashion and to accelerate pace and change.

The role of the great fashion houses began to diminish and there was a move from the monopoly which Society and Paris had enjoyed. These still furnished an indispensable foundation, but were supplemented by further very varied elements to which the cinema, the stage, the world of sport and motoring, the role of women within society, youth and the arrival of the pop scene, all supplied contributions.

Interest centres mainly on female dress, which witnesses far more rapid and drastic changes than male fashion. During the twentieth century there have been no major changes in the style of the male lounge suit, and standardization set in, accelerated by mass-production. Prior to 1939 there were specific rules for correct attire on certain occasions, although we are aware of a change in outlook beginning in the inter-war period. Informality became the overriding influence dominating male dress, and major changes were seen only in lapel shapes, number of buttons and length and width of trousers. Feminine dress, likewise, followed a more casual trend; by contrasting the styles of the early 1900s with following fashions, it can be seen that the period before the First World War witnessed an interesting transitional stage from early constriction to ease and informality. The war years and feminist movements throughout the twentieth century have made important contributions to the cut of female dress.

Whatever steps mankind may take, fashion is always in search of new and revolutionary trends. We have seen that fashion reflects the predominant mood of contemporary life; we can only speculate what form the cut of our clothes will take in future years.

Information on Patterns

All patterns are ⅕ scale. A grid of 0.5 cm squares is provided to assist in enlarging to full-size: one 0.5 cm square = 2.5 cm. More detailed instructions on enlarging are given in the following section.

Some general points:

1. A seam allowance of 6 mm (¼ in.) is included in male patterns, except at fronts and collar edges, since this is the most usual form of presentation in men's tailoring.
2. Seam allowances are not included for women's garments.
3. *All* patterns are cut without hem allowances, vents, plackets and facings.
4. Grain lines and pattern instructions are included on all pattern pieces. All grain lines are parallel to the edge of the page unless otherwise marked.
5. All patterns are based on the following standard measurements:

Women:

Bust	88 cm	(34–35 in.)
Waist	66 cm	(26 in.)
Hips	93 cm	(36–37 in.)
Back waist length (nape to waist):	39.5 cm	(15½ in.)
Height	165–170 cm	(5 ft 5 in.– 5 ft 7 in.)

Men:

Chest	100 cm	(38–40 in.)
Waist	82 cm	(30–32 in.)
Inside leg	81 cm	(32 in.)
Neck (collar size):	40 cm	(15½–16 in.)
Height	170– 78 cm	(5 ft 7 in.– 5 ft 10 in.)

Any deviation from the above is clearly indicated in individual pattern notes.

Specific instructions on the making-up of garments are not included; additional information and hints on construction are provided in the accompanying text where relevant.

Listing of suitable fabrics and colours becomes increasingly difficult as each year progresses due to the wider variety available. Only the most popular are therefore mentioned.

The patterns follow the basic principles of pattern cutting appropriate to the period. For the most part, men's and ladies' tailored styles have been taken from surviving garments and contemporary tailoring books and magazine articles. Alterations may be required in some instances to retain the correct proportions appropriate to the era, and in relation to the wearer. It should be stressed that tailored clothes for both men and women require skilful cutting and manipulation of the fabric through stretching, shrinking, easing, padding, interfacing and inner construction details, to achieve perfect fit and balance. It is not recommended that the inexperienced attempt such styles without expert advice and assistance.

It is advisable to cut all costumes directly from measurements taken from the wearer's figure, over the appropriate foundation garments. This is of particular importance with the intricate construction at the turn of the century and tightly fitting or bias-cut styles. The patterns are provided as a basis on which to build further adaptations to suit the requirements of the costume, and in relation to the figure of the person for whom the garment is intended.

Undergarments change simultaneously with fashion – indeed, they are essential to it – and must be selected with the same consideration and attention to detail as the outer garments. A dress from the 1920s, however carefully constructed, will lack the feeling and colour of the times if it is dressed on a nineteen-eighties figure. The clothes must be worn as they were worn, if a truthful representation of the fashionable figure is to be achieved. Details of underclothes and accessories are provided throughout the text.

Instructions on Enlarging Patterns

1. Trace the appropriate pattern using stout tracing paper.

2. Position the tracing paper over the grid provided and secure with paper clips or reusable adhesive putty (Figure 1).

3. A new grid should be drawn up with squares five times the size of the squares on the grid provided (i.e. 2.5 cm), and the pattern can then be redrawn to full scale, using the squaring method. It is advisable to work with only one pattern piece at a time (Figure 2).

The use of a metric pattern cutting board or metric pattern paper will make this task easier.

NB To enlarge using imperial measurements, trace the pattern on to a grid of 1/4 in. squares. The pattern may then be enlarged to full scale, using the method outlined above and a grid of 1 1/4 in. squares.

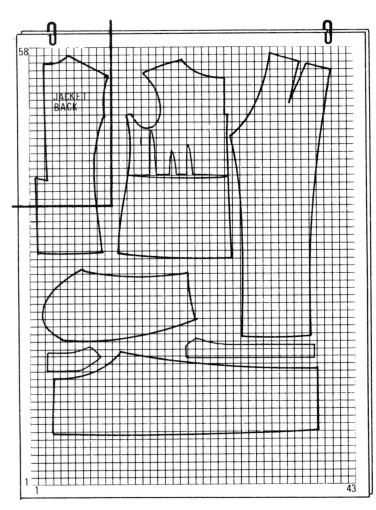

Figure 1

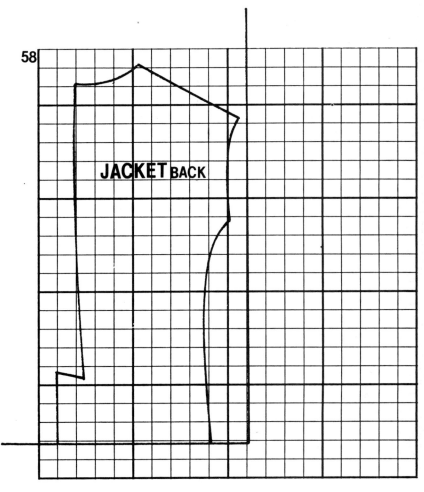

Figure 2

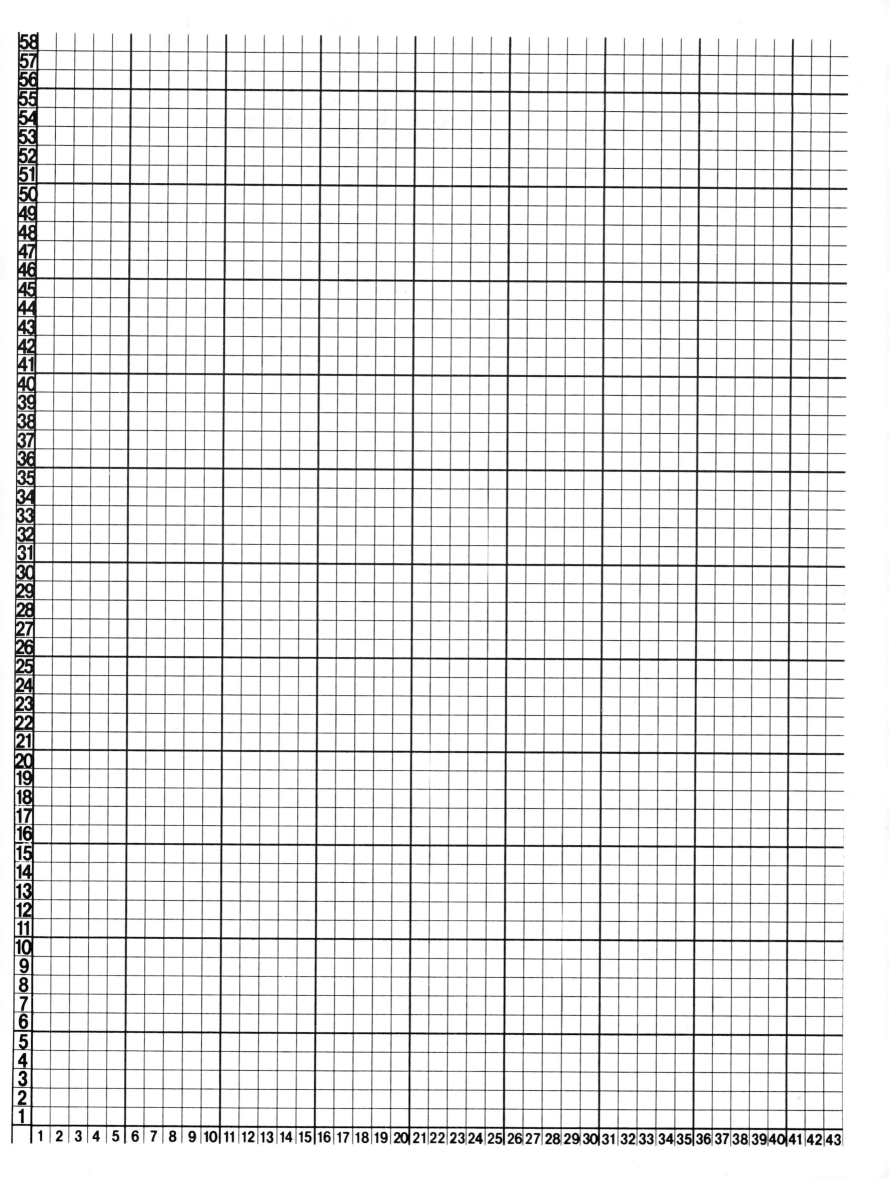

The First Decade 1900~1909

The turn of the century witnessed the passing of the Victorian age with the death of Queen Victoria in 1901. In the same year Marconi developed radio telegraphy and sent the first wireless signal across the Atlantic, the first electric tram cars ran in Britain, and two years later the Wright Brothers made the world's first powered flight – all memorable events and forerunners of a century of change and innovation.

The turn of the century, then, neatly marks the end of the Victorian era; fashion did not change overnight but significant movements did occur with the coming of the Edwardian age. Female fashion, with its flamboyant, extravagant character, adhered to strict rules of dress which placed it well out of reach of all but select high society. Male costume likewise remained tied to convention, with the cut and quality of fabric formulating the essential detail. Paris dictated the new modes and remained unrivalled in the influence it exerted. The very cut and detail of women's clothes defied successful imitation, and dressmaking with its many empiecements made mass-production in any form impossible. The importance of the overworked and underpaid dressmaker remained paramount. By its very nature fashion demanded time and money, and was not yet established as a right of the masses; it remained exclusively a luxury and a status symbol.

Edwardian fashions were all expensive, elaborate and ultra-feminine, relying on numerous undergarments to shape the silhouette. A bell-shaped skirt trailing the ground rustled with the movements of the wearer, achieving the desired shape by the combination of many petticoats, flounced and frilled above the hem. Remaining smooth over the hips, such petticoats rivalled the outer costume with trimmings of ribbon and lace, the final layer of coloured silk correctly revealed as an important fashion feature as the lady walked. The bell-shaped skirt, often remaining longer behind, heightened the effect of the S-shape silhouette which favoured the figure of the mature well-built woman. The corset as the foundation of the mode supported the stomach from below, the front of the bodice being made absolutely straight by a rigid whalebone structure. All fullness was thrust forward and upward into the stomach and chest, emphasizing a waspish waist and large hips, and creating a curvaceous and unnatural bend at the back of the body. As James Laver, writing in 1937, suggested: 'the general effect was as if the female body had been cut in two at the waist and the pieces put together again after the upper portion had been pushed several inches forward'.

The size of the bust was further emphasized by the pouching blouse, embellished with tucks, frills, braids and laces, which hung over the corseted waistline, and appeared rather like an overhanging cliff. Boning in foundation garments, and in the dress, moulded, or more accurately, contorted the figure to its essential rounded line. Stiffened supports incorporated in the bodice also controlled the high neckline of the blouse, compelling women to stand with the head inclined slightly upwards. The stance balanced the top-heavy bust and supported wide-brimmed hats worn far forward on the head, projecting almost as far as the bust line. During the day a lady's clothing covered her from head to toe, with *décolletage* reserved for the evening gown and falling very low to reveal a large expanse of the female bosom, and sometimes, indeed, the shoulders.

The efforts which the morning dress ritual inevitably entailed may seem to us in retrospect quite exhausting, and require us to consider the spirit of the age and the purpose to which these energies were directed: that is, an outward display of rank and position in society. We may become even more intrigued when we understand that the fashionable lady adopted several modes throughout the day according to occasion, time and place. These might include breakfast and matinée gowns, walking dresses, travelling coats, sports suits, frilly tea gowns, and luxurious ball and dinner gowns. The list is by no means exhaustive, and each change of clothing possessed an entirely different character inextricably linked with custom according to the hour of the day.

Men's dress, too, was governed by the law of the hour, which necessitated a change of costume maybe three to four times a day. Men's formal wear at the turn of the century included a frock or morning coat with silk top hat, for morning – as the name implies – or business wear, worn usually with striped trousers and contrast waistcoat. A lounge suit or Norfolk jacket provided a more practical alternative for informal or sports events, and men always changed for dinner, even in their own homes, a dress coat or the increasingly popular dinner jacket completing the correct evening attire. Rigid high collars echoed those of their female counterparts, trousers were narrower than previous fashion and without turn-ups, except for country and sport. A sharp crease in the trouser leg also became a more common sight with the introduction of the trouser press in the final years of the nineteenth century.

Until the First World War men's clothes remained tied to strict conventions with little loosening of existing rules of etiquette. However, signs of change were present which led to small, but significant movements towards a less formal mode of dress. Edward VII exerted a great influence on men's fashion by the care and interest he so obviously took in his own appearance. He occasionally wore the lounge suit, which was establishing itself as the standard male day dress, instead of the frock or morning coat. The frock coat, however, still remained correct for formal and city wear. The lounge suit would usually be worn with matching striped or check trousers, contrast waistcoat, high collar, bow tie, boots and soft felt hat, and was favoured by younger gentlemen. In summer a boater-style straw hat might be worn, and there began a vogue for lighter fabrics and colours, a trend even more significant in female dress, which chose not to confine the use of cream, eau-de-nil, and pastel blues and greens to the summer months alone – a reaction perhaps to the unrelieved dark, sombre colours of the Victorian age.

Women, too, like the younger men with their increased activity and interest in sport, looked to adopt an alternative costume. A new generation of women had taken up clerical or shop work, typewriting or telephone operating, and middle-class girls had abandoned leisurely home life to train for professions. Domestic service as the traditional occupation of the working-class woman began to decrease steadily from 1900 with the introduction of gas-fires, plumbing and new forms of heating and lighting in wealthier homes. The tailor-made suit for travelling and walking fitted the needs of the 'New Woman' and was one of the first fashions initiated in the British Isles. The outfit consisted of a full ankle-length skirt, blouse or masculine collar and tie, worn with a straw boater, or – for more special occasions – a wide-brimmed hat. The silhouette remained the same as for the main fashion trend, with a wide, stiffened belt tightly encircling the corseted waist. The basic suit could be adapted for cycling, golf, or tennis, with the jacket usually discarded for the latter. There was also a separate costume for motoring, but this became almost divorced from fashion, bowing to separate rules and requirements. However, true comfort was not yet established, and dusty roads led to the adoption of voluminous dust coats by men and women alike. For women flat caps, secured by veils, and sometimes enclosing the head completely, protected the complexion of the fair English rose. By the end of the decade private car ownership had increased, aided by Henry Ford's mass-production techniques from 1903. Significantly, many road surfaces were to be tarred and a Road Highways Act of 1903 required registration of motor vehicles and restricted the speed limit to 20 miles per hour.

The more active female began to question her role in society on a social and political level. In 1903 Emmeline Pankhurst formed the Women's Social and Political Union to demand votes for women; this became increasingly militant when demonstrations alone failed to have any impact. In 1908 suffragettes chained themselves to the railings at 10 Downing Street and 280,000 attended a demonstration at Hyde Park.

Women were demanding changes to their traditional role and during the 1900s much was beginning to be achieved in developments at other levels of society. The Liberal government introduced a number of reforms which brought an improved standard of living to ordinary people. The Education Act of 1902 established free elementary education to the age of 13, and in 1907 school meals were set up in British schools. In 1909 an Old Age Pension was given to all over seventy with an income of less than ten shillings a week. Better washing facilities, cleansing powders, antiseptics, toothpaste and soaps brought higher levels of hygiene, and new devices such as the phonograph, vacuum cleaner and electric washing machine, from 1907, although they had little impact at the time, promised an easier existence. Improvements in public transport with the first motor buses, electric trams and trains, provided mobility and increased freedom of movement.

The latter half of the decade also brought subtle changes to the cut of female dress, which from 1908 saw the extreme of the fashion modified, and the effective straightening of the female silhouette. The bust became less pronounced and skirts narrowed at the hem. Hats remained large, however, and continued to increase in width.

A positive and forward-looking age, the Edwardian era staged the final scenes of fashion dictated solely by society. In the year that closed the decade a hundredweight of suffragist leaflets were scattered over London from a balloon and Blériot flew the English Channel. We can now view the age in the wider context of the twentieth century, and are aware that although pursuing a slow course, the signs of progress indicated undercurrents of the wave of change which was to affect British fashion and society in ensuing years.

1901

Predominant fashion features

Women

Silhouette softer, lighter and more feminine in contrast to rigid Victorian fashions. Straight-fronted corsets provide the essential hour-glass figure, flattening below the waist and accentuating the bust and hips. Bell-shaped skirts grow progressively tighter over the hips, trailing the ground and usually longer at the back, with the exception of the walking or sports skirt which just clears the ground. Fussily trimmed corsage with blouse pouching over waist and high neckline. For full evening dress the neckline is cut low, either squared or rounded, the full, trailing skirt often made of diaphanous, flimsy fabrics over a silk or satin foundation.

Fabrics: Softer and lighter in character; alpaca, mohair, lawn, fine velvets, silks, fine facecloth, chiffon, faille. Universal use of lace, and lace trimmings.
    Dust coats and sports wear – gabardine, heavy wools and tweeds.

Colours: Pale pinks, blues, peach, eau-de-nil.

Undergarments: Straight-fronted whalebone corset, laced at the back with stocking suspenders attached. Silk replacing linen for luxurious underwear (lingerie). Chemise or vest of fine linen, muslin, batiste or lawn, worn under the corset. Camisoles or corset-covers shaped to the waist in batiste or fine muslin, worn under the blouse.
    Petticoats essential to bell-shape effect of the skirt, with frills and flounces at the hem. Sometimes buttoned to lower edge of corset.

Footwear: Pointed or round-toed shoes, high-laced shoes for winter wear, leather, suede or kid. Black, beige or bronze court shoes with louis heel for evening.

Stockings: Black ribbed lisle or cashmere for winter. White with white shoes for summer. Lace insertion for evening.

Hair: Drawn on to the top of the head over pads. Hair softly waved with additional fullness at sides and dressed high and full. For evening, hair decorated with ornamental combs, flowers, feathers and false hair pieces.

Hats: Always worn. Small and high, lavishly trimmed with feathers, flowers, birds, lace, ribbons, buckles and worn straight on the head. Toques, straw boaters. Hats secured with decorated and jewelled metal hatpins.

Accessories: Short gloves of black leather or suede for day wear. Full length gloves in soft kid or silk for evening with long button fastening. Small leather bags for day, embroidered silk or beadwork for evening, with metal chain. Small fans of lace, embroidered or painted silk; feather fans popular for evening. Parasols and umbrellas of lace, silk or moiré. Rings, clip earrings, bracelets and neckbands to enhance the low evening *décolletage.*

Movement: Upright poise with head held high above stiffened neckline. Upper carriage thrust forward and shoulders down. Skirt lifted with the fingers at one side while walking, with the hand resting on backward thrust of the hip, displaying the lower edge of the petticoat.

Men

Menswear remains tied to strict conventions. Lounge suits increasingly worn as practical alternative for day or informal wear, fronts of jacket occasionally rounded. Short, pointed lapels with the jacket cut slightly longer and shaped to the waist. Worn with contrast waistcoats in colour and fabric. Trouser legs are narrow with a crease down the front, slightly wider with morning coat. Trousers sometimes feature turn-ups for country or sports wear.

Fabrics: Fine worsted suitings – alpaca, flannel, mohair.

Colours: Soft blues and greys, small checks and stripes, pale grey for summer wear.

Undergarments, underwear and socks: As 1902.

Footwear: Boots – two-tone with cloth tops; round-toed, lace-up Oxford-style shoes in black or brown calfskin or patent leather. Tan or white buckskin for summer. Light-coloured spats fastening with buttons and buttonholes.

Hats: Always worn outdoors. Silk top hat with morning or frock coat. Bowler hats for city and business wear. Trilby in soft felt, velour or straw, and straw boaters for summer.

Hair: Short with centre parting, smoothed with hair creams and oils.

Accessories: As 1902.

Movement: Straight and dignified poise with head held proud due to high collar. Stance determined by formality of occasion.

Details of illustrated patterns

Woman

Lady's afternoon dress consisting of a separate bodice and skirt. The bell-shaped skirt trails the ground, being longer at the back than the front, and fits smoothly over the hips. The blousing of the front bodice is very pronounced, and undersleeves are gathered into a cuff. The overbodice meets at the centre front with bell-shaped, set-in sleeves and turn-back roll collar, extending over the sleevehead and to shoulder-bone at back bodice.

Fabrics: Dress and bodice – alpaca, crêpe, lightweight woollen materials.
    Bodice blouse front and sleeve ends – silk crêpe de Chine, jap silk, nun's veiling.
    Heavy cotton fabric for underbodice.
    Heavier silk fabric for front bodice foundation.

Colours: Soft subdued tones – powder blue, pink, pale grey, eau-de-nil.
    Front bodice – ivory, pink, sky blue.

Decoration: Bodice collar and sleeves are faced in silk taffeta in a deeper tone than the main fabric and edged with pleated taffeta frills. Matching frills are also applied above the hemline of the skirt with taffeta strappings.
    The bodice front pin-tucked across its entire width with ivory insertion lace and small frills at centre front. Narrow black velvet ribbon edges the high tucked collar and cuffs. Neck jabot of ivory lace.

Hat: Straw hat with upturned brim, decorated lavishly on the underside and crown with artificial flowers and petersham ribbon.

Man

Double-breasted frock coat with three buttons on each side and buttonstands. Lapels are faced in silk, with buttonholes parallel to the top lapel. An outside breast pocket may be present (not illustrated). The coat has a waist seam and centre vent at the back with two hip buttons at the top. The straight sleeves are slit at the cuff, fastening with three buttons. The frock coat is usually worn open, revealing single-breasted waistcoat with collar and lapels. Double-breasted waistcoats are also popular with frock coats. Black-and-white-striped trousers.

Fabric: Wool gabardine, worsted, or barathea.

Colour: Black.

Hat: Silk top hat.

Notes on construction of garments

Woman

Make up the underbodice of heavy cotton fabric; this fastens edge to edge at the centre front. The bloused front bodice panel is tucked along lines indicated, then mounted on to front bodice foundation of heavier silk. The raw edges of bodice and foundation are joined at the lower edge, gathered and bound with 2.5 cm (1 in.) wide taffeta crossway strips.
    The entire front panel is stitched to the underbodice on the right side and fastens with hooks and eyes at the left (the position is indicated by dotted line on the underbodice pattern), concealing the foundation. The collar is tucked along lines indicated, stiffened and boned, fastening at the left shoulder seam.
    Construct the main bodice separately, the collar cut in one with the front and faced in taffeta. The lower edge of the front bodice is pleated and gathered in to the lower bodice panel to give a pouched effect; this then fastens at the centre front.
    Sleeves are also faced in taffeta at the lower edge. Sleeve-ends of ivory silk are attached to the sleeves under the faced section.
    Position of boning on bodice seams is indicated by heavier black lines. The bodice is attached to the skirt with hooks and eyes at centre back, marked **X** on pattern.
    The skirt is sewn to a narrow waistbamd with concealed placket in right front seam.

Petticoat: Cut on the same lines as skirt.

Man

Face lapels with ribbed silk fabric, as illustrated. Adapt waistcoat pattern from 1906/1907.

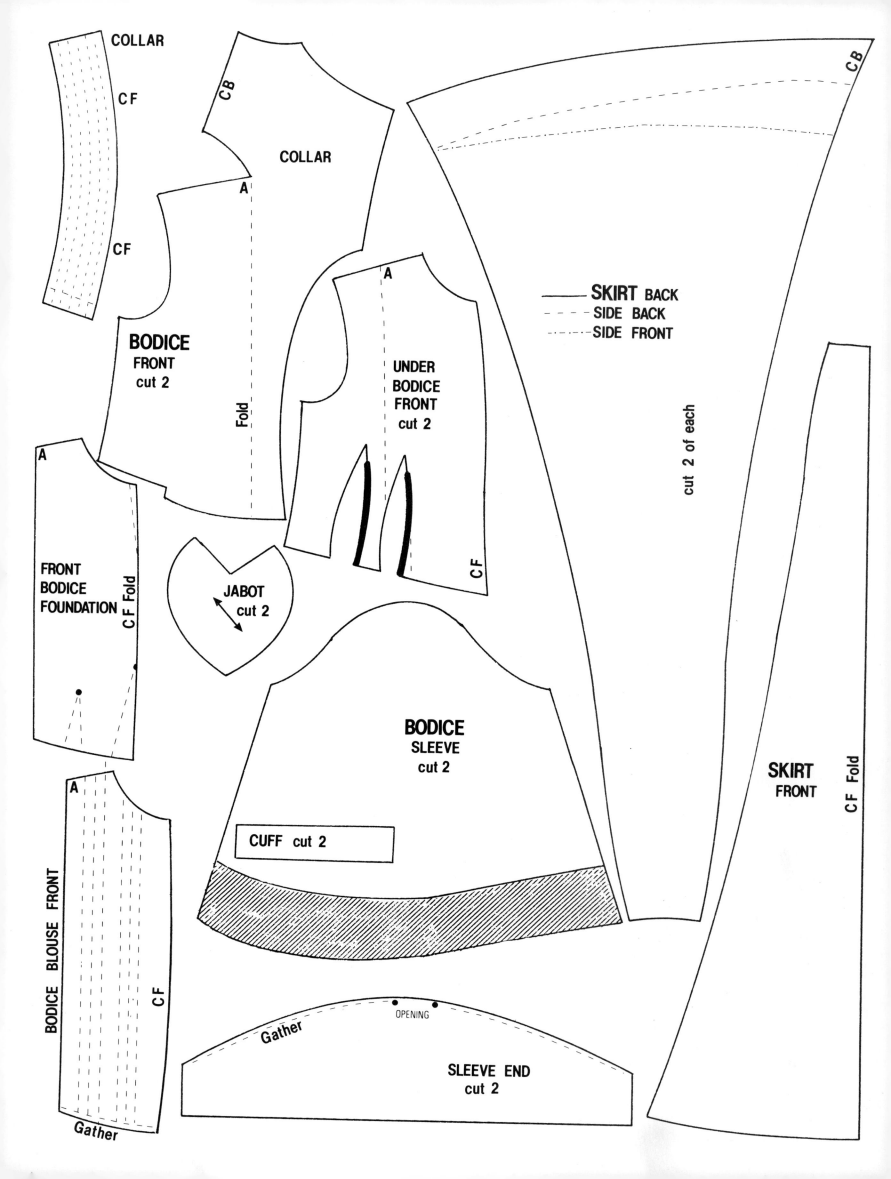

COLLAR

CF

CF

COLLAR

CB

A

SKIRT BACK
— — — SIDE BACK
— · — · — SIDE FRONT

CB

BODICE
FRONT
cut 2

A

Fold

UNDER
BODICE
FRONT
cut 2

cut 2 of each

A

FRONT
BODICE
FOUNDATION

CF Fold

JABOT
cut 2

CF

SKIRT
FRONT

CF Fold

BODICE BLOUSE FRONT

A

BODICE
SLEEVE
cut 2

CUFF cut 2

CF

Gather

Gather

OPENING

SLEEVE END
cut 2

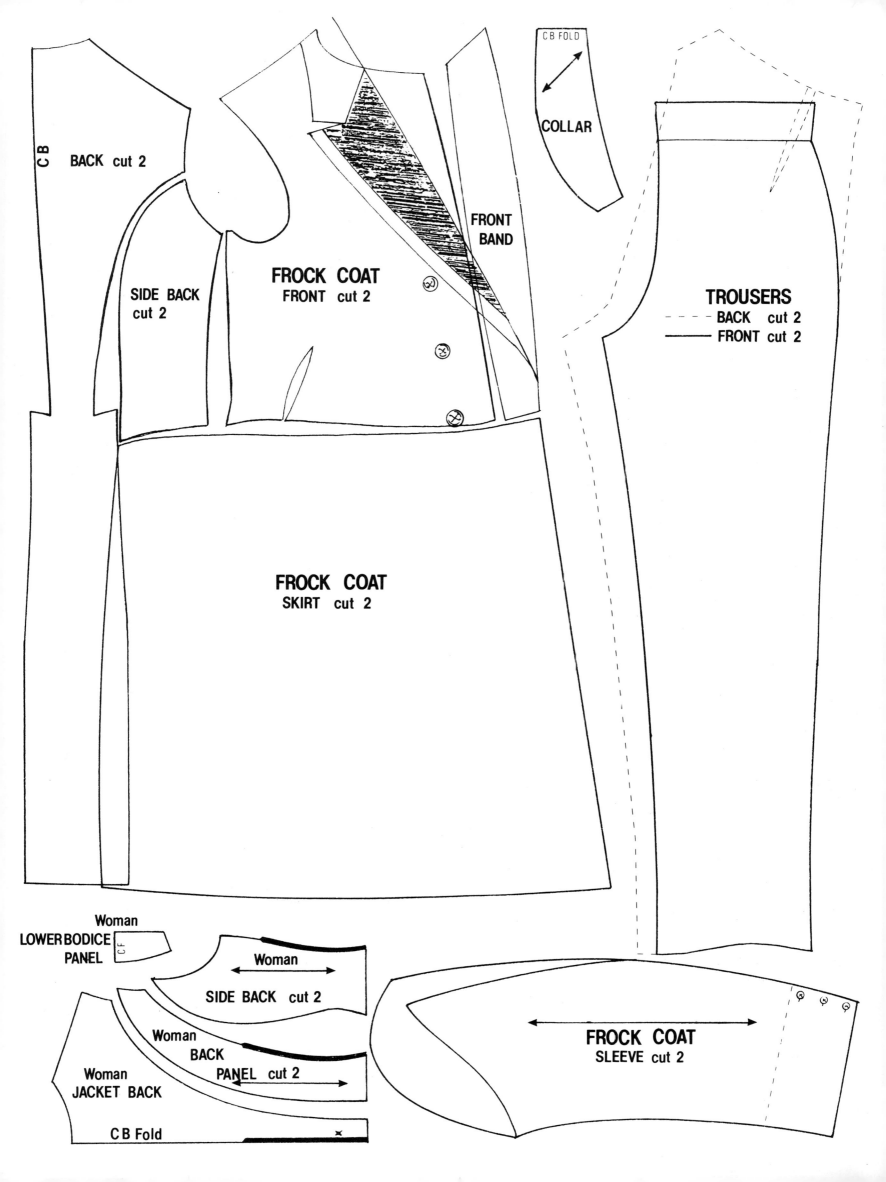

C B

BACK cut 2

SIDE BACK
cut 2

FROCK COAT
FRONT cut 2

FRONT
BAND

FROCK COAT
SKIRT cut 2

CB FOLD

COLLAR

TROUSERS
- - - BACK cut 2
—— FRONT cut 2

Woman
LOWER BODICE
PANEL

CF

Woman
SIDE BACK cut 2

Woman
BACK
PANEL cut 2

Woman
JACKET BACK

CB Fold

FROCK COAT
SLEEVE cut 2

1902

Predominant fashion features

Women

'It was the age of the 'fine' woman, of the mature and well-rounded contour and every fashion of the period might actually have been designed to set her off to advantage and to handicap the young girl.' (Laver, *Taste and Fashion*)

All fashion expensive, elaborate and ultra feminine. 'S-shape', Gibson Girl silhouette – straight front; full, heavy, protruding bust; hips pushed backwards.

Pouching blouse exaggerated, deep lace, embroidered yokes, higher necklines, boned to just under the ears. Skirts continue to tighten over the hips.

New corselet skirt, boned and extended above the waistline, usually worn with shorter bolero.

Fabrics: Similar to previous fashion. For day wear – velveteen, velvets, silk, organdie, gauze, muslin, gingham, net, serge, alpaca, taffeta, tussore, cashmere, satin, linen, batiste.

For evening and tea gowns – frothy lace, chiffon faille, Breton net, ninon, voile, crêpe de Chine, *mousseline de soie*.

Colours: Pale, delicate shades, eau-de-nil, shades of green and blue, soft greys, browns, navy for tailor-mades. White and pastels for evening. Blouses usually white or écru.

Velveteens – greens, emerald, sage green; reds – tulip, geranium and poppy.

Cream serge for country, also grey, fawn, and pale blues.

Decoration: Embroidered and hand-painted fabrics; ubiquitous use of lace – guipure, Cluny, Brussels. Ornamental strappings and stitching, dull metallic buttons, gold and silver braids, ribbon velvet, ruched and pleated silks. Blouses heavily tucked, with lace insertion.

Undergarments: Straight-fronted corset with long metal stays and hook fastening gives long, sloping bust-line, the bend of the narrow waist accentuated at the back above smoothly curving hips. Empire corset, short above the waist and just covering the bust. Suspenders are attached to the corset, replacing garters.

Bust-improvers add emphasis for the less well endowed.

Chemise and camisole as previous fashion. Many petticoats, flounced and decorated at the lower edge, continue to support the bell-shaped silhouette. The top petticoat (underslip) in brighter colours – pink, green, peach and luxurious fabrics – taffeta, satin, glacé silk, moirette, rustling with the movements of the wearer.

Shoes and stockings: Similar to previous fashion.

Hats: Slightly larger, with small crowns, tilted with the brim upturned and decorated, as in the previous year. Lavishly trimmed, tricorne shapes and toques remain popular. Fur hats and trimming for winter.

Hair: As previous fashion, with hair fuller at the sides.

Accessories: Similar to previous fashion; round muffs and fur stoles in fox or sable for winter wear. Increasing amount of jewellery worn.

Movement: Poise determined by rigidity of corset and high neck stays, as previously. Head thrown back to balance carriage of body. Movement is further restricted by tightness of skirt over the hips. Petticoats 'swish' with movement.

Men

Similar to previous year. Lounge suits with slightly longer jackets.

Overcoats – calf-length chesterfield style remains popular, either single-breasted with fly front, or double-breasted, slightly waisted with back vent, and with collars, and sometimes cuffs, faced in velvet. Ulsters, raglans and caped overcoats continue to be worn.

Fabrics: Alpaca, grey flannel, narrow-striped fabrics for summer lounge suits.

Colours: As previous fashion.

Undergarments: All shirts tunic-style. Coloured shirts acceptable for day wear, with linen front and cuffs, white or coloured to match the shirt. Detachable rigid collars, 8 cm (3¼ in.) in height, of white linen or celluloid (for poorer classes). Wing collars (with the points turned down) are worn with evening dress. Polo or double collar popular for day wear.

Underwear: Undervest and long pants of knitted wool, wool and silk mix or cotton for summer. Combinations and shorter 'drawers', ending just below the knee, are also worn.

Footwear: Similar to previous fashion.

Socks: Reaching to mid-calf and held up with suspenders.

Hats: Similar to previous fashion. Straw panama styles popular for summer, and stiff felt Homburg styles with indented crown and curled brim.

Hair: As previous fashion.

Accessories: Neckties – variety of styles worn, silk bow ties popular, white with evening dress suit or tails. Fancy Ascot cravat with morning suit. Plain, striped or spotted ties worn with lounge suits.

Suede, leather or kid gloves always worn outdoors. White kid or buckskin gloves for evening wear.

White handkerchief worn in breast pocket, for decoration. Umbrella or walking stick.

Collar studs and cuff links made to match in mother-of-pearl or onyx. For evening wear, links match studs on dress shirt.

Details of illustrated patterns

Woman

Floor-length walking skirt and matching bolero jacket. The skirt extends above the natural waistline, with decorative front panel, and is attached to a silk foundation, boned at the waist and pleated at lower edge. There are four panels, flaring from slim hips. The panelled jacket meets at centre front, with high-rolling shawl collar and three-quarter-length sleeves, gathered tightly at sleevehead. A cream, silk blouse, with high boned collar and button front, completes the outfit.

Fabric: Facecloth.

Colours: Pale apple green.

Decoration: Panel seams of jacket and skirt are trimmed with a very fine black silk piping. Heavy metal buttons and rouleau loops are applied between curves of these seams. Cuffs and collar are faced with pleated black silk taffeta and cream hopsack fabric, separated by a line of top fabric and piping. The shaped top panel of the skirt is edged with black piping and top-stitched to the skirt; it is decorated with mock gold braid buttonholes.

Hat: Straw hat with shallow crown perched well forward on head. Lavishly decorated with artificial flowers and grosgrain ribbon.

Man

Double-breasted close-fitting chesterfield overcoat with four-button fastening. The lapels are soft rolling, with buttonhole on each side and upper collar of velvet. The close-fitting skirt has centre back vent and slanted welt pocket at hip. Two-piece straight sleeves are slit at the cuff with four-button fastening. Worn with striped trousers.

Fabric and colours: Oxford and medium grey cheviots and velours, black-and-white feather designs.

Hat: Silk top hat.

Notes on construction of garments

Woman

The bolero should fit the figure snugly with all seams boned for 10–14 cm (4–5½ in.) from lower edges.

Sleeves are strapped with self-fabric from centre of sleevehead and tucked into shaped facing at lower edge.

Skirt waist is boned for 10 cm (4 in.), or use wide-boned petersham ribbon to face top edge.

Petticoats cut on same lines as skirt; add extra flouncing and pleating at lower edge to support skirt hem.

Man

Use trouser pattern from 1901; adapt waistcoat pattern from 1906/1907.

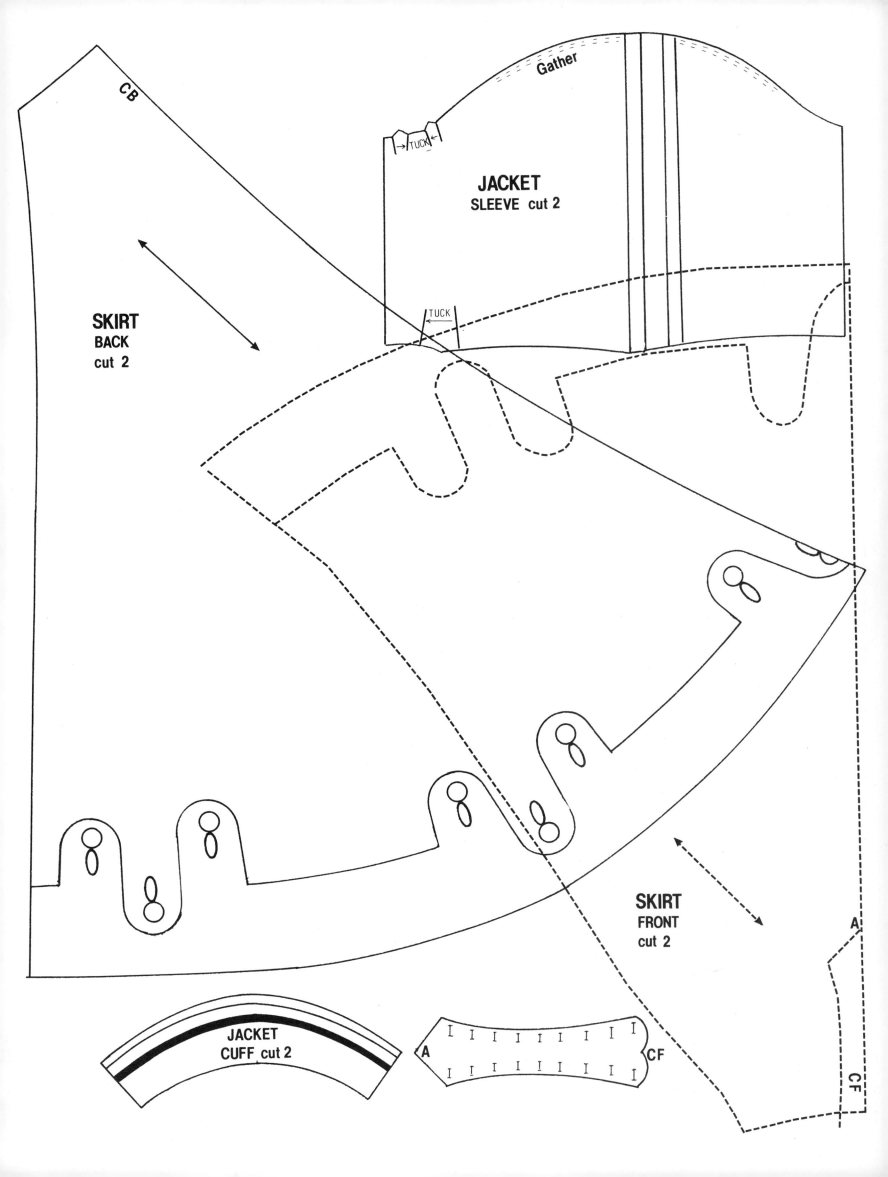

CB

Gather

TUCK

JACKET
SLEEVE cut 2

TUCK

SKIRT
BACK
cut 2

SKIRT
FRONT
cut 2

A

JACKET
CUFF cut 2

A

CF

CF

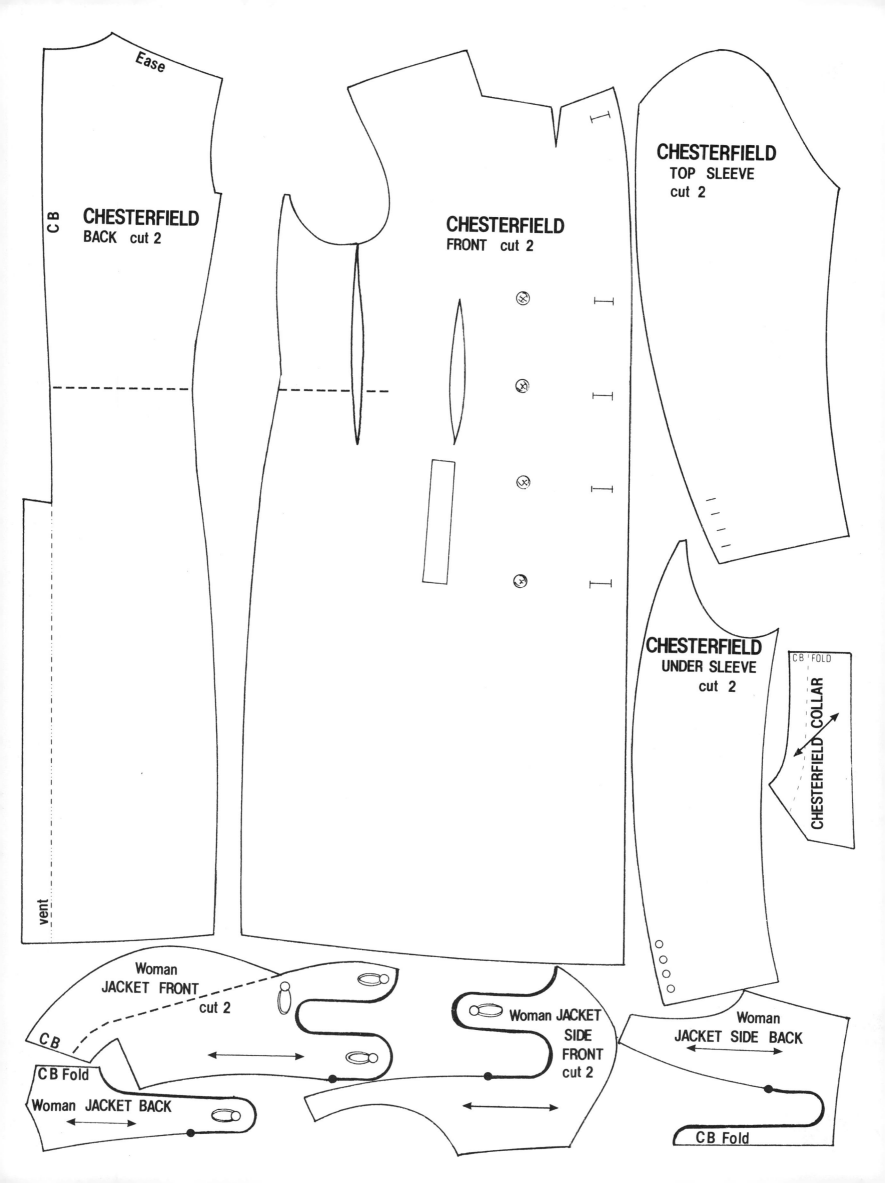

Ease

C B

CHESTERFIELD
BACK cut 2

vent

CHESTERFIELD
FRONT cut 2

CHESTERFIELD
TOP SLEEVE
cut 2

CHESTERFIELD
UNDER SLEEVE
cut 2

CB FOLD

CHESTERFIELD COLLAR

Woman
JACKET FRONT

cut 2

C B

CB Fold

Woman **JACKET BACK**

Woman **JACKET
SIDE
FRONT**
cut 2

Woman
JACKET SIDE BACK

CB Fold

1906~1907

Predominant fashion features

Women

Boleros and skirts remain popular, with full sleeves, semi-gigot style to wrist. Corselet skirts extend well above natural waistline. Walking, sports skirt 5 cm (2 in.) from ground.

Bust less exaggerated and blouses no longer pouched, with straighter front, remaining highly decorated with tucks, embroidery and lace. Empire line, with raised waist effects. Evening dresses cut with low *décolletage* at front and back.

Afternoon or tea gowns – made in one piece in princess or Empire style.

Skirts, pleated, gathered or flounced. Ribbon sashes at the waist. Tailor-mades continue in popularity with wider shoulders, and closer-cut sleeves from 1907. Three-quarter-length sleeves popular.

Fabrics: Woollen checks, fine herringbone, serge, facecloth for tailor-mades.

Afternoon – summer linens, heavy lace, muslin, chiffon, tussore, alpacas, shantung; striped fabrics popular.

Undergarments – cambric, lawn, batiste, glacé silk, moirette, nainsook.

Colours: Black, white and pastel shades.

Decoration: Tassels on stoles, jackets and evening wear; velvet pompoms in black and brown; velvets, fur, feathers, embroidery. 1907 – crochet lace in vogue.

Undergarments: Underclothes slim down; Empire line, princess-style petticoats with higher waist and straighter skirts. Narrow ribbon, lace trim and insertion.

Corsets shorten above waist, longer below.

Footwear: As previous fashion.

Hats: Becoming wider, still lavishly trimmed, fuller crowns and brims, worn tilted forward or to one side (right) with face veils. Tweed hats or caps for sports and country.

Hair: Coiffure similar to previous style although fuller and more puffed. Permanent Marcel waving.

Accessories: Gloves – gauntlet style for outdoor. Evening gloves long to elbow in light kid or buckskin, or silk; feather boas and fans.

Large fur muffs and stoles for winter.

Accessories generally larger.

Movement: Poise more natural but remaining rigid with front carriage thrust less far forward. Head still held high above boned collar and to balance wider hat.

Men

Day wear – lounge suits generally worn in place of frock coat, except by older gentlemen. Proportions remain similar to previous fashion. Soft-fronted white shirt replacing starched front for business, and coloured for less formal occasions, with the collar remaining white and rigid. Dress shirt fronts often tucked.

Informal and sports wear – double-breasted, straight-cut reefer jackets or lounge jackets. Tweed sports jackets worn with flannels or matching trousers or knickerbockers.

Norfolk jackets with separate or attached belt and box pleats, popular for shooting and golf.

Knitted jumpers, cardigans or waistcoats might also be worn, and breeches or knickerbockers.

Fabrics: English wools for overcoats and suitings.

Trouserings – vicuñas, serge, worsted. Overcoats, Melton cloth. Tweeds, herringbones for sports jackets.

Zephyr and Oxford shirting fabrics.

Colours: Grey or brown shades of twill, check or stripe. Heathers and soft browns, small checks with coloured thread forming overcheck in great evidence.

Relief from grey, in favour during the first part of the decade. Wide herringbone or feather designs, striped or overchecked with bright coloured twist threads. Grey with slight tinges of blue.

Undergarments: All shirts tunic-style. Soft-fronted shirt fronts as noted above. Collar height shortened from 7.5 cm (3 in.) to 5 cm (2 in.).

Flannel shirt with linen polo, or stand collar for sports. Underwear in previous style.

Socks: As previous fashion. Patterned in checks or stripes with knickerbockers or breeches.

Footwear: As 1901. Short garter-spats for town and country – usually light grey, fawn, buttoning at one side and fastening under instep with buckle and strap.

Hats: For day wear as previous modes. Tweed hats, deerstalkers and pleated caps for sports.

Hair: Side-parting becoming more usual than centre-parting.

Accessories: Similar to previous fashion; walking sticks.

Movement: Movement and posture determined by formality of occasion and clothes. Rules of etiquette in fashion become less rigid.

Details of illustrated patterns

Woman

The outfit consists of a long, belted Norfolk jacket with full-length two-piece sleeves, pleated into sleevehead and narrow at the wrist with shaped cuff. Front and back jacket are strapped with crossway self fabric, remaining unstitched at waist-level to act as belt carriers. The jacket is single-breasted with high lapel opening, the upper collar faced in silk or velvet.

The gored skirt just clears the ground, with inverted pleats at the base of each seam. Seams are strapped with shaped self fabric.

The outfit is worn with stiff masculine collar and tie and large tweed peaked cap.

Fabric and colours: Checked tweed or plain serge in subtle browns and greens.

Man

Norfolk jacket with high lapel opening, attached belt and box pleats to waist level at front and back. The jacket skirt is close-fitting with large, expanding flapped pockets and centre back vent. Two-piece sleeves are slit at the cuff with one-button fastening.

Knee-length knickerbockers are in matching fabric and fasten under the knee with strap and button. They are looser in fit than breeches.

The outfit is worn with peaked cap, long woollen stockings, boots and short gaiters.

Fabric: Checked brown tweed.

Notes on construction of garments

Woman

Cut 2.5 cm (1 in.) wide strips of bias fabric to cover jacket seams – position of strappings is indicated by broken lines. Straps are left free over the waistline.

Bone all jacket seams, breaking at the waistline.

The skirt is sewn to a waistband, with concealed placket in left front seam. The skirt should fit the waist and hips smoothly. The petticoat is cut on the same lines as the skirt, with additional flouncing to support the weight at the lower edge and allow for easy movement.

Add pleat extension to all skirt seams as illustrated on skirt front.

Broken lines indicate position and pattern of self fabric decoration, cut on bias of fabric.

Man

Broken line on front jacket indicates position of pleat. Expand the pattern 8 cm (3 in.) to allow for 4 cm (1½ in.) box pleat, as on jacket back.

Construct pockets with additional 2.5 cm (1 in.) pleats at outside edges to allow for pocket expansion.

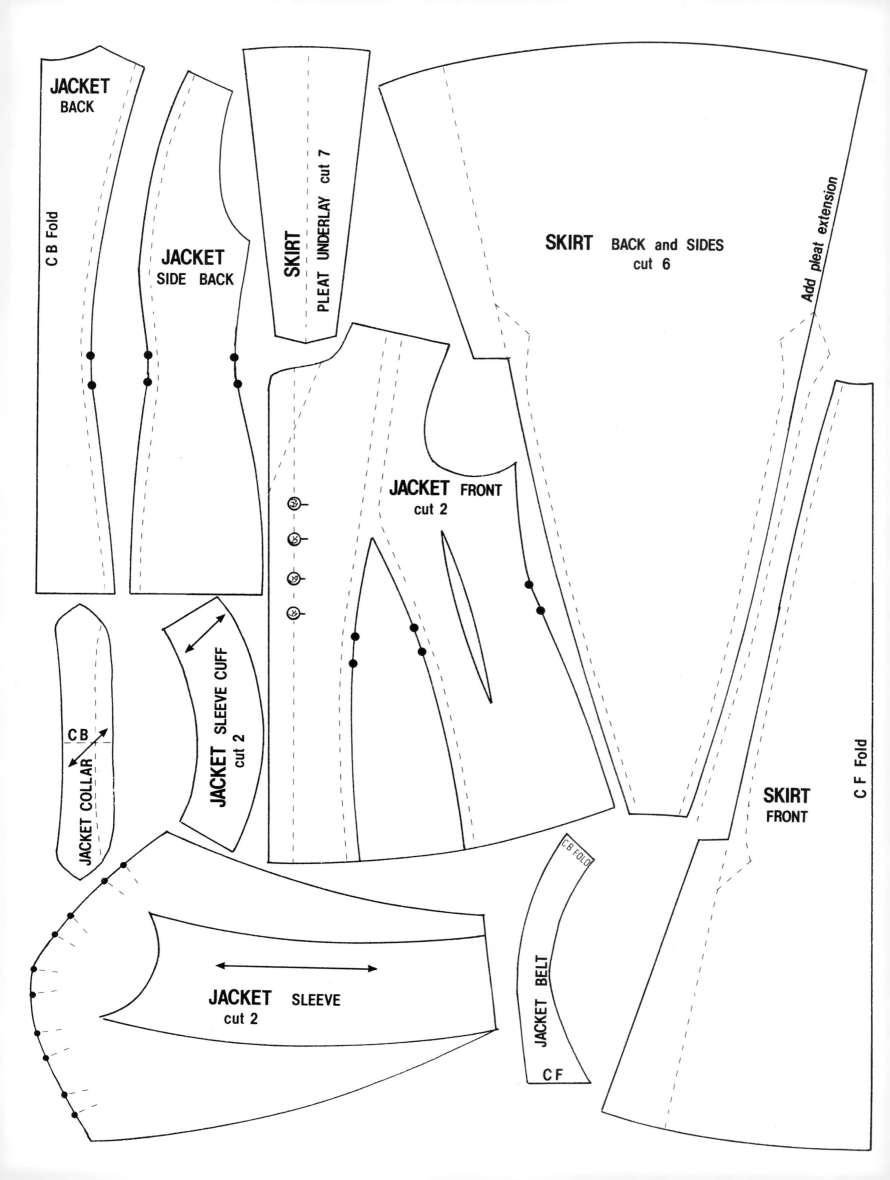

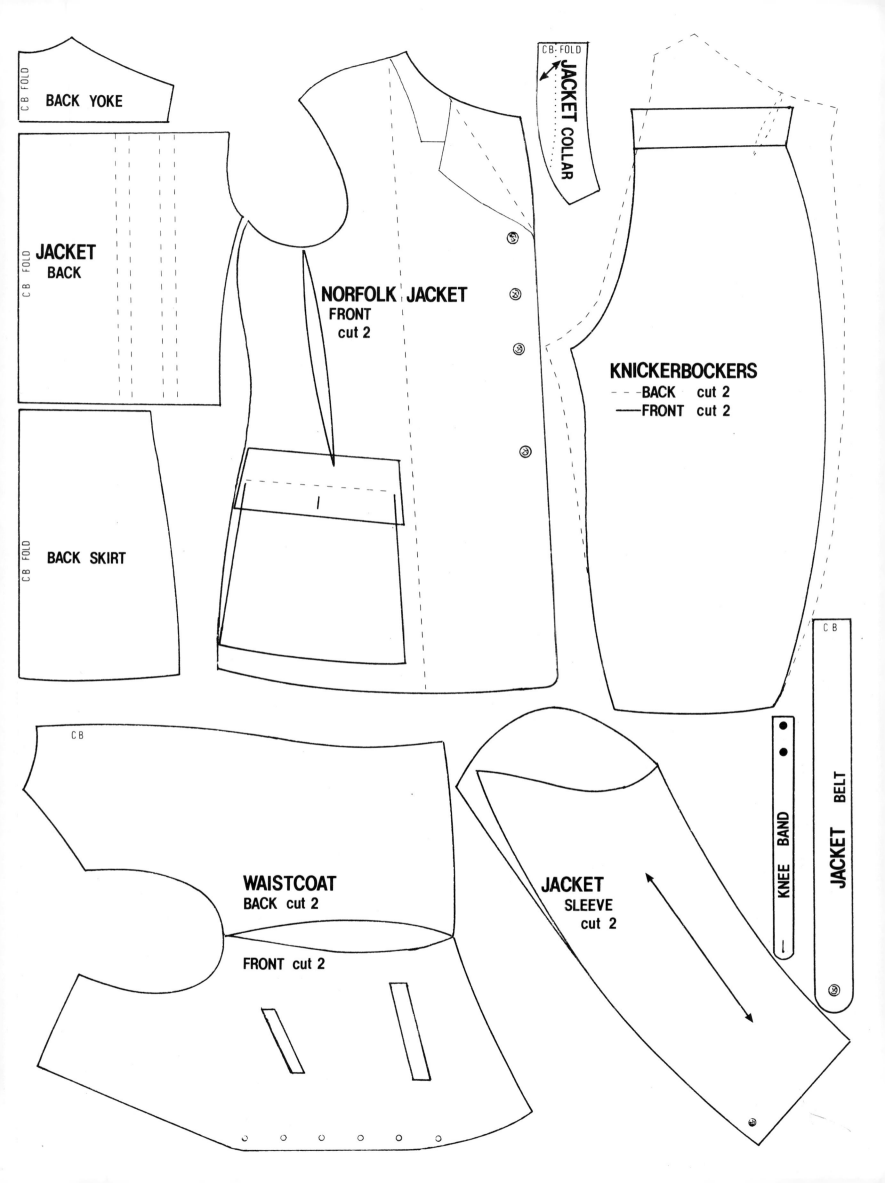

BACK YOKE

C B FOLD

JACKET
BACK

C B FOLD

BACK SKIRT

C B FOLD

NORFOLK JACKET
FRONT
cut 2

CB·FOLD

JACKET COLLAR

KNICKERBOCKERS
- - - BACK   cut 2
——— FRONT   cut 2

C B

CB

WAISTCOAT
BACK cut 2

FRONT cut 2

JACKET
SLEEVE
cut 2

KNEE BAND

JACKET   BELT

1908

Predominant fashion features

Women

Change in line, with the extreme of Edwardian fashion modified; bust and waist are less exaggerated, with a closer-fitting tubular silhouette. Collar remains stiff and higher than in previous modes. Empire or *Directoire* line affects all fashion.

Décolletage remains low for evening wear, squarer and with the shoulders covered, and usually consisting of transparent fabrics, partially lined.

Outdoor wear — longer coats worn over the slimmer skirt, jackets lengthen generally, with the bolero jacket, popular since the turn of the century, no longer worn. Coats or jackets and skirts often differ in both fabric and colour.

Redingote — long, Empire-line coat.

Fabrics: Crêpe de Chine, shantung, georgette. Striped fabrics are seen everywhere.

Undergarments — fine linen, muslin, batiste, lawn.

Colours: Evidence of renewed interest in colour — yellow, peach, blue, brown and pastels.

Tea gowns — greens, lavender, warm greys, orange.

Decoration: Ruching for lighter tea gowns and evening dresses, chiffon flowers and embroidery.

Braids, strappings and decorative buttons. Tassels on stoles, jackets and evening wear. Feather trimmings on hats.

Undergarments: As skirts narrow at the hem petticoats slim down, losing their fullness and 'rustling' qualities. Trimmings and decoration still restricted to the lower edge. Empire style continues.

Chemise — Empire style, narrow shoulders, wide neckline, cut close to figure. Skirt knickers replace combinations.

Corsets even shorter above the waist and longer below, 50.75 – 63.5 cm (20 – 25 in.) in length.

Ribbon corset — 3–4 widths of satin ribbon 2 in. (5 cm) wide, lightly boned at the sides, front fastening, back lacing, for sport and general wear.

Petticoats and corsets sometimes combined.

Footwear: High boots to the knees, either buttoned or laced, with higher louis heels.

Stockings: No major changes.

Hats: Generally flatter in crown, with significantly wider brims. Trimming remains lavish, restricted to the crown and top of the hat, rather than under the brim.

'An extremely wide hat always seems to have the effect of narrowing the width of the skirt, as if there were some natural law that forbids the feminine figure to be wide at both ends at once.' (Laver, *Taste and Fashion*)

Hair: Middle parting with coiffure widened at the sides, and hair styled more to the back of the head than on the crown, to accommodate larger millinery fashions.

Marcel waving.

Accessories: Generally large — fur muffs, stoles. Evening gloves long to elbows.

Movement: Similar to previous year.

Men

No significant changes from previous year in style or fabrics. Bottom button of waistcoat with lounge jacket usually left undone, a trend which continues throughout the twentieth century. Collarless styles become more frequent, with opening cut lower.

Fabrics: Viyella — new unshrinkable flannel for shirts.

Colour: Shades of green popular for shirts, with white linen collar.

Undergarments: For full evening dress, white shirt with high wing collar, starched dress front in piqué or marcella, pleated front, 22.75–25.5 cm (9–10 in.) wide. Square cuff.

Viyella shirts, slightly shaped at waist. Less high collar continues. Rounded cuffs. Soft-fronted flannel or cambric shirts in summer. Length of stiff-fronted business shirt reduced.

Undervest — natural-coloured wool, wool and silk mix or cellular cotton in summer, with long or short sleeves.

Drawers or pants — in similar fabric to undervest, with button front and tape loops at waist for braces. Pants — to ankle or mid-calf; drawers — below or above knee.

Hats: Previous modes continue. Popular styles: bowler - hard felt hat with bowl crown and narrow brim, curled upwards for city or business. Homburg — stiff felt hat with indented crown and silk-bound brim, worn with lounge suits. Trilby — similar to Homburg in softer felt with no trim on brim.

Hair: As previous year.

Footwear: As 1901.

Accessories: As previous year. Evening dress shirt worn with white tie, 1–3 mother-of-pearl studs and links.

Details of illustrated patterns

Woman

Directoire evening dress with draped bodice and low square-cut neckline, forming V at centre back. The skirt is straighter than styles of the early 1900s and less fussily trimmed. A wide velvet sash accentuates the high waistline. The dress fastens at the centre back with placket and hook-and-eye closure. Double sleeves of transparent net and chiffon are gathered into velvet ribbon shoulder straps.

Fabrics: Bodice and skirt composed of layers of satin, net and chiffon over a firmer silk foundation.

Colours: Black, ivory, midnight blue.

Decoration: Dress bodice of draped black net is covered with tiny pearl beads, which also decorate the net overskirt, combined with silver embroidery above hemline. Pearl trimming edges the neckline and black velvet sash, which is finished with silver embroidery and tassels. A silver and pearl buckle under the bust further accentuates the raised waistline.

Accessories: Silver and lace fan with silver tassel trim; long kid gloves; wide silver and pearl choker and hair bandeau of velvet and pearls. The hair may also be decorated with trailing flowers, ribbons, combs or feathers.

Man

Full evening dress consisting of tail coat, white waistcoat and trousers.

The coat has square-cut fronts with closely fitting, knee-length tails cut in one with the lower forepart. The collar is stepped, and the lapels faced with silk. Two-piece sleeves are slit at the wrist with three-button fastening and silk piping set into mock cuff seam. The coat is always worn open.

Trousers are slightly narrower in the leg than for contemporary daytime fashions and trimmed with silk braid on outer leg seams.

The single-breasted waistcoat of white piqué with low-cut, curved lapels fastens at centre front with four pearl buttons, with cuff links and shirt studs to match.

White dress shirt with starched front, high stiff collar and white bow tie. Black tie correct only with dinner jacket, which might be worn with soft-pleated shirt front.

Fabrics and colours: Black wool worsted. White piqué.

Shoes and socks: Black patent leather shoes with rounded toes and ribbon bow decoration; black silk lisle socks.

Notes on construction of garments

Woman

Construct bodice foundation of firm silk and bone all seams as indicated by darker lines on pattern. The foundation meets edge to edge at centre back with hook-and-eye closure. It is entirely covered by draped overbodice of two layers of net and chiffon, gathered and held in position with pearls and invisible stitching at side seams. An overlap is required on the right side of the overbodice only, to conceal back fastening. The upper edge is trimmed with velvet ribbon and pearls, in the same fashion as the upper sleeve edge.

Make up sleeve and oversleeve separately, each consisting of a layer of net and chiffon, and ease, as one, into shoulder band of velvet trim.

The overskirt of two layers of net and chiffon is gathered on to the skirt foundation of firmer silk and joined to the bodice, leaving a short opening at centre back. The waist seam is concealed by the velvet belt and the latter secured at centre back. The position of the belt is indicated by dotted lines on bodice pattern.

Pleat ends of sash along broken lines indicated on pattern, before applying to underside of belt at centre front.

Man

Tail coat and trousers should fit closely to the figure — expert cutting and construction are essential to achieve correct proportion and balance.

Make up waistcoat back in cheaper lining fabric with strap and buckle, to enable closer fit at waistline.

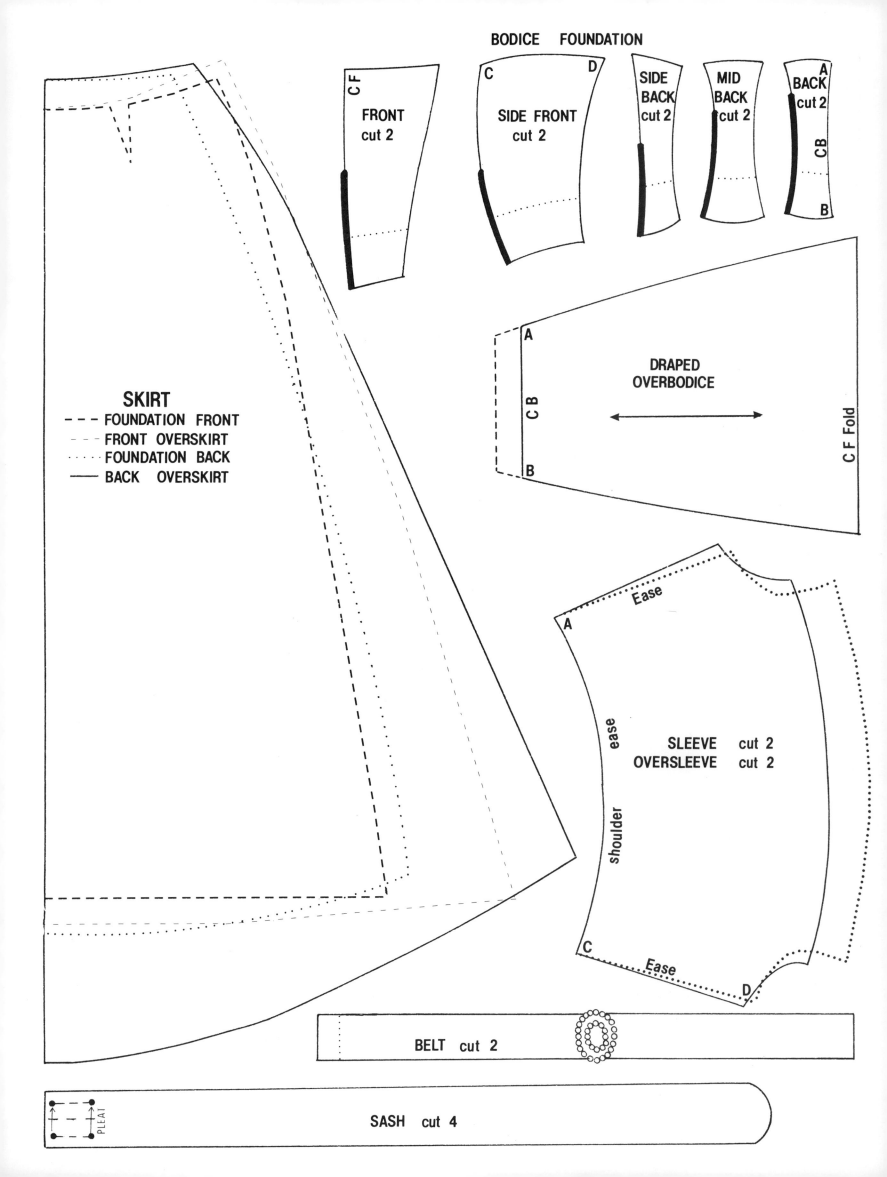

BODICE FOUNDATION

CF
FRONT
cut 2

C   D
SIDE FRONT
cut 2

SIDE
BACK
cut 2

MID
BACK
cut 2

A
BACK
cut 2
CB
B

SKIRT
- - - FOUNDATION FRONT
- - - FRONT OVERSKIRT
.... FOUNDATION BACK
——— BACK OVERSKIRT

A

C B   DRAPED
OVERBODICE

B   C F Fold

Ease

A

ease

shoulder

SLEEVE   cut 2
OVERSLEEVE   cut 2

C
Ease
D

BELT cut 2

PLEAT

SASH cut 4

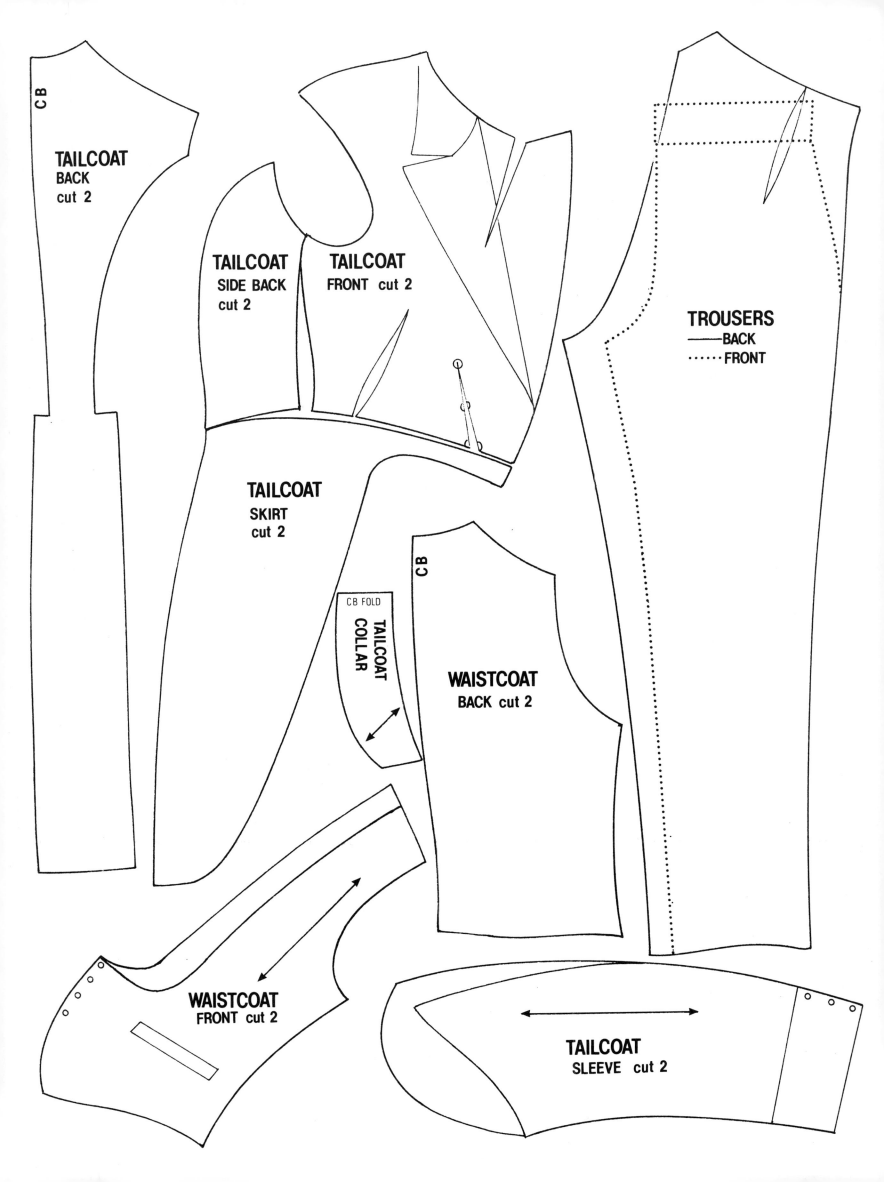

TAILCOAT
BACK
cut 2

CB

TAILCOAT
SIDE BACK
cut 2

TAILCOAT
FRONT cut 2

TROUSERS
——— BACK
········ FRONT

TAILCOAT
SKIRT
cut 2

CB

CB FOLD

TAILCOAT
COLLAR

WAISTCOAT
BACK cut 2

WAISTCOAT
FRONT cut 2

TAILCOAT
SLEEVE cut 2

The Second Decade
1910~1919

1910 witnessed the passing of the Edwardian age, with the death in May of King Edward VII. The new reign of George V, which was to last until 1936, was to be troubled with world war with its unprecedented loss of life, and unemployment on a destructive scale; alongside this, improved technology and the rise of new industry led Britain forward. Fashion was to form part of that industry.

Between 1910 and 1914 many new fashions were introduced, their effect stifled by the declaration of war. Many of the fashions of post-war Britain have been entirely credited to the impact which war itself had on society. We will see that war did have far-reaching effects, but must not distort the true picture by ignoring movements immediately prior to it.

1910 was an important and reactionary year in the history of fashion which witnessed a fundamental change in the female line. The silhouette straightened out completely and women moved from the S- to the I-shape. Skirts narrowed to the extent that they appeared to hug the ankles, the waist slackened, and the bust resumed a normal proportion. The line was essentially tubular, and far removed from the full flowing skirts of the previous decade. The fashions were inspired by oriental art and, more importantly, by the French designer Paul Poiret and the *Ballet Russe*, which toured Europe with a show of vivid and revolutionary costume. The ballet was a riot of colour, with orange, cerise, blues and golds combined in oriental designs. The immediate mode which arose from these fresh influences was the 'harem' skirt, which became the hobble of 1911. The skirt was aptly named, for the narrow hem restricted the movements of the wearer to the extent that the lady could only hobble, or, at least, walk with tiny steps. Many *Punch* cartoons focused on this intriguing and amusing mode, which was considered the height of femininity at the time. A slit was later introduced to give greater freedom, sometimes extending as high as knee level, necessitated particularly by the craze for ragtime dancing towards the middle of the decade. With the narrow skirt, hats remained large and became flatter and wider, reaching the extreme of the fashion by 1912. Every theatre had its notice requesting ladies to remove their hats; with her large cartwheel hat, still laden with excessive trimming, a woman now more accurately resembled the letter T! From 1912 hats became smaller and higher, often in a turban style with single or double plume trimming.

The effect of the tubular look was often heightened by the vogue for using the same fabric throughout the dress, replacing the more usual blouse and skirt. However, the tailored suit, which had been so popular, remained in a looser form, with the walking skirt shortened to just above the ankle, and vibrant colours replaced the traditional blue serge. Over the tubular dress from 1912 a tunic or drape became popular, often combining the use of rich and plain fabrics, or gold for evening wear. Colour in fashion was thus made possible. The tunic line, and more precisely the 'lampshade tunic', which flared out over the clinging dress, became the uniform of fashion until 1914.

With the start of the new look necklines had remained high, but by 1913 the fussy corsage was replaced by the V-shape. The abandonment of the high-necked blouse or bodice brought sharp comment and criticism, which is surprising when we look back at the low *décolletage* of the Edwardian evening gown.

Fashions of the day favoured the younger, slimmer figure, the closer-fitting, sheath-like dress inevitably leading to a fundamental change in the line and embellishment of undergarments. Numerous petticoats became obsolete, for beneath the tight skirt a tubular slip hugged the hips and finished above the ankle. It was no longer considered exciting to show your petticoat, or daring to display an ankle when lifting your skirt to cross a street. The corset retained its straight front but was worn far lower on the female figure, often extending as low as the knees and losing height above. As the corset was now short above the waist, a *cache-corset* often replaced the camisole, which might be boned to give additional support to the large figure. New ribbon straps are surely indicative of the lighter character of lingerie.

By 1914 the male silhouette had changed to the line it was to follow, with slight alterations, throughout the twentieth century. Indeed, the formal male suit has changed very little, although other fashions introduced alongside it can hardly be considered as standardized. Between 1910 and 1914 there were no startling changes. Jackets were generally cut looser and straighter, and trousers wider, sometimes with pleats from the waistband. Since the trousers remained narrow at the hem, this created a kind of peg-top effect. Knitted cardigans were introduced for golf, and shoes were preferred to boots for sports and informal dress by the younger set. For summer a blazer might be worn with flannel trousers, although this was not always considered to be in the best of taste. Moustaches and high collars remained fashionable. With the declaration of war in 1914 the majority of men adopted a uniform – examined more closely in the pattern section.

For women, ostentatious fashion and unnaturally tight corseting appeared to be things of the past. However, the new fashions, freer and healthier, can hardly be attributed to the new woman's search for emancipation, for the fashion of the day restricted the female in a different way, by constricting the legs. Peaceable means had failed to win attention for the cause of women's suffrage. Women smashed windows and chained themselves to railings in order to be imprisoned and gain recognition. In prison the suffragettes continued their cause with hunger-strikes, and in 1912 the movement claimed its first martyr when Emily Davison threw herself in front of the King's horse on Derby Day.

By the outbreak of war the movement seemed no nearer to realizing its aims, and the suffragettes rechannelled their agitation into encouraging women to take part in the national effort. This undoubtedly played an important part in enabling women to exploit opportunities opened to them by war. In May 1915, the shortage of munitions led to the setting up of a special Ministry of Munitions, while a shortage of soldiers led in January 1916 to the conscription of single men, and in May to universal male conscription. The enforced withdrawal of men from the domestic front provided the critical impetus towards full-scale employment of women in all types of jobs.

Expansion of job opportunity was a central phenomenon of women's war work, and, as will become obvious, was fundamental to the changes which took place in fashion, not so much as regards the more obvious aspects of economy and utility in dress, but in relation to a wider view of women's role in society and preconceptions of their capabilities. Few of the women who took up new types of employment during the war, whether as WAACs (Women's Army Auxiliary Corps), conductresses, munitionettes, or land workers, were consciously working for women's rights. Yet simply by doing new jobs and doing them well, they achieved a great deal.

On a purely simplistic level, women's war work illustrated the necessity of adopting functional clothing, at least during working hours. There can be no doubt that in this respect the war was largely responsible for the disappearance of the corset – that is, in the form of a rigid whalebone structure. Before 1914 covered steel had begun to replace whalebone, and a vulcanized rubber foundation garment was introduced with no boning; this was worn universally during the war.

The predominant tunic line of 1914 provided a convenient means to move away from the impractical fashions of the day. The tunic had been considerably lengthened before the war, standing away from the figure over the narrow skirt. The skirt was discarded and the tunic lengthened, resulting in a rather flared skirt which reached below the calf. Worn with high-laced boots, this became the overriding fashion of the war. The fashion world remained dormant over the war years, for a demonstration of wealth was not in keeping with the times. Strategically placed posters were a constant reminder that 'to dress extravagantly in war-time is more than bad form: it is unpatriotic'. Economy was the watchword of the day, with petrol rationing in June 1917 and ration cards issued for meat, sugar, butter and other foodstuffs in 1918. The government set up the Women's Land Army to gain optimum use from our agricultural resources, the recruits assuming a uniform of breeches, smocks and gumboots. A khaki uniform styled on contemporary dress was adopted by the WAACs, formed in 1916. British women joined the armed forces for the first time in history, and although uninvolved in active service, further proved their capabilities and simultaneously strengthened their cause. Women not only demonstrated their adaptability, but, more importantly, were earning on their own account, and thus gained a measure of economic and social freedom. In consequence there was more money available to spend on personal appearance. The average woman was still a long way from social and financial independence, but in the absence of men the war had removed some of the more tiresome constraints. It was during the war that the age-old tradition of the chaperone died. As the *Daily Mail* commented in 1915: 'The war-time business girl is to be seen any night dining out alone . . . Formerly she would never have had her evening meal out unless in the company of a man-friend. But now with money and without men she is more and more beginning to dine out.'

War work not only brought women greater economic and social freedom; it also led to the questioning of their political role. As the time approached for a general election it became more difficult to defend denial of the vote to men with restricted or no voting right before 1914, who were now at the front. The same, said the suffragettes, should apply to the army of female patriots.

It was the consideration of the problems of votes for men which inevitably brought the question of votes for women into full view. The Representation of the People Act, 1918, included women over thirty as well as all males over twenty-one, the age bar on women being on the grounds of their numerical majority in the population. Although the Franchise Reform Act did mark a significant step forwards in the political history of women, the impact of the Act was limited, for it did not enfranchise the younger woman, who, as Graves and Hodges remark, had 'done the hardest and most thankless war work'. With the increased freedom the war had given these women, the fight for political emancipation seemed to recede and assume a secondary importance.

The political and legal story of women's rights is relatively straightforward, with important developments being achieved during this and the following decade. After the General Election of December 1918, when the mainly Conservative coalition government under Lloyd George took office, the Government brought in a Sex Disqualification Act which opened nearly all the public offices and professions to women. It also made clear that there was, in law, no barrier to their full membership of the ancient universities of Oxford and Cambridge. Various other measures of emancipation followed in the twenties.

In the years immediately following the war there were many cross-currents, as if fashion were unsure whether to continue from 1914 or begin again with renewed vigour. The barrel line of 1918 displayed the shortest skirt, six to eight inches from the ground, yet in becoming narrower towards the hem exhibited pre-war characteristics. Other fashions resulted directly from the war: the British Warm and the trenchcoat, practical overcoats for men and women alike. The tubular figure, which was to become the foundation of the nineteen-twenties, originated towards the end of this decade. Women's undergarments now consisted of a shapeless camisole bra and girdle or hip-belt, the bra compressing rather than supporting the breasts. The youthful line predominated; 'Never has the skirt been so youthful and irresponsible in charater,' noted Vogue in 1919.

Dancing was a particularly popular pastime in the period immediately following the First World War, and is often seen as part of the reaction against the restrictions it imposed. Yet, like many other features associated with the high-life of post-war Britain, it was established in the early war years. Dancing gained popularity during the war with troops on leave, and by the end of 1919 many new dance clubs and halls were opened. By the beginning of 1920 jazz was well established, and the dancing mania was a familiar topic in press articles and women's journals.

The type of dancing involved a new closeness and since it called for increased movement inevitably demanded greater freedom of dress. As Vogue commented: 'Now a long skirt and a minuet may go comfortably together, but the dancers of the moment decline with scorn to contemplate any unjust impediments in the shape of superfluous length. And so, of course, nothing was left to the skirt, but to conform.'

In brief, the early years of the decade might be seen as a transitional period, as fashion became less ostentatious and less staid. By 1919, fashion had set the course it was to follow for the next decade. Young men and women who had experienced the harsh realities of war looked forward to enjoying a lighter side of life. The war experience offered a unique opportunity for bringing about changes in the structure of society, evident on a number of levels; not least it precipitated a society in which women were to gain importance socially and economically. Similarly, it provided the essential impetus which accelerated the acceptance of new fashions. The many developments of the war, as will become obvious, not even those directly associated with fashion, emancipated dress in post-war Britain.

1911

Predominant fashion features

Women

The waistline continues to rise and the skirt narrows progressively, achieving a straight, tubular silhouette, advancing quickly towards the hobble skirt. The trend reaches its extreme at first in evening wear, with the legs shackled either with additional bands of fabric or by drawing in the existing skirt hem, at the lower edge or at any point below the knee. Skirt length reaches the instep. Harem skirt, short-lived fashion of full divided skirt drawn in at ankles; worn with overdress — forerunner of the tunic line.

Dresses are now more usually constructed in one piece rather than the previous bodice and skirt, heightening the straight-line effect. Skirts are plainer in comparison to lavish decorations of previous decade. One-piece dresses for summer feature looser bodices with Magyar or kimono sleeves.

A more masculine trend is observable in tailor-mades, with the new longer jacket, plainer, more fitted sleeves with cuffs, loose-waisted and with the walking skirt shortened to the ankle. Other forms include the wrapover, knee-length tunic, fastening at one side, and the Zouave (bolero) jacket and Empire skirt.

Necklines remain high for day wear, lower and often rounded for evening.

Fabrics: Velvet, crêpe, georgette, shantung, satins. Linens for summer frocks.

Woollen facecloth, broadcloth, serge for tailor-mades, commonly striped, worn with Oxford and zephyr shirting fabrics, traditionally masculine.

Undergarments — lighter fabrics: muslin, nainsook, cambric, lawn, batiste, crêpe de Chine. Fine black-and-white stripes or checks.

Colours: Soft colours: pinks, peach, apricot, silver grey, snuff browns.

Decoration: Elaborate braiding and strapping, large decorative buttons. Tassels on evening wear, stoles and to edge jackets. Wide belts and sashes, frequently with tasselled ends.

Undergarments: Slimmer petticoats necessitated by tubular skirt, narrowing towards the ankles. Princess petticoats remain popular, retaining light flouncing at lower edge, and broderie Anglaise and ribbon trim.

Corsets less heavily boned, longer over the hips and shorter above the waist – creating slim hips and freeing the waist and bust to some extent. *Cache-corset* (corset cover) might be boned to give additional support to the fuller figure, often laced at the back.

Hobble gaiters made of braid worn below the knees prevent the lady from taking too long a stride.

Footwear: Boots worn in winter reaching to mid-calf — two-tone with gabardine, kid, or suede tops in light colours. Heels higher and curved or straight.

Coloured gaiters buttoned over patent leather, pointed shoes. Shoes fastened with instep strap, low vamps and court styles.

Stockings: Black for day wear in lisle or cotton; coloured silk for evening. Most fashionable to match the dress with which they are worn.

Hats: Reach extreme in width, creating a top-heavy effect. Exotic trimmings begin to move upwards with decorative satin flowers, wide ribbons, ostrich plumes.

The crown is full, fitting lower on the head. High toques with large satin rosettes.

Hair: Coiffure increasingly simplified and flatter on the crown and sides with centre or side parting. Hair swept backwards, coiled or braided towards the back of the head.

Accessories: All large. Long, broad stoles in fur or black satin, tasselled ends.

Velvet, suede or tapestry handbags with clasp or flap closure and long cord straps.

Day gloves wrist length.

Longer jewelled hatpins with butt to protect sharp point. Long bead necklaces.

Movement: Restricted by narrowness of skirt at ankle, causing women to move with tiny steps – to hobble. The body assumes an upright position with the head held high to balance the large hat.

Men

Similar to previous fashion, with three-piece lounge suit increasingly popular for day wear. Frock and morning coats still worn by older gentlemen, harking back to the Edwardian era. Trousers reach to the instep, or ankle length when worn with turn-ups.

Overcoats — previous styles continue; chesterfields, ulsters, raglan. Loose-fitting single-breasted sack coat to mid-calf.

Evening — dinner jackets/tail coats and dress coats with white piqué waistcoat, occasionally black waistcoat with black dinner jacket. Trousers match jackets, with no turn-ups, and with braiding on outer leg seam.

Fabrics and colours: Similar to previous decade — flannel, worsted suitings, coarser tweeds, herringbones for sport and country.

Finely striped shirting fabrics.

Undergarments: Shirts continue to be classed as undergarments, never exposed when ladies are present, except for the specially prepared front. Starched front of formal white shirt shortened significantly, worn with wing or double collar, now approximately 5 cm (2 in.) in height. Striped shirts popular with white linen collars and cuffs. Dress shirt worn with full evening dress, with pleated front and wing collar most common; square cuffs. Vests with long or short sleeves, drawers, pants and combinations.

Footwear: Shoes more usual than boots for younger gentleman. Light-coloured cloth or suede spats.

Socks: Lighter in weight, of thinner wools and cotton. Available in a variety of colours for wearing with shoes.

Hats: Similar to previous decade.

Hair: Side-parting remains popular, slightly fuller and brushed back from the hairline. Short clipped or walrus moustaches, waxed for stiffness.

Accessories: Similar to previous decade, tightly rolled umbrellas, walking sticks.

Movement: Similar to previous fashion.

Details of illustrated patterns

Woman

Straight-line costume consisting of double-breasted, panelled jacket with low eight-button fastening, set on decorative contrast braiding. Broad lapels are also edged with contrast braid, and set-in sleeves narrow at the wrist with mock button fastening. This decoration is also employed in centre back panel.

The ankle-length corselet skirt extends above the natural waistline and is constructed in six panels, with the lower side skirt pleated to the hemline. Button and braid trimming unifies the skirt and jacket.

Lace blouse with high, stiffened collar, centre back fastening and jabot front.

Fabrics: Fine woollen tweed, facecloth.

Colours: Grey and white, soft browns.

Hat: Large-brimmed hat lavishly trimmed with black lace, grosgrain ribbon and ostrich feathers.

Man

Single-breasted morning coat with fronts cut well away from the stomach and tails ending at the knee. The waist is cut on the short side with medium skirt room over the hips. Low lapels roll from two-button fastening, with notched collar and buttonhole on left lapel. Two-piece sleeves are finished with turn-back cuff and slit fastening with three buttons. Cuffs and coat edges are braided or ribbon bound. Back vents with pleats end at the waist with buttons. Pockets may be included in the pleats as well as a breast pocket and inside ticket pocket.

The single-breasted waistcoat may match the coat, or be made in contrast fabric.

The outfit is most frequently worn with striped trousers, without turn-ups.

Fabrics: Wool worsted.

Colours: Shades of grey – dark for more formal occasions and winter, light for summer.

Undergarments: Soft-fronted tunic-style shirt with starched wing collar and cuffs.

Shoes: Black leather Oxford shoes with light-coloured spats.

Hats: Top hat correct with morning coat.

Accessories: Four-in-hand or Ascot tie. Handkerchief in breast pocket for decoration only.

Notes on construction of garments

Woman

Pad jacket softly over chest and shoulders and stiffen collar, front and cuffs. Trim lapel edges with flat silk braid.

Skirt – construct concealed placket at left side seam. Bone all seams for 19 cm (7½ in.) from top. Expand lower side skirt panel to form horizontal pleats to hemline.

Petticoat – adapt foundation skirts from skirt pattern.

Man

Use back waistcoat pattern from 1908.

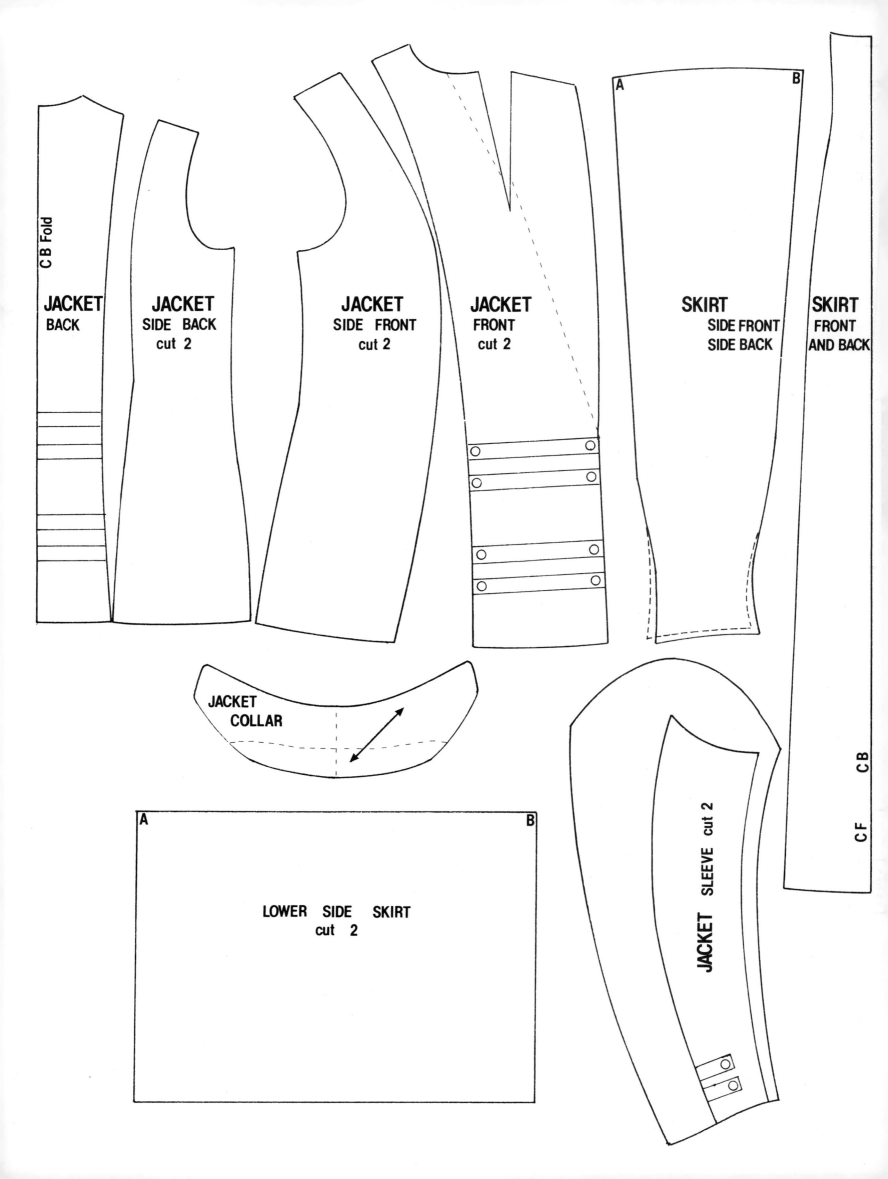

CB Fold

JACKET
BACK

JACKET
SIDE BACK
cut 2

JACKET
SIDE FRONT
cut 2

JACKET
FRONT
cut 2

A   B

SKIRT
SIDE FRONT
SIDE BACK

SKIRT
FRONT
AND BACK

JACKET
COLLAR

CF   CB

A   B

LOWER SIDE SKIRT
cut 2

JACKET SLEEVE cut 2

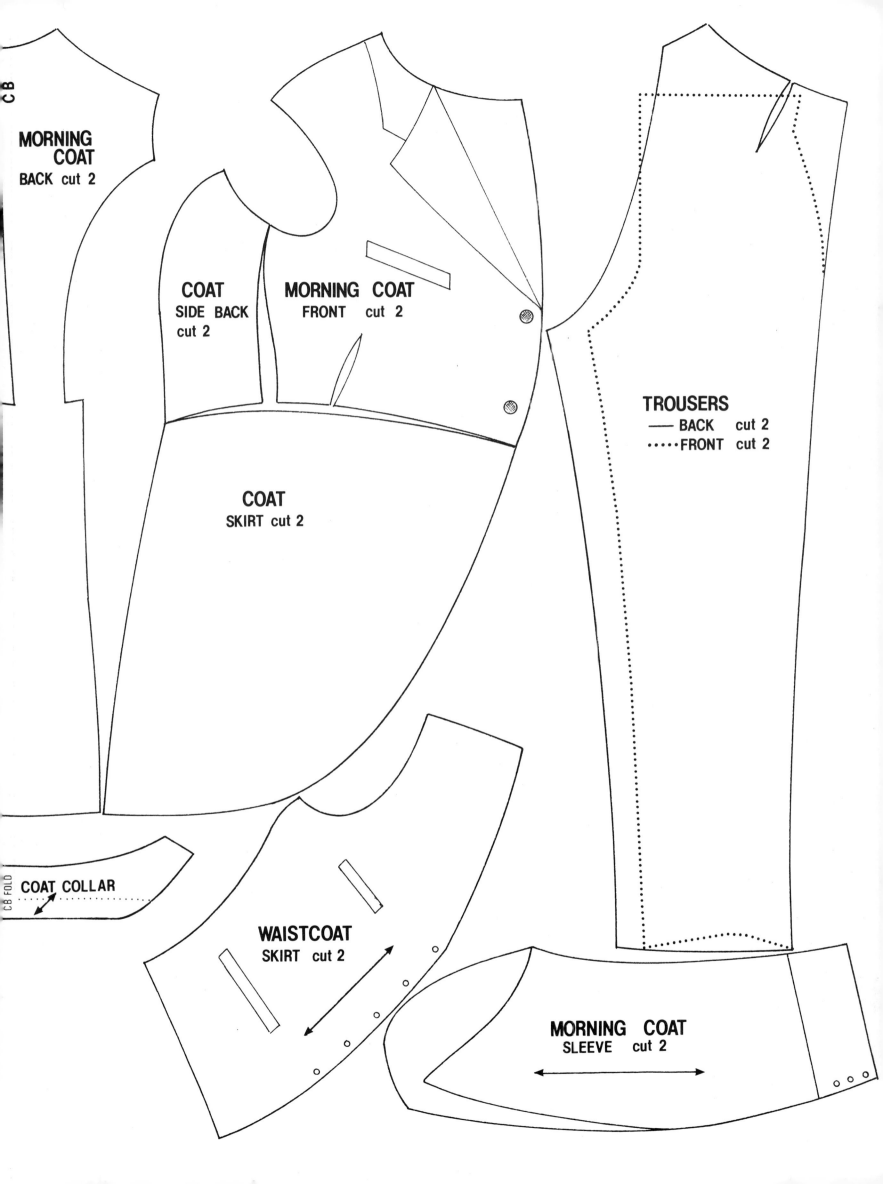

CB

MORNING
COAT
BACK cut 2

COAT
SIDE BACK
cut 2

MORNING COAT
FRONT   cut 2

COAT
SKIRT cut 2

TROUSERS
—— BACK   cut 2
······ FRONT cut 2

CB FOLD

COAT COLLAR

WAISTCOAT
SKIRT cut 2

MORNING COAT
SLEEVE cut 2

1914

Predominant fashion features

Women

Pre-war hobble skirt, narrow to the ankle, incorporating side slits or buttons which might be left undone. Peg-top – i.e. with fullness at the waist – worn with cut-away coats.

Tailor-mades are short-waisted with Magyar or kimono sleeves cut in one with the bodice, evidence of a looser fit. The vogue for wrapover styles, buttoning to the left, continues. The tailor-made is sometimes worn with fancy waistcoat of brocade or moiré silk.

Tunic styles predominate. Necklines drop dramatically with the new V- or U-shapes and softer flat or roll collars.

All blouses feature the new open front with large limp or Medici collar (standing high at the back of the neck), and stand-up frills of tulle to edge a plain neckline.

Afternoon and evening dresses commonly feature overdraping tunics, combining rich and plain fabrics, and skirt split almost to the knee for dancing.

Décolletage at the back of dancing dresses is extreme, cut to the waist at times.

From 1915, due largely to the impact of war, skirts become fuller and shorter, approximately 20 cm (8 in.) from the ground. This is partly achieved by abolishing the underskirt and retaining the tunic, which had become fuller and longer prior to 1914 – the 'lampshade tunic'.

Skirts become progressively shorter during the war – 25 cm (10 in.) from the ground in 1917; they are worn with calf-length laced boots and dark-coloured cotton or wool stockings, white in summer. Jackets are looser, too, cut in military style with large patch pockets. Hair is drawn into a loose bun or coil at the back of the neck.

Fabrics: Crêpe de Chine, chiffon, georgette, brocades, firm satins. The vogue for striped fabrics continues.

Evening wear – plain or embroidered brocades, satins, silk, tulle, lace, charmeuse, marquisette.

Serge, broadcloth, hopsack for tailor-mades.

Undergarments – crêpe de Chine, cambric, broderie Anglaise, ninon. Underskirts in satin, taffeta, moirette.

Colours: Brighter colours – cerise, orange, yellow, bright blue, emerald. Coloured underskirts – scarlet, navy, purple, blue.

Decoration: Fur and velvet trimmings on cuffs, collars, pockets and jacket edges.

Ribbon, embroidery, decorative buttons on sides and hem of skirts and jackets. Much draping of fabrics.

Bead fringing, tassels, satin sashes with large bows and flowers for evening.

Undergarments: 'Princess' petticoats in Empire style continue, tubular and flounced or pleated from the knee. Hobble petticoats grip the knees. Waist-length petticoats (underskirts).

Harem-style petticoats for dancing consist of two wide legs, fastened with button and loop to one side of the split skirt.

Rubber-coated steel or celluloid replacing whalebone to stiffen corsets, which continue short above the waist and long below.

Camisoles with fine ribbon straps. French knickers with wider frilled legs or *Directoire* knickers, drawn into bands at the knee. Modesty vests fill in low V-neckline.

Footwear: Shoes laced or buckled, with higher, straighter heels, pointed toes and bar-and-button closure. Stitching decoration, buckles, ribbon bows and punched designs on court shoes. Elastic used to achieve higher, closer fit. Coloured shoes, matching the outfit, are fashionable.

For dancing, satin slippers with ribbon ties.

Stockings: Similar to previous fashion.

Hats: Smaller, with higher crowns and narrower brims popular in turban style with single-plume trim, wired vertically or backwards. High toques, berets, tam o'shanters in straw, velvet, furs.

Hair: Dressed higher on the crown with soft curls falling on to the face. For evening, hair decorated with wired feather decorations fastened to velvet or jewelled bandeaux.

Accessories: Gloves – long to elbow for day or evening wear with short sleeves, gathered from the wrist upwards for evening – in kid, buckskin and silk in light colours; white for evening.

Large black fox muffs and stoles. New dyes for other furs; coney and sealskin increase their use in fashion.

Oriental influence brings fringed silk sunshades and silk fans in bright colours.

Movement: Walking remains restricted due to narrowness of skirts at ankle.

Men

Major change is in cut of trousers, worn clean-fitting about the waist with ample ease over the seat, created by pleating from the waistband, from which the legs taper to more or less peg-top form. Average size for knee and bottom 48.25 cm (19 in.) and 40.5 cm (16 in.) respectively, with deep turn-ups. Trousers made with waistbands eliminate the need for braces.

Jackets to lounge suits also more generously cut, with wider shoulders and deep-cut armhole.

Single-breasted lounge jackets more usual.

Fabrics: As previous fashion, black-and-white check very popular, and black-and-white check silk neckwear.

Colours: Grey browns, soft browns, snuff and tobacco, subdued greens for sports and country; black and white.

Undergarments: Soft-fronted, coloured tunic shirt with soft, detachable collar, sometimes matching, provides practical alternative for more casual wear, especially in summer. Collar height continues to decrease. Underwear similar to previous fashion.

Shoes: Similar to previous fashion.

Socks: Similar to previous fashion.

Hats: Previous styles continue; slightly wider brims.

Hair: Similar to previous fashion.

Accessories: Similar to previous fashion.

Movement: More relaxed poise in comparison to Edwardian era. Heads held less rigidly with lower collars.

Details of illustrated patterns

Woman

Finger-length tunic-style jacket with V-neckline, cutaway skirt and button and rouleau trim at centre front fastening. The jacket is gathered at sides and held in at raised waistline with attached three-quarter belt.

Sleeves cut on kimono pattern fit snugly over elbow, flaring at the wrist with pleated inset and finished with button and rouleau loop.

Side-fastening ankle-length hobble skirt narrows towards the hemline, with two unstitched pleats at centre front seam for draped effect.

Blouse – full-length kimono sleeve, fitting tightly from elbow to cuff. Medici collar with low V-opening and pearl button fastening.

Toque of stiffened faille worn straight on head and decorated with single wired ostrich plume and jewelled trim.

Man

Single-breasted lounge suit with three-button fastening, squared lapels and curved lower edges. Two-piece sleeves slit at the wrist with three-buttons and slit cuff. Flap pockets at hip level and left breast pocket. The jacket is cut with centre back seam and vent and with ample length to cover the seat.

Peg-top trousers, pleated into front waistband, with ample ease over the hips and upper thighs, narrowing to the instep with turn-ups. Sharp centre crease.

Waistcoat – single-breasted with V-opening and six-button fastening; the last button is usually worn undone. Two welt pockets at waist level and breast pocket at left side only.

Fabrics: Tweed.

Colours: Black or grey and white.

Undergarments: Tunic-style shirt with detachable starched square cuffs and polo collar.

Shoes: Black leather Oxford shoes with light-coloured felt spats.

Hat: Felt Homburg.

Accessories: Four-in-hand tie; handkerchief in breast pocket with double points showing; grey buckskin gloves, gauntlet style.

Notes on construction of garments

Woman

Jacket – slit jacket front from **A** to **B** and gather upper section to fit; stitch with narrow seam. Cover seam with belt, attach with single button either end and catch at side seams.

Narrow hem and accordion-pleat sleeve inset along broken lines indicated on pattern; a seam allowance of 1 cm (⅜ in.) is recommended. Slit jacket sleeve from **C** to **D** and attach inset using 1 cm (⅜ in.) tapered seam (dotted line). Finish with button and rouleau loop trim.

Skirt – add placket at left side seam for opening.

Man

Use back waistcoat pattern from 1908. Add vent to centre back of jacket.

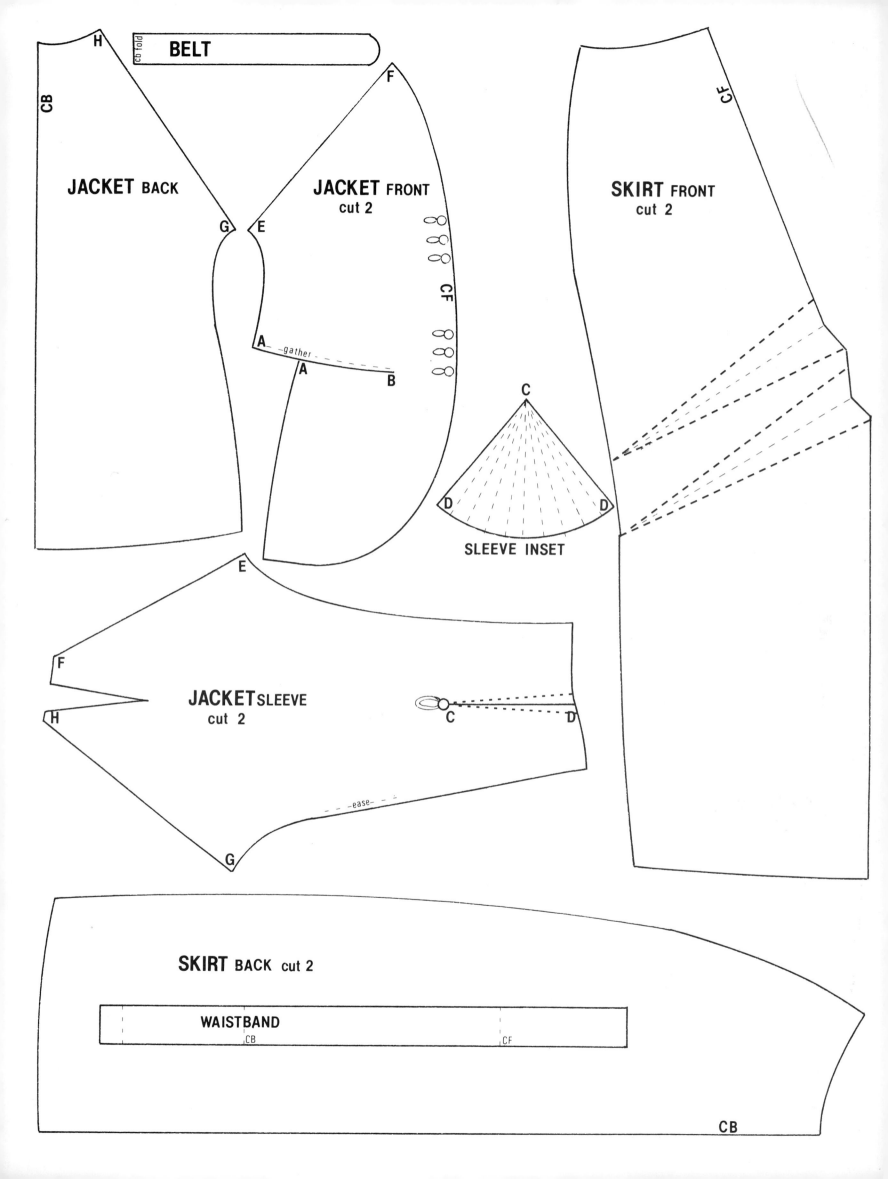

BELT

JACKET BACK

JACKET FRONT
cut 2

CB

H

CF

A _gather_ A B

G E

E

SKIRT FRONT
cut 2

CF

C

D D

SLEEVE INSET

F

H

JACKET SLEEVE
cut 2

ease

G

C D

CB

SKIRT BACK cut 2

WAISTBAND

CB CF

CB

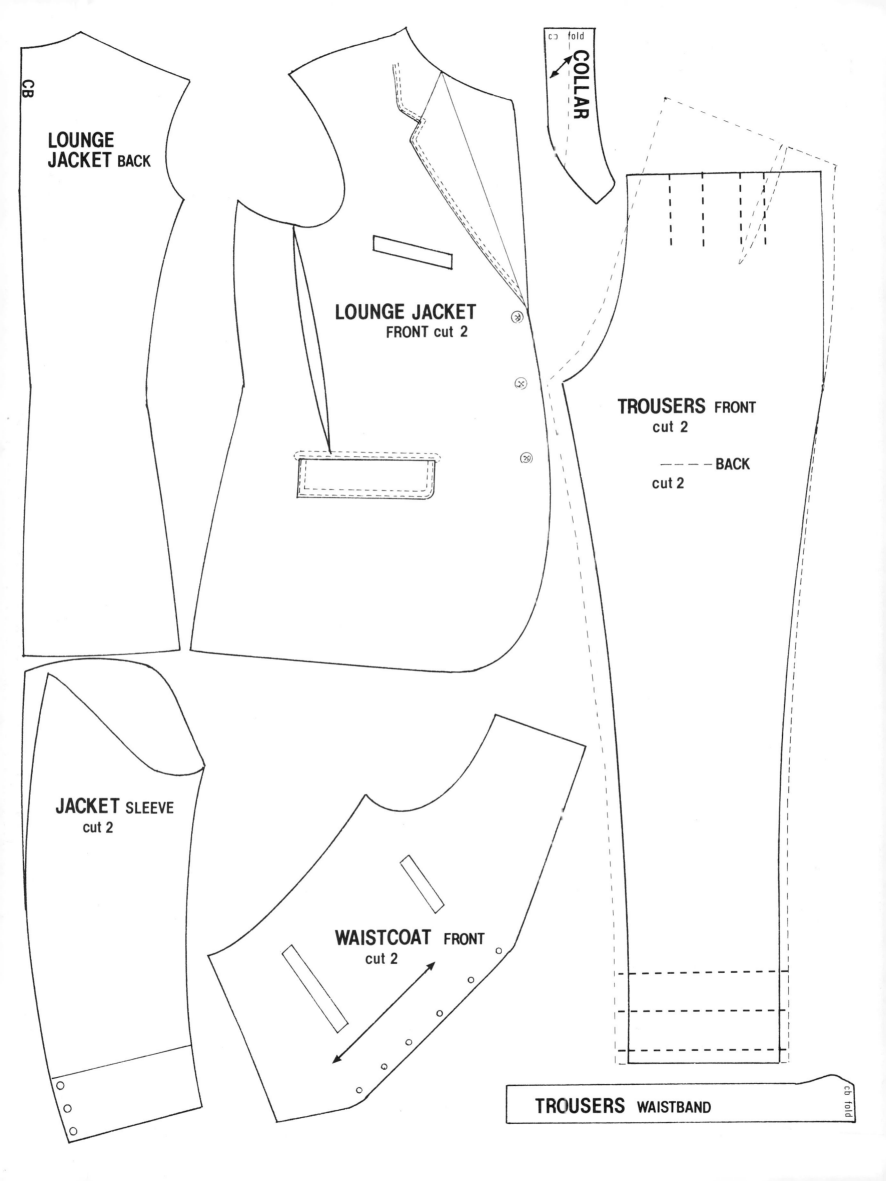

LOUNGE JACKET BACK

CB

LOUNGE JACKET
FRONT cut 2

COLLAR

cb fold

TROUSERS FRONT
cut 2

— — — **BACK**
cut 2

JACKET SLEEVE
cut 2

WAISTCOAT FRONT
cut 2

TROUSERS WAISTBAND

cb fold

1917

Details of illustrated patterns

Note: Imperial measurements precede metric equivalents in the case of war uniforms, as they relate to exact specifications laid down by the War Office.

Woman

Officer's uniform, WAAC (Women's Army Auxiliary Corps), formed December 1916.

Military-style loose-fitting jacket buttons to left and features step-collar front, three 1 in. (2.5 cm) military brass buttons and detachable belt of matching fabric. Shoulder straps carrying badges of rank fasten in the scye at the shoulder and button at the neck. WAAC badge in gilt metal is worn on the collar. Unstitched pleats at front and back of tunic are held in position at the waistline with buttons and fastened to buttonholes on belt. Expanding pockets of cross fabric below the waist 6½ in. (16.5 cm) wide at the top and 9¼ in. (23.5 cm) at the bottom, 2¼ in. (5.75 cm) deep flap fastened with a small brass button. Two-piece fitted sleeves with two-button mock fastening and braid insignia of rank stitched on top sleeve.

Skirt – moderately full, often made up in different fabric to jacket, features full-length centre front 2 in. (5 cm) stitched tuck, concealing opening at top. The skirt is gathered into the waistband at the back. Side seam pockets have flaps extending over back skirt.

Fabric: Jacket and skirt – khaki (military term is 'drab') serge, facecloth, or drill. Silk lining to match colour of cloth for jacket.

Shirt – khaki Viyella or plain cotton.

Undergarments: Khaki Viyella shirt and tie. The shirt is cut in male tunic style with detachable collar, shoulder yoke and back tucks.

Hat: Pudding-basin-style velour hat with soft brim 2¼ in. wide (5.75 cm). Metal badge worn at front.

Shoes and stockings: Black woollen stockings; laced leather boots.

Gloves: Brown or black leather.

Man

(Standard pattern of garment worn by all officers of the British Army.)

Length of jacket skirt 13 in. (33 cm) varies in proportion to height. Step-collar front fastens with four buttons of regimental pattern. Two breast patch pockets, 6 in. (15.25 cm) wide at top and 7 in. (17.75 cm) deep to top of flap, to fasten with small button. Two expanding pockets below waist 10½ in. (26.75 cm) at top, and 11½ in. (29.25 cm) at the bottom, 9¼ in. (23.5 cm) to top of pocket under flap, also fastened with small button. Shoulder strap on shoulder seam to carry badges of rank. Two-piece sleeve and shaped shoulder yoke. Fitted waistbelt 2 in. (5 cm) wide.

Breeches – leather reinforcement on inside legs, concealed front-fly button opening. Waistband buttoned at top edge to attach braces. Six-eyelet fastening at lower edge.

Fabric: Jacket – khaki drill, serge, or facecloth. Silk lining to match jacket.

Breeches in khaki cavalry twill or Bedford cord in lighter shade than jacket.

Shirt – heavy cotton or Viyella khaki.

Underclothes: Tunic-style khaki shirt in heavy cotton or Viyella with shoulder yoke, detachable collar, tails and shaped cuff. Pleated box front and tucks into back yoke.

Cap: Peaked cap with stiffened top and piped edge; top 10½ in. (26.75 cm) diameter, 2 in. (5 cm) stand, 2¼ in. (5.75 cm) peak; leather chin strap.

Belt: Sam Brown leather belt and straps.

Footwear: Close-fitting brown leather boots with 1 in. (2.5 cm) heel, 18 in. (45.75 cm) in height, with pull-on tabs.

Gloves: Leather gauntlet style.

Notes on construction of garments

Woman

Expanding pockets and flap of jacket, flap of skirt and waistband, cut on cross fabric.

Inner skirt band of boned 2½ in. (6.25 cm) petersham, two-hook-and-eye closure.

Skirt pocket bag indicated by dotted line.

Add 4 in. (10.25 cm) to centre front of right skirt to form stitched tuck. Leave open above small dot for opening to fasten with five large press studs.

2 in. (5 cm) hem stitched through front skirt. Length of skirt 32 in. (81.25 cm).

Man

Use plain seams throughout.

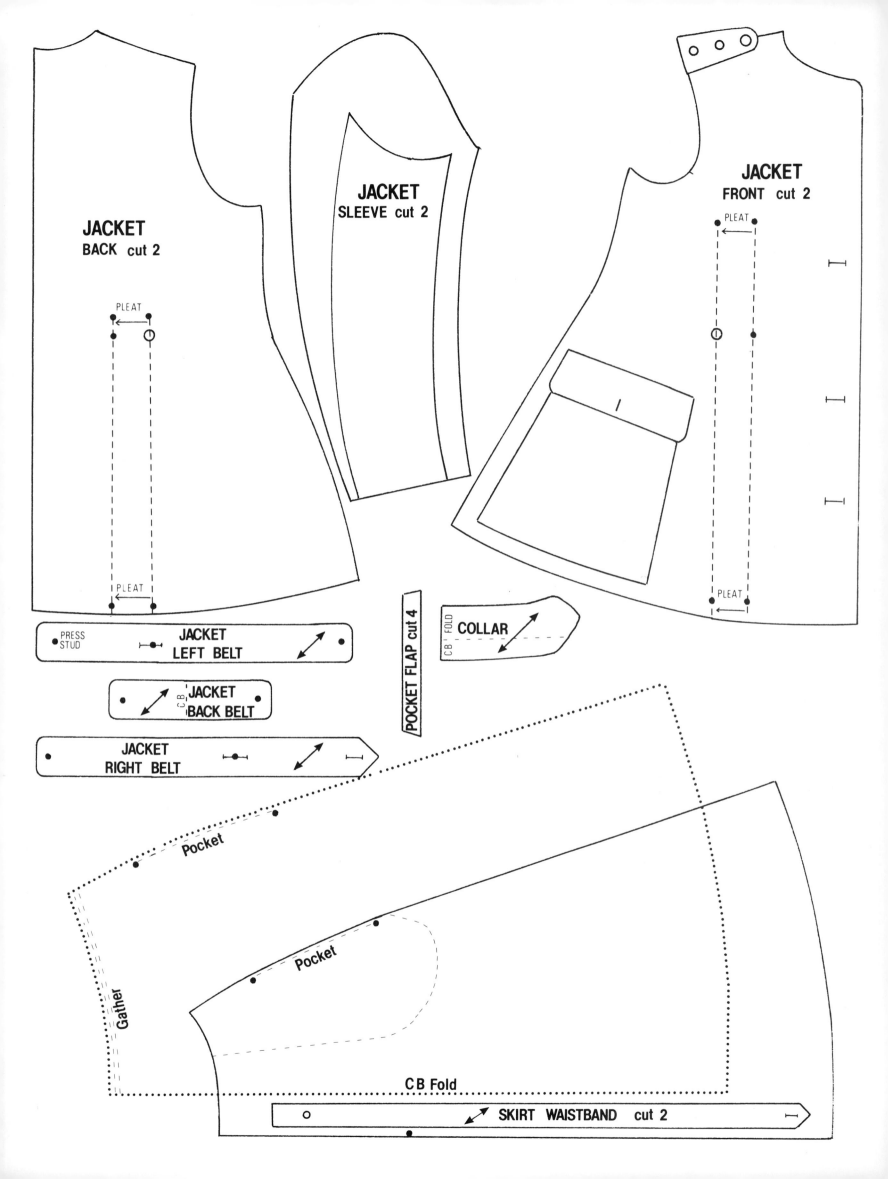

JACKET
BACK cut 2

PLEAT

JACKET
SLEEVE cut 2

JACKET
FRONT cut 2

PLEAT

PLEAT

PLEAT

PRESS
STUD

JACKET
LEFT BELT

C.B. JACKET
BACK BELT

JACKET
RIGHT BELT

POCKET FLAP cut 4

C.B. FOLD COLLAR

Pocket

Pocket

Gather

CB Fold

SKIRT WAISTBAND cut 2

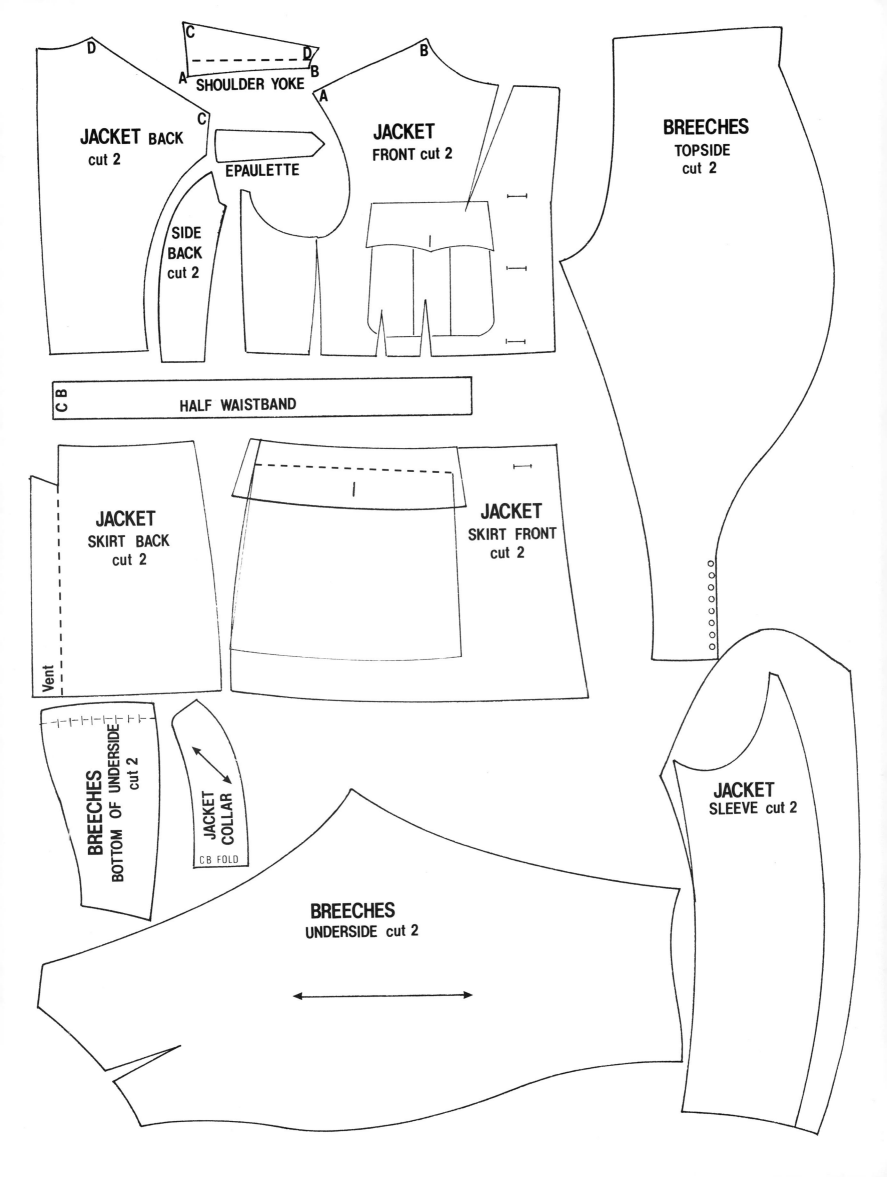

1918

Predominant fashion features

Women

With the end of the war skirts lengthen once again, 15 – 20 cm (6–8 in.) from the ground. The barrel line, curving towards the skirt hem, is reminiscent of the pre-war hobble skirt. The most significant feature is the absence of the 'figure'; the waistline is not emphasized, is usually high and never pulled in tightly. Garments are loose and easy-fitting. 'The silhouette. . . is not sternly masculine, it is boyish. Indeed with straight, waistless garments for day wear, slim women look more like their own sons than anything else.' (Women's Wear Fashion, 14 November 1918)

Ready-to-wear begins to emerge more forcibly after the war with the coat frock, the first real ready-to-wear garment, which had been adapted as a practical alternative to the coat and skirt during the war; V- or square neck. Long pleats and outside pockets are characteristic.

Costume coats worn with plain, narrow skirt and waistcoat. Blouses loose-fitting with deep V-neckline, often pouched into the skirt waistband. Jerseys worn over the skirt. Sailor collars popular.

Outdoor garments – overcoats follow barrel line. British Warm and trenchcoat adapted for civilian use from war-time, loose-fitting with deep collar, revers, large pockets and belt.

Fabrics: Gabardine, Melton cloth for overcoats. Artifical silk, wool or silk stockinette for jerseys. Bedford cord suitings, check suitings, overcheck tweeds.

Colours: Soft and subdued maize, soft greys, fawn, cream, black, navy and white.

For evening – brighter colours – rose pink, saxe blue.

Decoration: Top-stitching on panel seams, sparse embroidery, tassels, sash or drapery essential with evening dress.

Undergarments: Corsets continue long over the hips and short above the waist, lightly boned with little constriction at the waist. Petticoats simpler, in princess-style trimmed with lace and ribbon. Shapeless camisole bra and girdle or hip-belt, suppressing rather than supporting the bust. Cami-knickers.

Footwear: Boots with cloth top, fastened with laces or buttons, cover the calf completely, the top of the boots covered by the skirt. High, straight heel, 5–7 cm (2–2¾ in.). Pointed shoes with high vamp. Leather brogues for informal day or sports wear.

Stockings: Black cotton or woollen hose for winter, white silk for summer.

Hats: Tricorne, toques, berets, also wide-brimmed hats with little trimming, fitting low on the head – cloth, soft felt, velour.

Hair: Coiffure continues to be drawn to the back of the head with bun or coil worn low on the crown. Hair is more tightly waved and 'bobbed' by the younger woman.

Accessories: Gloves – long, white silk or buckskin for evening, fastening with buttons. Gauntlet-style for day, knitted for winter. Leather handbags, clasp fastening.

Movement: Relaxed and natural.

Men

Lounge suit established as ordinary day wear, cut slightly shorter, with centre back vent and seam. Single-breasted styles more usual with 2–4 buttons. Jackets are shaped into the waist with darts. Piped or bound (jetted) pockets replace flaps.

Waistcoats now made up in same fabric as the suit, with the back in lining fabric with adjustable half-belt and buckle.

Trousers wider in the leg although still narrower at hem than knees, without turn-ups and retaining pleats into the waistband.

Light flannel suits for informal wear.

Overcoats – British Warm and trenchcoat adapted for civilian use and cut on lines of officer's greatcoat: loose-fitting, double-breasted, with additional flap-yoke over the shoulders and belted. Raglan coats in rubber or waterproofed materials, fly fronts. Ulsters made in thicker, warmer fabrics, looser-fitting, with full or half-belt.

Fabrics: Suiting fabrics similar to previous fashion: flannel, alpaca, worsteds, wool and silk mixture fabrics. Melton cloth for British Warm.

Colours: Black or dark grey suitings (for business lounge-suits). Camel or fawn for British Warm and overcoats. Lighter colours, grey and buff for light flannel suits.

Undergarments: Shirts similar to styles of 1914; also underwear.

Footwear: Laced leather brogues in brown or black. Oxford-style lace-up shoes with more pointed toes, worn by younger gentlemen. Older gentlemen favour boots with suede or cloth tops, covering the ankle.

Socks: Brightly coloured for wearing with shoes, sometimes striped.

Hats: Less worn by younger men. Bowler, trilby, and Homburg most popular hat styles.

Hair: Centre-parting again popular, with hair combed back. Brilliantine hair ointment gives smooth, silky look.

Accessories: Long ties with knot, known as four-in-hand. Gloves, gauntlet style with button fastening. Silver and gold tie pins, and cuff links. Walking sticks less fashionable. Wrist watches, worn before the war, now more common.

Movement: More relaxed, although some retaining military stance.

Details of illustrated patterns

Woman

Loose-fitting top coat with wide lapels rolling from raised waistline, single-breasted centre front button fastening and attached belt. Shaped panel seams at back and front incorporate deep pockets at side front, accentuating the hips. Two-piece, set-in sleeves fasten at slit cuff with single button. Coat hemline is stitched through to right side, finishing 10.25 cm (4 in.) above skirt hemline.

Barrel-line skirt reaching to lower calf in four panels, worn 19 cm (7½ in.) from the ground.

The outfit is worn with soft-collared, loose-fitting shirt and tie.

Fabrics: Coat in heavyweight gabardine; skirt – medium-weight twill wool.

Colours: Soft browns, fawn.

Hat: Straw, deep crown trimmed with grosgrain ribbon and shaped brim, worn straight on head.

Man

Knee-length raglan raincoat falls loosely from the shoulders with split sleeve and button and flap trim at cuff; high-fastening neckband, fly front and slit welt pockets, allowing the hands to reach inside trouser pockets.

Centre back seam and vent allows for easy movement.

Fabric: Rubberized or waterproofed gabardine.

Footwear: Low, laced brown calfskin boots, knee-length cloth leggings, buttoning over instep.

Hat: Felt trilby with down-turned brim.

Notes on construction of garments

Woman

Cut coat pattern along solid lines to separate side back and back pattern pieces. Separate side front and front in the same manner; the inserted pocket may be cut grown-on to the side front and stitched through to right side of fabric. Fine broken lines indicate position of belt. Ease back to front at shoulder seam. 5 cm (2 in.) hem is stitched through to right side.

Skirt – form concealed placket opening in left side seam.

Man

Add vent to centre back of coat, 5 cm (2 in.) wide and 50.75 cm (20 in.) from hemline.

Add fly strap to left coat front to conceal buttons and buttonholes.

Slit welt pockets in lining fabric, to allow access to trouser pockets when worn.

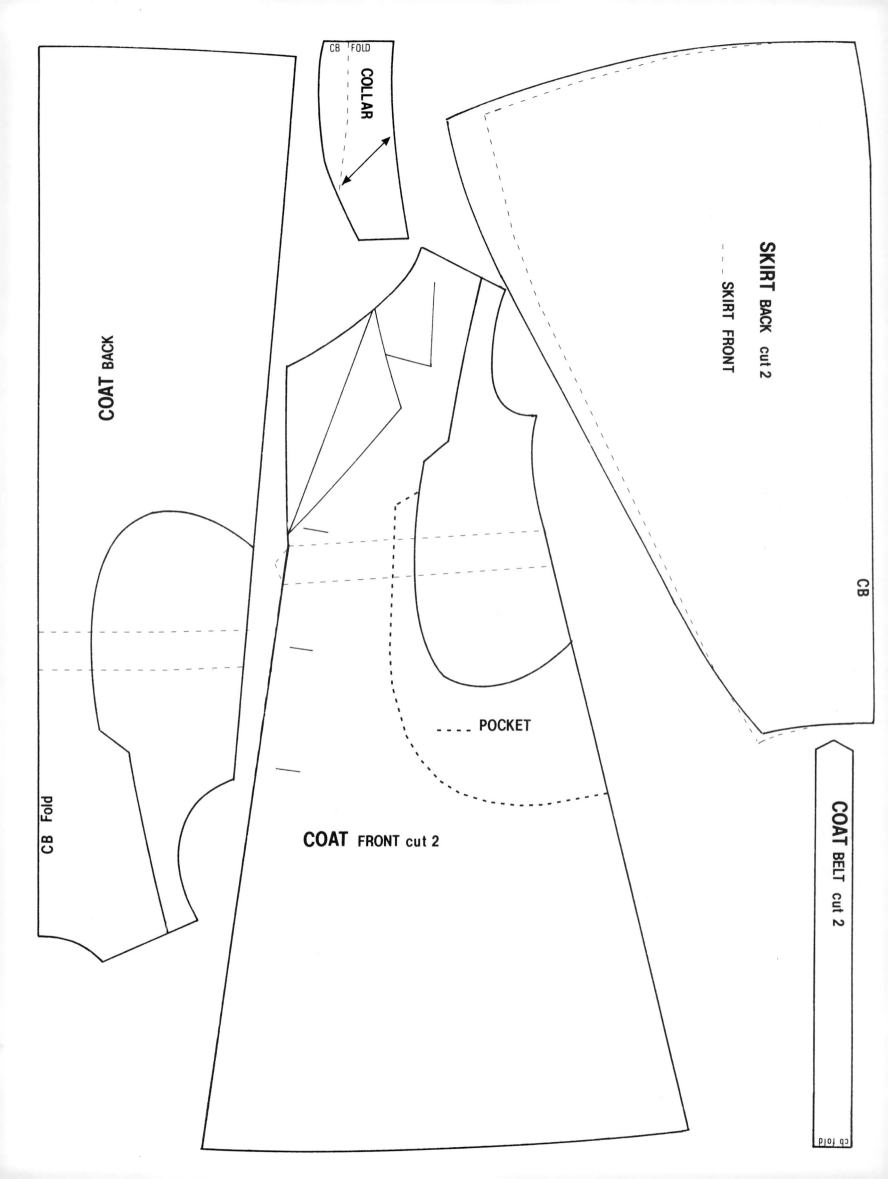

COLLAR

CB FOLD

SKIRT BACK cut 2

SKIRT FRONT

CB

COAT BACK

COAT FRONT cut 2

POCKET

CB Fold

COAT BELT cut 2

cb fold

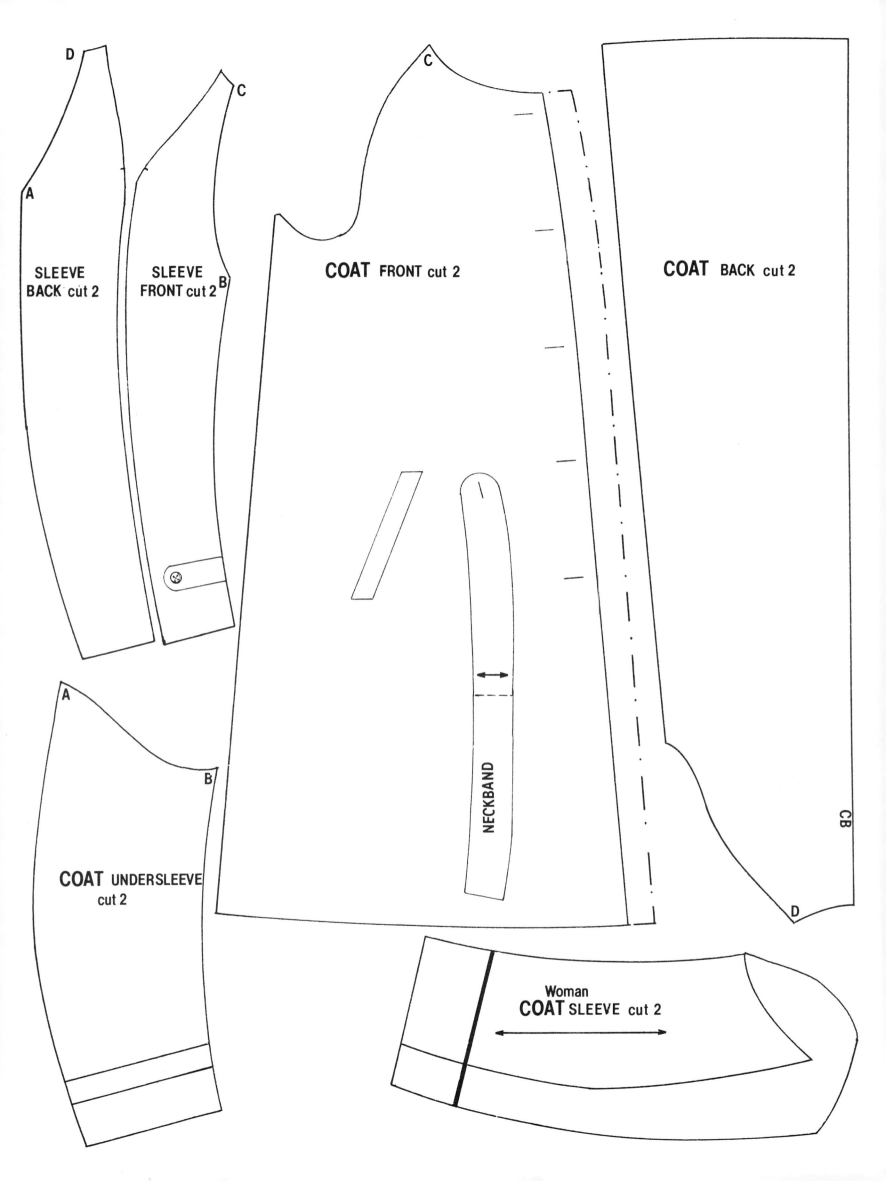

SLEEVE
BACK cut 2

SLEEVE
FRONT cut 2

D

A

C

B

COAT FRONT cut 2

COAT BACK cut 2

C

D

CB

NECKBAND

COAT UNDERSLEEVE
cut 2

A

B

Woman
COAT SLEEVE cut 2

1919

Predominant fashion features

Women

The slim silhouette with straighter line for day wear and slightly longer skirts, frequently pleated, especially for sports, with flannel blazer or jacket.

One-piece frocks increasingly popular, with loosely accentuated waist. Hips are emphasized with gathers, drapery or sashes in all forms of fashion. Shorter sleeves for summer.

Evening dresses flimsy in character, retaining the barrel line, wide over the hips and drawn in above the ankle. *Décolletage* is frequently horizontal, with fine bodice straps, and a sash of contrast or matching fabric often drawn over the shoulder and falling to the floor at the back, creating the effect of a train. Diaphanous bodices open to the waist at the front and back of the dress, over a straight-cut underbodice, with high-waisted sash.

Outdoor garments – barrel line retained for coats, large patch pockets emphasizing the hips.

Fabrics: For evening crêpe de Chine, crêpe georgette, printed chiffon taffeta, satin charmeuse, voiles, foulards, velvet. Diaphanous, semi-transparent fabrics combined with satins, brocades, etc.

Striped silks, ninon, zephyrs in checks, stripes and plain colours. Serge, tweeds, merino.

Colours: Soft, subdued tones – salmon pinks, coffee, navy, putty, amethyst, sky blue, emerald, saxe, soft greys; silver and gold lamé. Brighter colours for evening – fuchsia, violet, lace pink.

Decoration: Evening dresses fringed for dancing – ostrich, swansdown and beaded edgings, velvet ribbons, silk tassels. Gold embroidery. Satin and chiffon sashes or drapery, tasselled and hanging to the front, sides or back, are essential to the evening dress.

Undergarments: Petticoats straight-hanging with flounce at lower edge.

Knitted 'undies' in silk tricot, elastic-waisted. Satin underskirts. Dainty lawn chemise and knickers decorated with tucks and trimmed with broderie Anglaise lace and narrow ribbon. Lightly boned or woven elastic corsets enclose entire torso, with suspenders and straps, little constriction at the waist.

Shapeless camisole bra and girdle or hip belt, suppressing rather than supporting or emphasizing the bust.

Shoes: Pointed toes, high heels with jewelled buckle trim or strap fastening. Black patent for day.

Stockings: Black usual for day wear, silk or artificial silk, matching the dress for evening.

Hats: Wider at the sides, with turned-down brims, worn low on the head. Pleated tulle, ostrich feather (glycerined to ensure the correct droop), ribbons and veils. Soft 'pudding-basin' styles.

Hair: Tightly waved, drawn forward on the forehead and cheeks in curls. For evening the hair is often drawn to the back of the head and held with combs.

Accessories: Long, buttoned gloves for evening, light-coloured in silk or buckskin. Small handbags in tapestry, silk, brocade; metal and cord chains. Large ostrich-plume fans.

Clasps, brooches, bracelets, rings and earrings all worn. Jewelled, diamanté or velvet forehead bands.

Make-up: Discreet rouging of the lips and cheeks becomes more acceptable and less associated with the stage and immorality.

Movement: As 1918.

Men

No major changes from previous year.

Details of illustrated patterns

Woman

Ankle-length evening dress with square-cut *décolletage* at front and back, and shaped hemline, accentuated by skirt drapery. The waist is cut fairly high, with jewelled clasp at right side seam, and side drape falling in folds to extended train. Hanging sleeves of soft contrast fabric trimmed with gold beading and tassels at shoulders and points.

Fabrics and colours: Pink-and-gold brocade; rose-pink charmeuse contrast.

Accessories: Large ostrich-feather fan; hair bandeau with single wired plume and centre jewel; long double pearl necklace.

Man

Full evening dress consisting of dress coat, white waistcoat and trousers. The coat is close-fitting with swallow-tails and high waist seam forming a continuous run to the front points. Two buttons are placed on the waist dart in front. The peaked lapel is finished to turn to the waist and is faced with silk to the edge. The skirt of the tail coat is long and smartly rounded away, and is not now cut with a strap. The entire length of the front is cut in the forepart, and the lapel is also cut in one with it. The lapel is of medium width with horizontal step, whilst the outer edge is shaped with very little curve. Two-piece set-in sleeves finish with slit cuff and two-button fastening. The tail coat is worn on all the more dressy occasions, but for the theatre or an informal dance the dinner jacket is worn. The latter is more usually worn with black waistcoat (vest), although for those who like just a little 'swank', a white or delicately coloured waistcoat is acceptable. All waistcoats are cut with long points in front and are well curved over the hips. The opening is generally U-shaped, but a V-style is also worn, especially when a heavier lapel is put on.

Dress trousers are usually finished with one or two rows of silk braid down the side. Two rows are more usual with dress jackets, and are placed approximately 6 mm (¼ in.) apart. Trousers are slightly narrower than for general day wear.

Fabrics and colours: Fine black worsted suiting. White piqué for waistcoat and bow tie.

Undergarments: Dress shirt with plain starched front and single stud fastening, white starched wing collar and cuffs.

Footwear: Black silk socks; patent leather shoes with rounded toes and ribbon bow trim.

Accessories: Matching shirt studs, waistcoat buttons and cuff links of onyx, pearl or mother-of-pearl on gold base, or plain gold; white cotton or buckskin gloves; signet ring. Black bow tie with dinner jacket, white piqué with full evening dress.

Notes on construction of garments

Woman

Leave opening at left side seam for hook-and-eye closure. Excess length is allowed at the waistline for draping of the fabric; catch in folds of fabric at side seam, and ensure a close fit. The bodice band is stretched to fit dress top and reduced in width in a similar manner to waistline, by stretching across the chest; finished width approximately 6.25 cm (2½ in.).

The entire dress is mounted on a firm foundation and boned over the bodice, as illustrated by solid black lines. Shoulder straps are stayed with silk braid below gold-bead edge trimming.

Catch stitch folds of skirt drape at centre and side seams, as indicated by dots and arrows on pattern, and insert ends into right side seam. Additional drapery from the waist conceals stitching line and extends into train.

A narrow roll hem is recommended on bias-cut edges.

Man

Tail coat and trousers should fit closely to the figure – expert cutting and construction are essential to achieve correct proportion and balance.

Make up waistcoat back in cheaper lining fabric with strap and buckle to ensure closer fit at waistline.

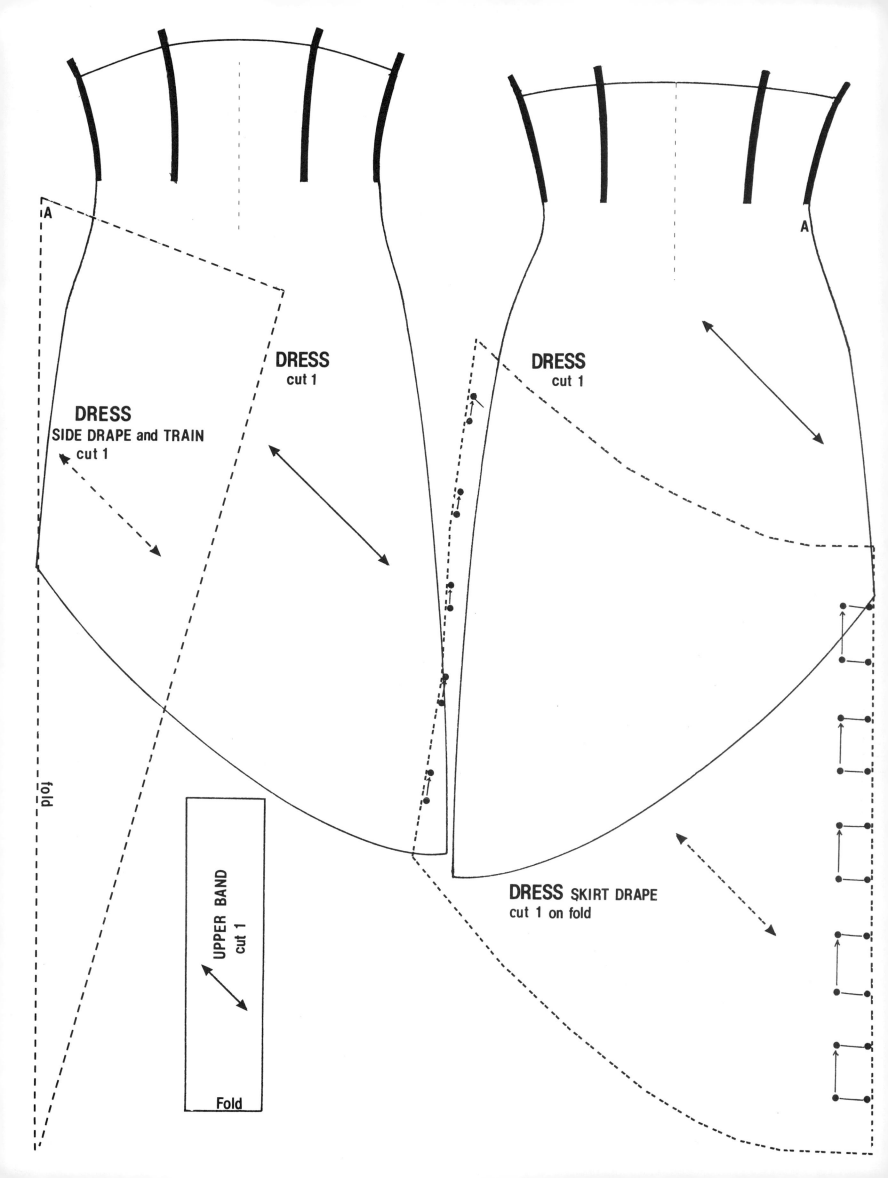

DRESS
cut 1

DRESS
SIDE DRAPE and TRAIN
cut 1

DRESS
cut 1

fold

UPPER BAND
cut 1

Fold

DRESS SKIRT DRAPE
cut 1 on fold

A

A

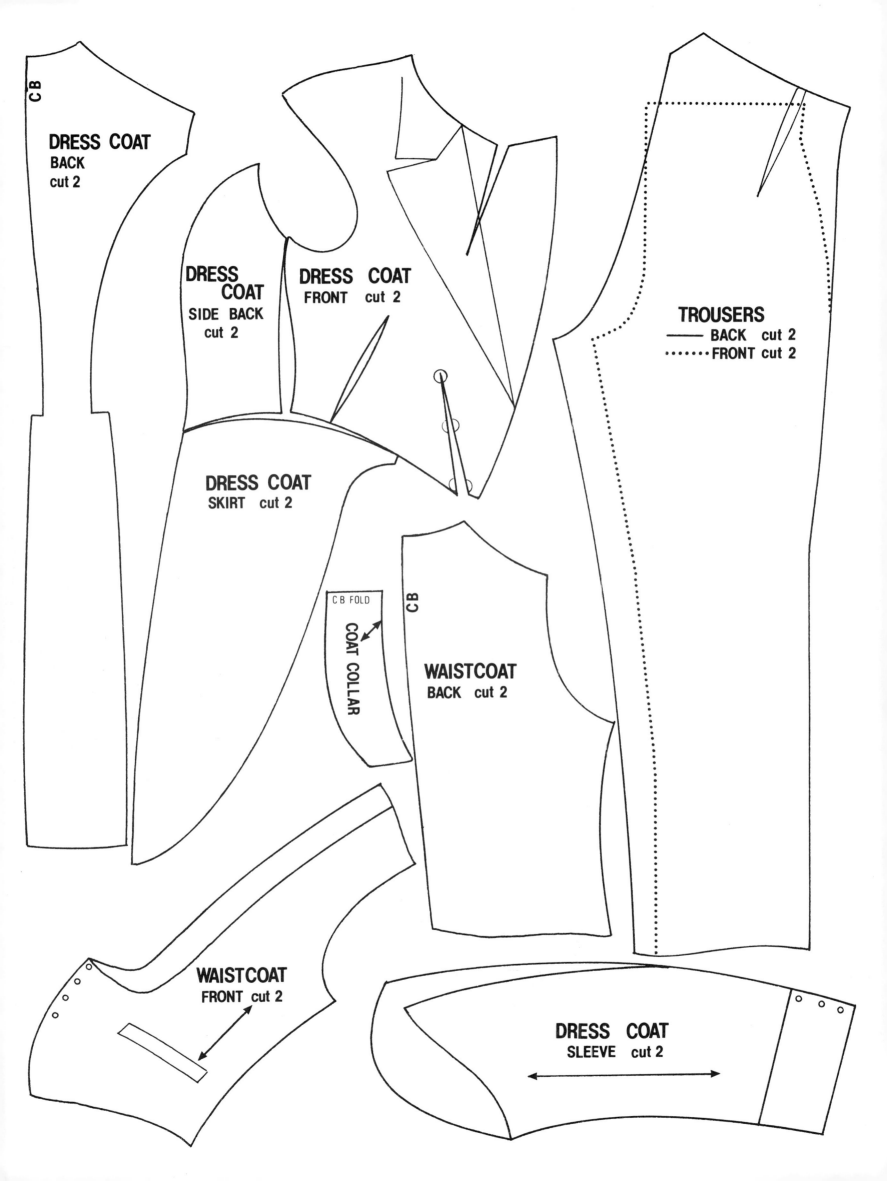

The Twenties

Fashion in pre-war Britain had always infiltrated into society from the older generation. Now, for the very first time, fashion was dominated by the young. It was an age which idolized youth and freedom. 'The Gay', 'The Roaring', 'The Reckless', are but a few of the many adjectives applied to the twenties, and as with any labelling of periods, they suggest the dominant flavour of the epoch. Both male and female fashions reflected the spirit of the age. The war had brought a new type of freedom and with it the abolishment of many pre-war social customs, particularly as regards formal morning and afternoon dress. It was at this time that the word 'casual' entered the fashion vocabulary.

Women's dress in 1918 had already set the standard to which it adhered throughout the twenties. With each successive year women's clothing became increasingly mannish in character, with flat chest and narrow hips. Shoulders became broader, the fit looser, and hair was cut in masculine proportions. Hair was short throughout the twenties. The bob was popular in the early part of the period, but was later followed by the shingle, a close, short cut with natural-looking waves. Finally, in 1927, came the Eton Crop, which made it even more difficult to distinguish between a woman and a schoolboy; make-up was her only feminine attribute. As *Vogue* remarked: 'if men and women have a similar outlook, it is natural that they should wear similar clothes'.

An often-cited reasoning behind the boyish, carefree cut was the new economic and social freedom enjoyed by women, and their fight for emancipation. Women seemed to be denying their femininity by appearing as two-dimensional as possible. Various measures followed the Act of 1918 which recognized women as morally responsible persons. Political emancipation was completed in 1928, when the Equal Franchise Act gave the vote to all women over twenty-one for municipal and parliamentary elections.

To say that the war brought votes for women is to make a very crude generalization, yet one which does contain essential truth. The suffragette movement may have come near to securing votes for women before 1914, yet the political advance of women was blocked by two major prejudices – the hostility of men and the reluctance, and indeed opposition, of many women. New developments during the war brought a new confidence to women and dissipated much of this apathy. Undoubtedly the replacement of militant suffragist activity by recruitment of women for the patriotic cause played its part as well, but more than this the war generated a tremendous mood favourable to change and innovation.

However, emancipation cannot be seen to give the full story of masculinity in dress, for it should be taken into account that immediately prior to the war, a time when suffragist agitation was at its height, fashion chose to restrict feminine movements to the minimum with the hobble skirt.

Another factor inextricably linked with the boyish ideal was the emphasis on youth. In March 1919 *Vogue* noted, 'never has the skirt been so youthful and irresponsible in character', and again in 1924, 'we shall be smart but not hard, there will only be one silhouette – the youthful one'.

Ankles, calves and knees became the new erogenous zones, with the bust suppressed in line with a younger figure. That women were baring more flesh is evident, the scantiness of their dress verified by the reduction in the quantity of fabric required for a complete outfit. This had declined from approximately nineteen to seven yards.

The drastic shortening of the skirt marked a startling innovation in fashion, and short skirts compelled all women to pay much more attention to, and spend more money on, shoes and stockings. Until this time very little had been seen of women's stockings, and black or some other dark shade was usual. All stockings now became flesh-coloured, or, at least, various tones of beige. This heightened the impression of nudity and caused further shock to moralists.

Although I have referred to the twenties as though fashion was uniform throughout the decade, a subtle change of style was apparent during the year 1925–6, which Cunnington describes as an essential change from a 'schoolboy' to that of a 'schoolgirl'. The skirt ceased to be tubular, with fullness introduced in the form of pleats or godets. We can almost watch, as the First World War receded, the process of growing up into maturity. The 'schoolgirl' era of the late twenties, with a greater accent on femininity, led almost inevitably to the reappearance of the natural waistline at the end of the decade.

During this period fashion enjoyed a greater democracy, characteristic of the irreversible changes witnessed by post-war Britain in the structure of society. There were fewer class distinctions – an outcome of the middle-class expansion – and the standard of living rose, partly because lower prices and a tendency for smaller families brought about an increase in spending on luxury products. Greater uniformity in society was reflected in a greater uniformity in dress, for fashion in post-war Britain became less a symbol of nobility and wealth, and effectively spread down the social scale. The period witnessed the birth of 'fashion for all' – 'all' being very much of a generalization since, in effect, it only related to those who could afford it. The title really referred to the increased proportion of the population for whom fashion was now attainable. In many respects, the availability of fashion in post-war Britain served to make an even greater distinction between the very poor and the middle classes. To the former, fashion was as inaccessible as it had been before the war.

Increased spending power was an important phenomenon in the growing uniformity which fashion acquired in this period, since less obvious class distinctions were the inevitable result. In previous eras it had not only been the finer quality of the clothes of the aristocracy which had distinguished them; more importantly, they possessed an entirely different character, and their greater complexity put fashion well out of the reach of everyday folk. In the twenties, clothes for women throughout the social structure were much simpler, and conformed to more or less the same essential character and line, providing the possibility of successful imitation.

The simplicity of 'high fashion' can be largely attributed to the influence of Gabrielle Chanel, whose distinctive style marked her out as the leading fashion designer. Her practical designs were easily adapted to the commercial market, as James Laver suggests: 'Chanel's originality lay in her introduction into high fashion of working-class modes.' She was largely responsible for the simple 'jumper' which suddenly became the day attire of almost every woman. This was the first garment to be used interchangeably by men and women. As universal as the jumper was the cloche hat, which was introduced in 1924 and continued in popularity throughout the decade. The cloche hat was particularly important, since its close fit finally compelled the majority of women to wear their hair short. In addition, it heightened the uniformity of fashion, since in the mid-twenties it came so low over the forehead as almost to cover the eyes. Make-up, too, tended to produce a standardized face.

Increased simplification of design not only brought fashion into wider availability commercially, but was also largely responsible for the increasing number of home dressmakers. Whereas previously dressmaking had been well beyond the capabilities of the average woman, women from all classes now began to make their own clothes. This development was given further impetus by the growth of the paper pattern industry.

This is not to say that fashion in the twenties was without its distinctions; these most definitely did exist, a fact clearly illustrated by the beautifully beaded and embroidered silk evening dresses of the wealthier set. Although machines had been developed for automatic beading, the cost of this technique was still relatively high, and the end product inaccessible to the majority of the population. Similarly, men's tailoring still relied on quality of cloth and cut, although it is significant that off-the-peg styles were more readily available.

The growing sophistication of man-made fibres during the inter-war years marked yet another leap forward in fashion for all. In the twenties the rayon industry was in its infancy, and although artificial silk had been in use since the early days of the First World War, the war had largely disrupted its development, and its influence in fashion at this time was negligible. The manufacture of artificial silk, which from 1927 came to be called by the less disparaging term 'rayon', expanded in various ways. New firms entered the industry, the most important of these in Britain being Courtaulds, ICI and British Celanese. New qualities and types of rayon were introduced; the best known was 'Celanese', which became very popular in the manufacture of women's underwear.

The rapid expansion of British textiles and fashion was aided by the 'Buy British' campaigns of the inter-war years, initiated by the government. Predominant among the methods used to recover from the war and deal with financial depression were the restrictions imposed on the freedom of world trade. Advertisers in all fields took advantage of the campaign to draw attention to the superiority of British products. Furthermore, duties on rayon imports in 1925 protected home producers against foreign imports and encouraged further growth of the industry. The British were thus able to close the gap between their products and those of foreign competitors which had grown during the war.

The availability of cheaper fabrics provided an essential impetus to the progress of ready-to-wear and the rise of the department store. Important changes were taking place in the patterns of trade and commercial activity which were to have far-reaching effects in the thirties, and more importantly, in the period following the Second World War.

Many of the new developments also owed a great deal to the progress of advertising, which was in turn dependent on improved means of communication, in particular through the press and the cinema. During this period fundamental changes took place in the structure of newspaper companies, which resulted in concentration of ownership as opposed to numerous private concerns. In short, as with fashion, newspaper ownership was largely democratized, and daily attained vast and nationwide circulation. To attract women readers, each paper had its fashion page, at least fifty per cent of which was devoted to advertisements for clothes and beauty. The style of presentation was also changing; from 1924, the new 'photo-tone' process enabled photographs to be produced more cheaply in magazines and newspapers. For the first time women in beautiful clothes could be recorded in detail, and the importance of the model became obvious.

In the twenties young people experienced a new freedom in dress synonymous with what seems to have been a complete change in attitude and outlook on life. This change was as much a result of the changing social status of young women as of their political independence, which undoubtedly had its roots in the war years.

In addition to the war experience, America also exerted a tremendous influence, and gave the lead in many social fashions. American tourists flooded into Britain in 1919, accelerating the infiltration of slang, smoking, jazz and cocktails. High heels, hitherto associated with the stage, Paris and immorality, came into general use, as did make-up. Beauty parlours were unknown in Britain in the early twenties, although cream and powder were already used by 'fast young ladies who powdered their noses in public'. (R. Graves and A. Hodges, *The Long Weekend*) Before 1914, only ladies of doubtful reputation had painted their faces. It took the stress and excitement of war, the affluence among the lower classes and the greater spending power of middle-class girls to bring about the heavier use of cosmetics.

Increased interest in health and sport among the young set helped bring about the union of sports and day clothes. Sports personalities, like cinema stars, became important dictators of fashion, and there can be no doubt that they led the field in the revolution in sportswear which took place, a revolution that had important effects on fashion generally.

Golfing and tennis enjoyed a great popularity after the war, becoming a favourite leisure pursuit of the upper and middle classes. Sports costume tended to be an adapted form of day wear, and men's golf saw the revival of knickerbockers, which by 1925 had become looser and fuller 'plus fours', teamed with a Fair Isle pullover and patterned socks. The Fair Isle is characteristic of the more colourful, freer nature of men's clothes, coinciding with the development of knitwear. Knitted garments for men had been introduced in the early 1900s, but their importance in the 1920s was beyond compare. One of the first unisex garments, this gained equal popularity with females, who were keen to adopt many items from their partners' wardrobes, including hats, shirts, neckties and golf stockings. *Vogue* tells us in 1926 that the modern woman 'in the country wears almost the same clothes as her husband'. A short tweed skirt, however, remained more popular than trousers, which were most acceptable in the form of beach or lounging pyjamas.

Coupled with the advance in sportswear, men's fashions generally experienced a more casual and younger-looking trend. Tweeds and checks remained popular, promoted partly by the Prince of Wales, who set the trend to enliven menswear. From 1922, flannel trousers without braces included a waistband and adjustable side straps, worn with a blazer and fine straw panama hat in the summer. Sports shirts with an all-in-one collar, often coloured and in soft fabrics, superseded the traditional tunic styles.

The most distinctive trend came in the trouser width, which provided a sharp contrast to the tapered styles of pre-war fashion. Trousers widened as the decade drew on, with Oxford bags reaching a hem width of 60 cm (24 in.) by 1926. During the latter years of the twenties the extreme of the fashion was modified, although trousers remained generally wide and pleated into the waistband. Jacket lapels and ties followed suit to correspond with the increased trouser breadth, and jackets were worn shorter for all occasions. This trend extended to the tails of the dress coat, which still remained the correct formal attire for dinner dances, with the collar and lapels faced in silk. A starched shirt front completed the outfit, although the vogue for the dinner jacket with soft shirt and turn-down collar increased in popularity, the waistcoat in the late twenties often replaced by a silk cummerbund.

A more casual outlook was evident by the greater frankness and relaxation of inhibitions on sexual topics. The morals and behaviour of the younger set seem to have undergone a thorough 'shaking up', related on the one hand to the new economic and social freedom, and on the other to the heightened intensity generated by the war and the colossal slaughter on the battlefields. The war marked a loosening of the standards of conventional morality. For many young women who had experienced freedom away from the sheltered home environment, a return to the old social customs would have been incongruous with the outlook on life and the opposite sex they had inevitably developed. Women were mixing freely with men without the chaperones of a previous era, and this, plus the wider availability of contraception, brought sexual liberty to women. This development was further aided by the work of Dr Marie Stopes, who set up a number of birth-control clinics in the East End of London.

An equally strong influence was exerted by the art world and was also indicative of a fresh approach and changing outlook. The *Exposition des Arts Décoratifs*, held in Paris in 1925, was far-reaching in its effect and set the modernistic and functional fashion. Taking its influence from cubism, the Bauhaus and the *Ballet Russe*, it introduced designs intended for mass-production in new materials and was not without its impact on design, architecture and furnishings, the rectangular futuristic designs characteristic of Art Deco replacing the luxuriance of Art Nouveau. Geometric patterns and the modern desire for functionality clearly showed its impact.

Thus the twenties witnessed more rapid fashion change, attributable to a number of fresh influences. As fashion began to spread downwards into all classes, large and commercial interests became involved. The pace of fashion accelerated, which may be seen as a manifestation of the generally increased rapidity of social and scientific developments. Flügel, writing in 1930, summed up this point:

Motoring, aviation, cinematography, the gramophone, the wireless, have all come into general use in the course of two or three decades. Corresponding to this rapidity in change in our environment, we have become less conservative, more intolerant of the old and more enamoured of the new, a mental tendency which can best express itself in changing tastes as regards fashion. The fashions may indeed be looked upon as symbolic of our changing outlook on many other things. (J.C. Flügel, *The Psychology of Clothes*)

1920

Predominant fashion features

Women

All styles follow the tubular line, with natural, loose waistline. Signs of a lower waistline towards the end of the year. Hips emphasized with large patch pockets, sashes, bows, draped and pannier effects. Sleeves long for winter, short in summer. Knitted jumpers, dresses, jackets and pleated skirts for casual wear.

Blouses – loose-fitting, with wide, flat collars, worn like a jumper over the skirt.

Coat-frock – a typical coat-frock might be plain at the back, with matching or contrast embroidered front panel, and square neck opening. A narrow belt constricts the waist very little. Patch pockets on either hip. Collar, lapels and turn-back cuffs and belt of lighter, contrasting cloth.

Outdoor coats – three-quarter length, fur trimming with large, floppy collars.

Evening wear – relatively close-fitting, retaining earlier fullness of the skirt for dancing. *Décolletage* horizontal, falling to the same distance front and back, uneven hemlines. Hems grow temporarily longer in 1921.

Fabrics: Silks, wool, stockinette, gabardine, satin, velvet, chiffon, georgette, cashmere, facecloth for day.

Silver and gold lamé, crêpe de Chine, printed chiffons and muslins, taffeta for evening. Transparent, diaphanous and firmer fabrics combined.

Undergarments – crêpe de Chine, muslin, lawn.

Colours: Duller and subdued: coffee, khaki, mustard, grey, navy blue. Brighter colours for evening, and black-and-white.

Decoration: Fringing, tassels, bead embroidery, gold braiding and embroidery. Fur cuffs and collars for coats – monkey fur and coney. Bold borders on jumpers.

Undergarments: Princess petticoats in flimsy fabrics, elasticated at the waist, trimmed with lace and appliqué. Cami-knickers, combining camisole and knickers. Corset similar to 1919.

Footwear: Buckled court styles predominant for day and evening. Oxford lace shoes for sports. Gaiters worn in winter.

Stockings: Black silk for day wear, coloured for evening.

Hats: Wide-brimmed soft hats in cloth, wool or velour, decorated with feathers, flowers, ribbon, pulled well down on to the forehead.

For evening, forehead bands and turbans embellished with feathers and beads.

Hair: Bobbed with side-parting, or long hair combed back into bun at the nape of the neck, brought forward on to the face to imitate a bob.

Accessories: Scarves, knotting low; long pearl necklaces. Ostrich-plume fans for evening. Headbands – brocade, velvet diamanté for evening. Wrist watches, leather and suede handbags.

Make-up: Similar to previous fashion.

Movement: Similar to previous fashion.

Men

Single-breasted lounge suit, similar to previous fashion, 2–4 buttons or link fastening, shaped into the waist with darts. Trouser and waistcoat styles remain unchanged, knee width approximately 56 cm (22 in.), 48.25 cm (19 in.) bottoms.

Overcoats: previous styles continue – chesterfield, raglan, ulsters – worn well below the knee in length, single- or double-breasted according to style.

Morning coat only for most formal occasions, e.g. weddings, usually grey, and worn with striped shirt, white collar and cuffs, bow tie or Ascot silk scarf.

Fabrics: Tweeds and checks in dark colours. Facecloth, gabardine, cashmere, worsteds. Oxford, taffeta and zephyr shirting fabrics.

Undergarments: wool, Viyella, Aertex cellular fabric.

Colours: Various shades of grey popular.

Undergarments: Shirts white, striped, coloured with white double collars, stiff or soft. Stiff-fronted shirt always worn with formal lounge suit and evening wear.

Vest and pants or combinations.

Footwear: Oxford-style lace-up shoes, moderately pointed toes. Laced leather brogues in brown or black.

Socks: Brightly coloured, sometimes striped.

Hair: Worn short-back-and-sides throughout the twenties, centre or side-parting. Hair may be flattened with hair cream.

Hats: Bowler (for city and business), trilby and Homburg most popular styles. Peaked tweed cap or trilby for sports and informal wear.

Accessories: Patterned, spotted, striped and paisley bow ties and silk scarves.

Umbrellas, wrist watches.

Movement: Relaxed.

Details of illustrated patterns

Woman

Smart coat-frock with shaped collar cut grown-on to the side front and faced in paler fabric. The contrasting centre panel underlaps side front, secured with a line of saddle stitching for ornamentation and to create the illusion of a separate coat and dress. Decorative stitching extends along hemline and is repeated at bodice, collar edges and on large, hip-level patch pockets. Rows of buttons accentuate embroidered front panel, divided by side-fastening belt at natural waistline, the latter indicated rather than emphasized. The back is cut whole with moderate flare. Two-piece, set-in sleeves end with attached cuff and two holes and buttons. The garment is loose-fitting throughout, allowing ample ease over the bustline and hips and creating the characteristic straight silhouette. Hemlines are raised slightly from previous fashions.

Fabric: Gabardine.

Colours: Coffee and cream.

Hat: Wide-brimmed soft felt hat with no trimming, worn straight on head.

Accessories: Small clasp-fastening leather handbag with metal frame, buckle trim and narrow cord handle; cream, wrist-length buckskin leather gloves, gauntlet style.

Man

Lounge suit demonstrates increasing trend of shapeliness, clearly defining the figure with a decided 'waisty' effect. The single-breasted, button-three jacket is cut shorter than formerly with pointed lapels, the roll is moderately low and the foreparts well rounded off at the bottom. There is a dart taken out of the forepart; an angled welt pocket on the breast and flap pockets on the hips are arranged slightly on the slant. Slit button cuffs and centre back seam without vent are features of the lounge suit now worn.

Top button of the single-breasted waistcoat is just visible between the lapels of the jacket.

The trousers are cut moderately wide in the legs and taper towards the bottom, with turn-ups. The back is cut higher to accommodate brace and buttons; buckle and strap to adjust waist measurement; side seam pockets and button covered fly.

Fabrics and colours: Fine, striped woollen suiting fabric in shades of grey.

Undergarments: Soft-fronted striped shirt with starched white double collar and cuffs.

Footwear: Black leather Oxford-style laced shoes and light-coloured spats. Spats less frequently worn among younger men.

Hat: Felt trilby.

Accessories: Plain four-in-hand tie, handkerchief in upper breast pocket for decoration only, gauntlet-style gloves, walking stick.

Notes on construction of garments

Woman

Ease back to front at shoulders. The collar is cut in one with coat fronts, with a single centre back seam, and faced in contrast colour.

Completed coat sides are attached to front dress panel using an overlaid seam, and saddle stitched 1.5 cm (5/8 in.) from front edge. Broken lines on pattern indicate position of stitching.

Shaded section of front panel is cut in main fabric and decorated with embroidery, as illustrated on sketch.

Man

Adapt waistcoat back pattern from 1919; the back is usually cut in lining fabric and includes buckle and strap fastening at waistline to ensure a closer fit.

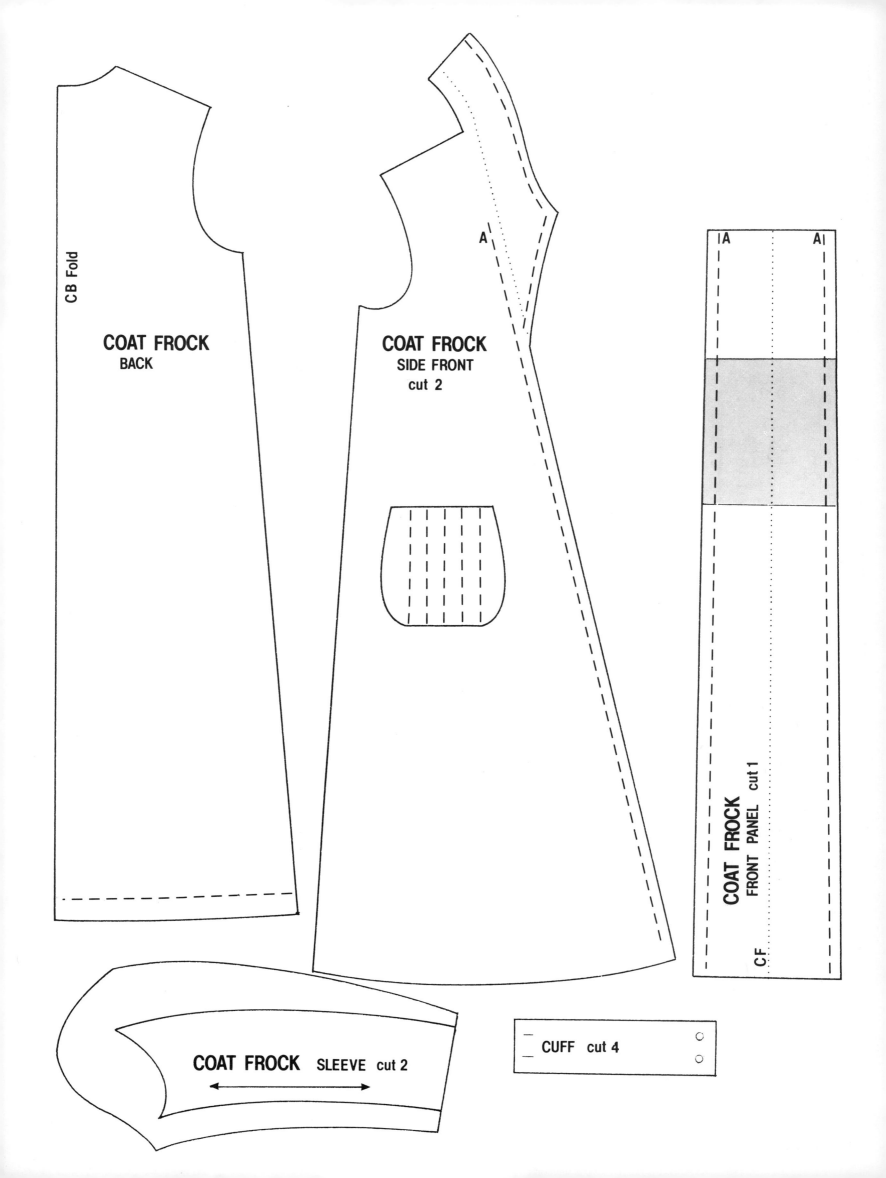

CB Fold

COAT FROCK
BACK

COAT FROCK
SIDE FRONT
cut 2

A

COAT FROCK SLEEVE cut 2

CUFF cut 4

A

A

COAT FROCK
FRONT PANEL cut 1

CF

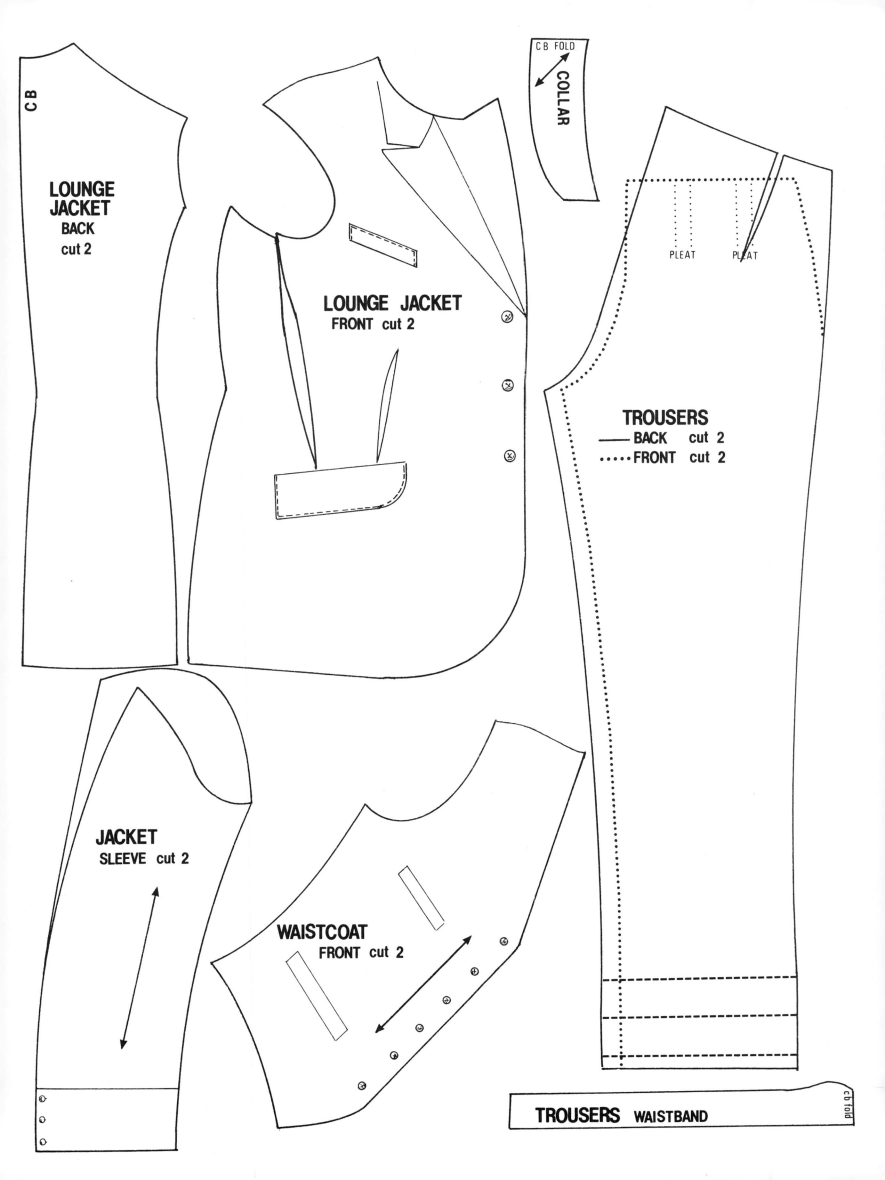

LOUNGE JACKET BACK cut 2

CB

COLLAR CB FOLD

LOUNGE JACKET FRONT cut 2

TROUSERS
—— BACK cut 2
•••• FRONT cut 2

PLEAT   PLEAT

JACKET SLEEVE cut 2

WAISTCOAT FRONT cut 2

TROUSERS WAISTBAND

cb fold

1924

Predominant fashion features

Women

'We shall be smart but not hard, there will only be one silhouette – the youthful one.' (*Vogue*, early autumn 1924)

Waistlines and hemlines lower after 1920, rising in 1923. From 1924 onwards the waistlines continue to lower while hemlines rise – 5 cm (2 in.) below the knee.

The straight silhouette is established – the skirt widened with pleats and godets. Blouses begin to be worn like jumpers, pulled over the hips, obliterating the natural waistline. The contribution of knitted fabrics is significant: jumpers, jumper suits, cardigan jackets, cardigan coats.

Two-piece costumes popular; straight, loose-fitting, hip-length jackets, buttoning low, worn over straight skirts.

Coats three-quarter or seven-eighth length without belts, buttoning to one side.

For evening, dipping and transparent hems herald the shorter skirt, with drapery and sashes at hipline, or over the shoulder. Low backs, dresses mostly sleeveless or with flimsy 'winged' effect.

Fabrics: Mostly plain fabrics, similar to previous fashion. Jersey and stockinette.

For evening, diaphanous, floaty fabrics – chiffon, crêpe georgette, crêpe de Chine, organza, voile, velvets, metallics, satins, beaded fabrics.

Colours: Beige and brown predominant, and fawn, grey, navy, black and white.

Brighter colours for evening – cerise, pinks, mauves, red, blue, black, apricot, green, cherry.

Decoration: Coloured scarves, beading, fringing, embroidery and ribbon lattice work. Fur cuffs and collars for coats.

Undergarments: Boneless, elastic foundation garments known as 'flatteners' take the place of corsets. Princess petticoats in crêpe de Chine.

Footwear: Russian boots for winter, wrinkled over the ankle, calf-length.

Court shoes with buckle, silver or diamanté for evening, straps for day wear. Snake, crocodile, lizard skin, all popular. Lower-heeled brogues for sport with rubber or crêpe soles.

Stockings: Fully fashioned shaped and seamed stockings. White silk, tan, beige, flesh, fawn, grey.

Woollen sports hose in check and plaid patterns.

Hat: Cloche hat first worn, pulled well down over forehead. Brims turn down at the back, upwards at the front. Some rolled upwards all round.

Hair: Bob is abandoned in favour of the shingle, a closer style with natural-looking waves. Fringes popular.

Accessories: Long pearls for day, silver fox fur stoles, coloured scarves essential fashion detail. Large shawls for evening wrap, chiffon scarves with evening dress draped from the shoulders or hips.

Handbags to match the outfit, beaded for evening. Jewellery important – long drop earrings, chokers, pearl necklaces, brooches and slave bangles.

Make-up: Rouge and lipstick, eyebrows plucked, eyebrow-pencil.

Movement: Less upright poise, with the shoulders hunched and pelvis pushed forward, creating an inward curve to the torso.

Men

Lounge jackets shorter, with no back vent, and sometimes worn without waistcoats. Wider trousers with turn-ups now the most popular form of menswear, worn for most occasions, except the most formal.

For business, dark lounge suits with striped trousers.

Oxford bags – wider trousers with turn-ups, up to 40 cm (15¾ in.) and worn long, i.e. over the instep, teamed with flannel jacket.

Flannel jackets and trousers, cut with a waistband, belt loops and adjustable side buckles. Tweed sports jackets or navy blazers with flannel trousers, grey or white in summer.

Overcoat as previous decade.

Knitted jumpers – Fair Isle or white with club colours replaces the waistcoat for sports.

Plus fours (looser and fuller than knickerbockers), with Fair Isle pullovers and patterned socks.

Fabrics: Tweeds, herringbones, dark suiting fabrics for formal lounge suit. Gabardine for raincoats.

Colours: As previous fashion.

Undergarments: Soft-fronted shirts with lounge or sports jackets, and coloured shirts with white double collar. Stiff shirt front with formal lounge suits, often striped. Essential to evening dress, always white.

Pants shortened to trunks. Sleeveless singlets with no fastenings replace buttoned vests.

Footwear: Shoes always worn in preference to boots by younger men. Brown or black leather, white buckskin with white flannels. Higher heels, patent leather Oxford shoe worn with lounge suits. Crêpe and rubber soles for sports shoes.

Socks: Brightly coloured, ribbed, patterned and striped socks. Mid-calf-length with plus fours, supported by elastic suspenders, fastening below the knee.

Hats: Trilby most popular style. Straw boaters or panama in summer. Tweed caps for sports and casual wear.

Hair: Short-back-and-sides, centre-parting with longer sideburns. Younger men clean-shaven.

Accessories: As previous fashion.

Details of illustrated patterns

Woman

Tennis costume consisting of a white pleated skirt and blue blazer. The blazer is cut without shaping, and shorter than contemporary costume jackets, with large patch pockets at hips and shaped pocket on breast. Wide lapels with step collar roll low, fastening with two gilt buttons. Two-piece, set-in sleeves finish with straight turn-back cuff.

The skirt with all-round knife pleats is set on a silk hip-yoke drawn in with elastic at the top edge.

A stockinette hip-length jersey with low rounded neckline extends over skirt hip yoke.

Fabrics and colours: Navy or royal blue flannel for jacket, white linen skirt. 'It is possible to make such a garment very attractive because of the possibility of the use of vivid coloured flannels and sharp contrast in the form of braid or ribbon for the edge.' (*Tailor and Cutter*, February 1924)

Footwear: Low-heeled laced sports shoes of white buckskin with crêpe soles.

Hat: Deep-crowned, pull-on type hat with turn-down brim, grosgrain ribbon and bow trim.

Man

Stylish double-breasted reefer jacket with a three-button front. It is close-fitting and a front dart is taken out of the foreparts. The revers are not too heavy, and the length of the turn is medium. Two slanted flaps at hip-level and outside welt pocket. The back is cut whole without seam or vent. Two-piece sleeves finish with slit cuff and two buttons and holes.

The waistcoat is of white or very light-coloured material and has five buttons or holes. It is visible between jacket lapels. The bottom button is always left open.

White flannel trousers with permanent turn-ups, although remaining fairly narrow in the leg, are wider than previous styles. Trousers are cut with waistband and buckles and straps placed at sides.

Fabrics and colours: Navy blue serge or flannel jacket; white flannel trousers.

Undergarments: Soft-fronted shirt with soft double collar, stiffened with celluloid tabs at collar points. It may be white or pale in colour.

Footwear: White buckskin shoes with four-eyelet fastening, crêpe soles and more pointed toes.

Hat: Straw boater.

Accessories: Striped tie. Hatband and tie may be in school, club or regimental colours. Walking stick, cuff links, signet ring.

Notes on construction of garments

Woman

Ease back to front at shoulder seams of jacket. Position of contrast braiding is indicated by solid black lines on pattern. The jacket is loose-fitting throughout.

The skirt is cut perfectly straight with all-round 2.5 cm (1 in.) knife pleats. A section of the skirt is given in the pattern section to illustrate spacing of the pleats. To construct the skirt, work directly on the cloth. Cut a piece of fabric depth 71 cm (28 in.) plus 5 cm (2 in.) hem allowance; width = 285 cm (112½ in.) (three times hips plus ease). It will be necessary to seam the fabric to create the full required width. Seams should be concealed at the inside fold of the pleats. Add seam allowance where required and to upper and outside edges.

The completed skirt is mounted on a silk hip yoke, elasticated to fit the waist at the top edge. To make up, cut a rectangle 12.75 cm (5 in.) deep by 95 cm (37½ in.) (hip measurement plus ease). Add seam allowances to side and lower edges and 2.5 cm to upper edge to form a narrow casing for elastic. Ease the lower skirt to fit hip yoke; it may be necessary to overlap top edge of pleats slightly.

Note: Measurements given are for a standard size 12.

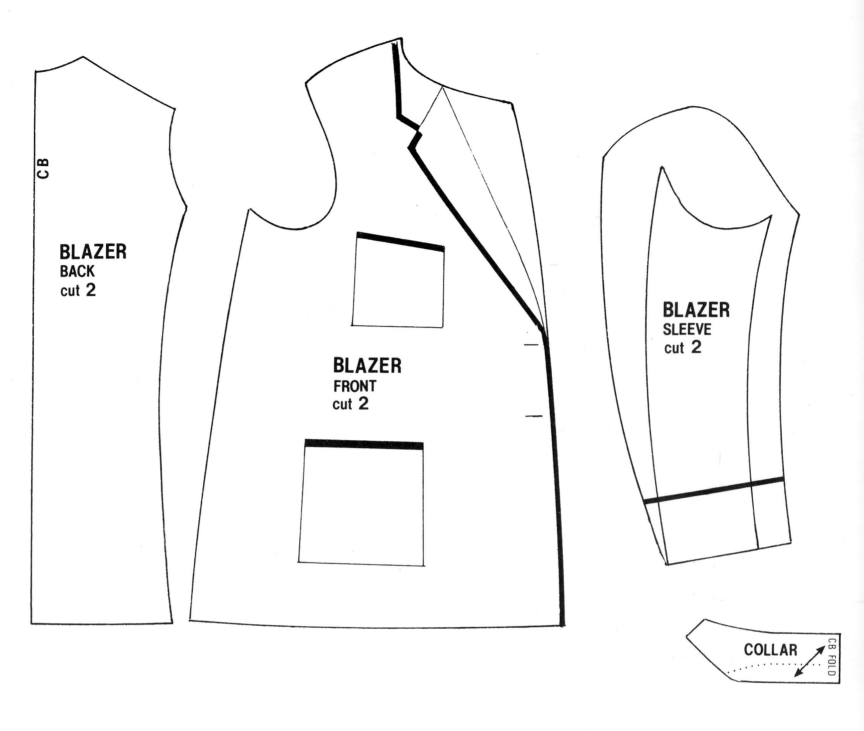

BLAZER
BACK
cut 2

CB

BLAZER
FRONT
cut 2

BLAZER
SLEEVE
cut 2

COLLAR

CB FOLD

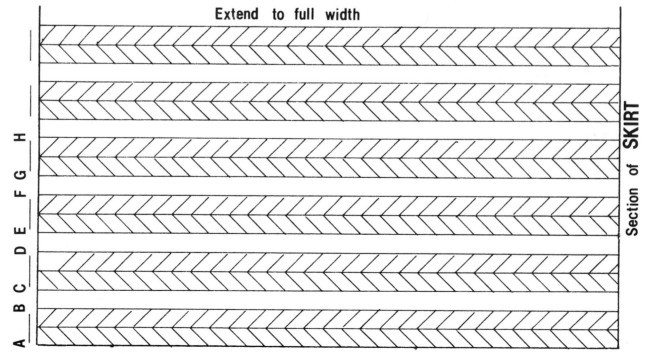

Extend to full width

A B C D E F G H

Section of **SKIRT**

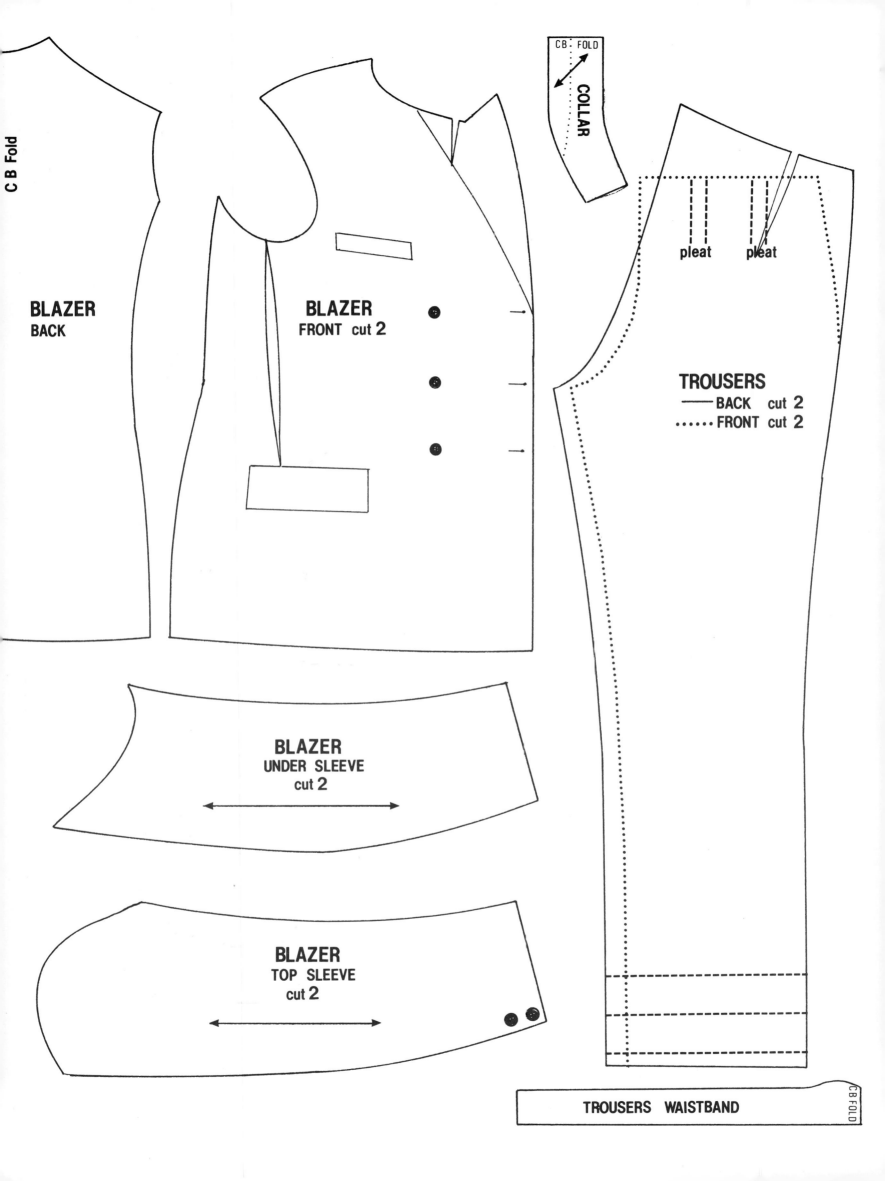

C B Fold

BLAZER
BACK

BLAZER
FRONT cut 2

BLAZER
UNDER SLEEVE
cut 2

BLAZER
TOP SLEEVE
cut 2

CB FOLD
COLLAR

pleat   pleat

TROUSERS
— BACK cut 2
····· FRONT cut 2

TROUSERS WAISTBAND

CB FOLD

1925~1926

Predominant fashion features

Women

Extreme of present mode reached. Skirts are straight, the knee revealed for the first time in fashion history; worn with straight, long tops, often sleeveless.

Many styles are adopted directly from men's tailoring – double-breasted waistcoats and jackets, link closure; shoulders are broader and the fit looser.

The years 1925/1926 also witness the first signs of change towards femininity in women's fashion. 'No longer are we all young boys... Yet we are not a day older; we are feminine before everything, slim as young birch trees, with a very real attempt to return to that old half-forgotten word – "charm".' (*Vogue*, early November 1926)

Hem width is emphasized with godets and pleats, the fullness apparent only with movement.

The trend of informality in day dress continues. Sports wear trends influence fashion.

Two-piece suits and costumes remain popular. Blouses and dresses with boat-shape necklines, flat Peter Pan sailor collars, pouched at the hip.

Coats very loose fitting, wider shoulders, fur trimming.

Evidence of change in evening dresses which begin to pouch at the 'waistline'; fuller in the skirt, often dipping at the back or sides. Low back *décolletage*.

One-sided designs dominate all fashions. *Trompe l'oeil* sweaters with scarves, bows, collars knitted into the design.

Fabrics: Crêpe de Chine, georgette, voiles, foulard, shantung, metallic laces, metallic cloths, beaded fabrics. Printed geometric and futuristic patterns. Tweeds and checks for daytime suits; knitted fabrics.

Furs – Persian lamb, astrakhan.

Colours: Bold colours – black, white, red, fuchsia, bright blue, orange, violet, jade. For evening all shades of purple, lavender, mauve.

Cream, brown, beige remain popular.

Decoration: Black lace, deep fringing, bead embroidery. Bold appliqué. Large, futuristic geometric and cubist patterns.

Undergarments: Light, flimsy fabrics, ninon, crêpe de Chine. Elasticated corsets compressing the breasts and hips; these are pulled up at the front and down at the back to increase flattening effect. Backless chemise for evening and strapless brassières. Cami-bockers combine camisole and closed *Directoire* knickers.

Shoes: Toes not so pointed, heels higher and curved, two or three straps popular. Shoes frequently combine two colours and materials – leather, suede, and skins: alligator, lizard, crocodile, snake.

Stockings: As previous fashion. Flesh tones, artificial silk and silk, silk and cotton.

Hats: Cloche hat universally worn, narrow-brimmed with close-fitting crown, pulled down well over the eyes like a helmet, and matching the outfit. Sparse trimming. Felts, velours and knitted styles all popular. Larger-brimmed hats for summer.

Hair: Eton crop, extreme of short hair, closely cropped style cut above the ears and close into the nape of the neck. Sometimes waved for softer effects. Women frequent men's barbers.

Accessories: Gauntlet-style gloves – suede, calfskin, buckskin. Envelope handbags, containing make-up, cigarette cases, long cigarette holders. Ties, tie pins, cuff links. Scarves – silk, for day fastened at one side with brooch. Fringed scarves for evening. Long bead necklaces. Costume jewellery, slave bangles, bracelets, long drop earrings, shoulder brooch.

Make-up: Orange rouge and lipstick, plucked eyebrows and pencilled brows create unnatural mask-like face.

Movement: Pelvis pushed forwards and shoulders rounded, one hand frequently resting on the hips. No emphasis is therefore given to the bustline.

Men

Menswear experiences more casual and younger-looking influence. Lounge jacket less defined at waistline. Lapels and shoulders widen to balance trouser width. Reefer jackets, blazers, sports jackets, flannel trousers – see previous fashion details. Oxford bags reach extreme in width, up to 62 cm (24 in.), lighter in colour than the jacket.

Overcoats – length shortened to just below the knee, velvet collars not so usual on chesterfields.

Sleeveless, knitted pullovers, shorter than jumpers in length, in brightly coloured Fair Isle patterns, worn with Oxford bags or plus fours. Flannel jackets and soft felt hats for sports and casual wear.

Fabrics: Tweeds and checks popular. Oxford shirting; light flannel or Viyella for sports shirt.

Colours: Oxford bags – grey, brown, beige, light navy. Light colours for shirts – blue, grey, peach tones.

Undergarments: Coloured shirts with new soft collars and detachable supports.

Shoes: Oxford style remains most popular. Co-respondent shoes in two colours, white and tan or black and white. Not always considered to be in the best taste.

Socks: Similar to previous fashion.

Hair and hats: Similar to previous fashion.

Accessories: Wider ties in brighter colours – patterned or spotted. Collar pins, tie pins, cuff links.

Details of illustrated patterns

Woman

Knee-length tubular evening dress drawn in at lowered waistline with gathered band under bodice. The bodice is loose fitting, with scoop neckline bound with main dress fabric, and shoulder decoration harmonizing with 'waistline'. Heavy metallic lace insertion at centre front, back and sides reveals silk foundation, meeting the hemline of matching scalloped lace. Narrow bands of finer insertion trim the lower skirt section. Deep, cut-away armholes are bound in the same fashion as neckline; the latter is cut low at the back.

Fabrics and colours: Gold crêpe de Chine, matching fine silk for foundation.

Footwear: Evening shoes of gold glacé kid with low vamp, pointed toes, curved heels and double T-straps.

Accessories: Gold bandeau worn around the head and across the forehead; much jewellery including slave bangles, pearl drop earrings, rings and choker necklace.

Man

Full evening dress consisting of dress coat, trousers and white waistcoat. The coat is close fitting, with tails ending above the knee and high waist seam, forming a continuous run to the front points. Three buttons are placed on the waist dart in front. The peaked lapel is finished to turn to the waist and is faced with silk to the edge. The entire front is cut in one piece and the lapel is cut in one with it. Two-piece sleeves finish with slit cuff and three-button fastening. The tail coat is worn for more dressy occasions, with the dinner jacket for informal evening wear. The latter is usually worn with black waistcoat and black tie.

The waistcoat, with deep U-shaped front and lapels, is cut with long points in the front and fastens with four buttons. A strap and buckle at the back enable a closer fit at waist-level.

Dress trousers are narrower than for day wear and without turn-ups. They are usually finished with one or two rows of silk braid down the side. The latter is more usual with dress jackets, and are placed approximately 6 mm (¼ in.) apart.

Fabrics and colours: Black wool worsted; white piqué for waistcoat and bow tie.

Undergarments: Dress shirt with plain starched front and single-stud fastening, white starched wing collar and cuffs.

Footwear: Black silk lisle socks; patent leather Oxford laced shoes with rounded toes.

Accessories: Matching shirt studs, waistcoat buttons and cuff links of onyx, pearl or mother-of-pearl on gold base; white cotton or buckskin gloves; signet ring; white bow tie.

Notes on construction of garments

Woman

Insert 6.25 cm (2½ in.) wide gold lace at front, back and sides of dress, and lower skirt. Position of lace is indicated by broken lines on pattern.

Gather at shoulders and lowered waistline, along broken lines, and stay with tape on wrong side.

Make up foundation and join to dress at neck and armhole edges with a narrow binding of self fabric, 6 mm (¼ in.) finished width.

Man

The dress coat fits closely to the figure. Trousers may be finished with a row of braid at side seams.

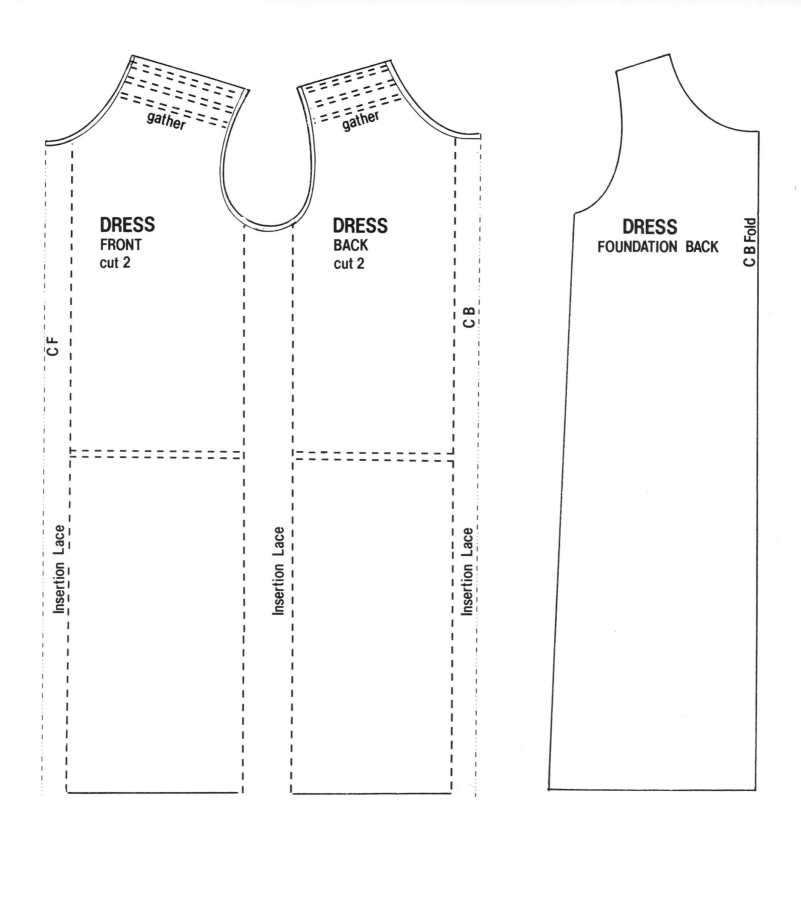

DRESS
FRONT
cut 2

CF

gather

Insertion Lace

DRESS
BACK
cut 2

C B

gather

Insertion Lace

Insertion Lace

DRESS
FOUNDATION BACK

C B Fold

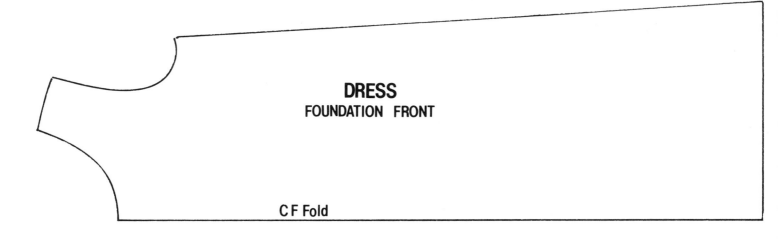

DRESS
FOUNDATION FRONT

C F Fold

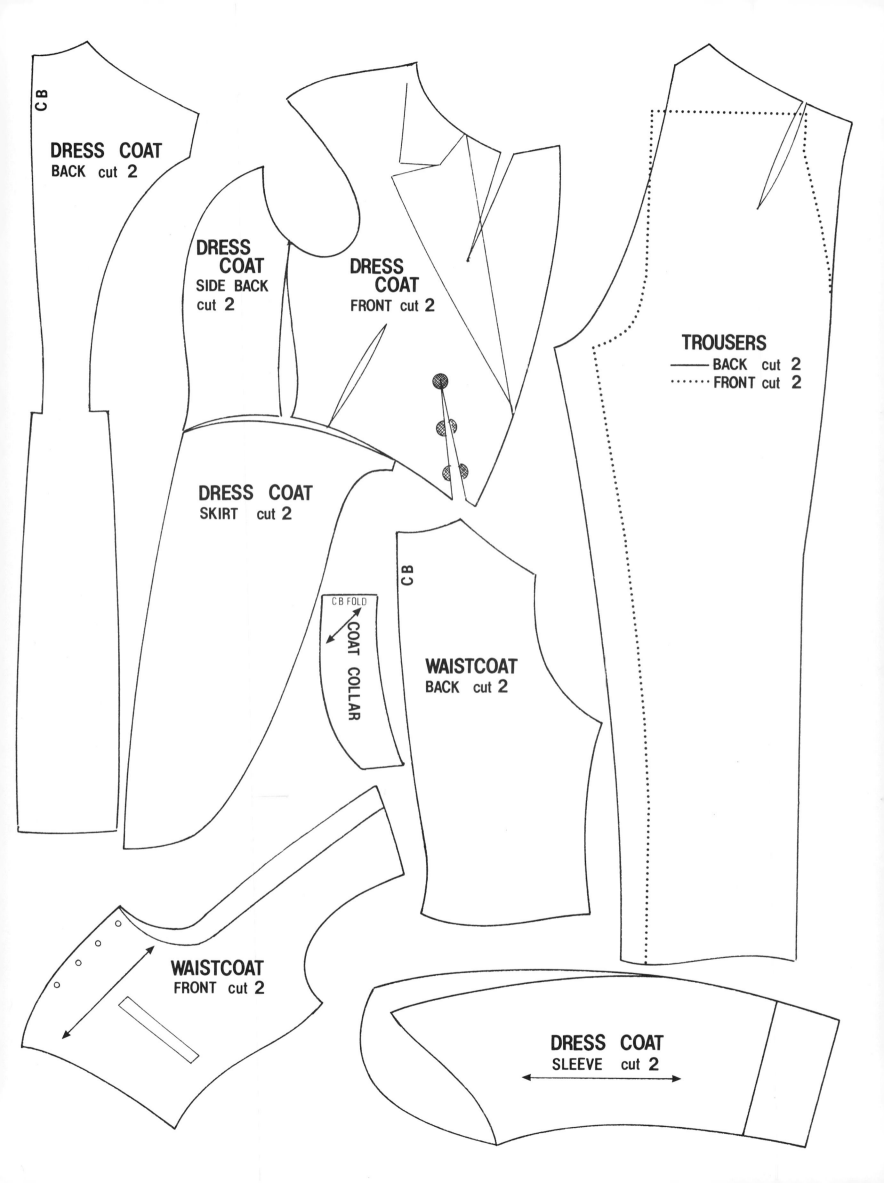

DRESS COAT
BACK cut 2

C B

DRESS COAT
SIDE BACK
cut 2

DRESS COAT
FRONT cut 2

DRESS COAT
SKIRT cut 2

CB FOLD

COAT COLLAR

C B

WAISTCOAT
BACK cut 2

TROUSERS
—— BACK cut 2
········ FRONT cut 2

WAISTCOAT
FRONT cut 2

DRESS COAT
SLEEVE cut 2

1927

Predominant fashion features

Women

Skirts knee-level, with pleats and godets. Length 38–40.5 cm (15–16 in.) from the ground. Blouses with softer sleeves. Gathers, pleats, darts, tucks beginning to appear on all garments.

Dresses – tunic style, tiered, drapery effects, especially in evening wear.

One-sided asymmetrical effects, *trompe l'oeil* sweaters.

Coats – three-quarter length, low revers, low buttoning with dropped waist, worn with short, pleated skirt. Long coats end just above the skirt hemline.

Satin pyjama suits for cocktails.

For golf – jumpers; tweed skirt culottes or plus fours. Leather sports coats.

Fabrics: Artificial silk, now known as 'rayon', manufactured by Courtaulds. Knitted fabrics, striped stockinette, fine silks. Tweeds and checks. Velvet and metallic fabrics, georgette, crêpe de Chine, lace.

Colours: Black and white, bold and pastel shades all popular.

Decoration: Silver fox fur, ruffles, jabots. Bold geometric designs.

Undergarments: White less popular than peaches and pinks for undergarments. Separate brassières constrict rather than support the breasts. Cami-knickers, cami-bockers.

Footwear: Suede, buckskin, crocodile, snakeskin, lizard; pointed toes, higher heels.

Stockings: Checked or striped woollen stockings for golf. 'Flesh-coloured' (beige) artificial silk or silk stockings.

Hats: Cloche hat is cut higher at the back, with the brim turned up on one side, linking with the asymmetrical nature of the dress.

Hair: Extremely short hair less popular. The shingle, a short cut with natural-looking waves, softer than previous fashion. False hair pieces add length to the back of the hair, if needed.

Accessories: Shoes and handbags match. Umbrellas with day costume. Costume jewellery.

Make-up: Plucked eyebrows, kohl to blacken eyes, rouge and lipstick. Suntanned skin fashionable.

Movement: As previous fashion.

Men

Styles are similar to previous fashion. Lounge jacket often cut straight at the hem. Single-breasted styles with three buttons; only the middle one fastened. Lapels and shoulder width increase. Permanently pressed turn-ups on trousers.

Oxford bags – less exaggerated trouser width. All trousers remain wider in the leg, pleated into the waistband.

Reefer jackets, blazers, sports jackets, flannel trousers – see fashion details 1924.

Evening wear – tail coats for formal wear. Collar and lapels faced in silk. Dinner jacket for less formal occasions. Black waistcoats, matching the suit, occasionally replace white, with the dinner jacket only. Trousers follow day styles, never with turn-ups. Sleeveless, knitted pullovers, shorter than jumpers in length, in brightly-coloured Fair Isle patterns, worn with Oxford bags or plus fours. Flannel jackets and soft felt hats for sports and casual wear.

Fabrics: Tweeds and checks popular. Oxford shirting; light flannel or Viyella for sports shirt.

Colours: Oxford bags – grey, brown, beige, light navy. Light colours for shirts – blue, grey, peach tones.

Undergarments: Coloured shirts with new soft collars and detachable supports.

Dress shirt with starched front of marcella or piqué, with plain, double cuffs or pleated front, worn with wing collar and white bow tie. Pleated shirts not usually worn with dinner jackets.

Shoes: Oxford style remains most popular. Co-respondent shoes in two colours, white and tan or black and white.

Socks: Brightly coloured, ribbed, patterned and striped socks.

Hats: Trilby most popular style; straw boater or panama in summer. Tweed caps for sports and casual wear.

Hair: Short-back-and-sides, centre-parting with longer side-burns.

Accessories: Wider ties in brighter colours – patterned or spotted. Gauntlet-style leather, suede or buckskin gloves, may be string-backed. Collar pins, tie pins, cuff links, wrist watches; umbrella with formal lounge suit.

Movement: Carefree, casual attitude of the 'bright young things', with their interest in sports and dancing, is reflected in their behaviour and movement.

Details of illustrated patterns

Woman

Hip-length lounge jacket of plain material, cut with panelled front and single-breasted fastening. Wide, pointed lapels roll from lowered waistline, with upper collar faced in velvet. Shaped patch pockets, with velvet trim and button tab, harmonize with collar. There is corresponding decoration at pointed cuffs of two-piece set-in sleeves.

The skirt is cut quite straight with single inverted pleat at centre front to allow greater freedom of movement.

A long-line, single-breasted waistcoat fastening from V-shaped neckline with a single row of closely spaced buttons, and a masculine collar and tie, complete the outfit.

Fabrics and colours: Fine woollen suiting fabric in tan, blue or grey shades.

Footwear: Snakeskin shoes with pointed toes, double T-bar straps and high curved heels.

Hat: Close-fitting cloche hat pulled down well on the head. Narrow brim turned up at the back, and braid trim.

Accessories: Pearl drop earrings; patent leather belt worn at lowered waistline; wrist-length, gauntlet-style kid gloves to match the outfit.

Man

Single-breasted blazer with wide, pointed lapels and three-button fastening. It is close-fitting, with a front dart taken out of the foreparts, and rounded lower edges. Two large patch pockets at hip-level and shaped breast pocket which may be embroidered with the crest or badge of club or regiment. Two-piece, set-in sleeves finish with slit and single gilt button, harmonizing with front jacket fastening. The back is cut with centre back seam and no vent.

White flannel Oxford bags are wide in the leg with turn-ups. They are cut with front pleats and belted waistband. Braces are not required.

A striped shirt, with white detachable soft collar, and striped club tie, complete the outfit.

Fabrics and colours: Navy flannel for jacket, white flannel trousers.

Hats: It is permissible for young men to go hatless.

Notes on construction of garments

Woman

A 6 mm (¼ in.) seam allowance is included in the pattern.

Jacket back is cut in one piece. Ease back to front at shoulder seams. Separate jacket front and side front pattern along panel line **A** to **B**. Add seam allowance to cut edges.

The pleated skirt is cut perfectly straight. If a seam or seams have to be introduced they are concealed at inner folds of pleats or at centre back. To cut the skirt work directly on the cloth. Cut a piece of fabric: depth = skirt length – 57 cm (22½ in.) plus hem and seam allowance; width = 95 cm (37½ in.) (hips and ease), plus a 32 cm (12½ in.) pleat allowance. Total width = 127 cm (50 in.), to which seam allowances must be added. The construction of the pleat at centre front is shown on the section of the skirt pattern illustrated.

The completed skirt is then mounted on to the silk bodice, which supports the skirt without bulk.

Man

The blazer may be bound with silk braid in club or regimental colours on outside edges, cuffs and pockets.

Oxford bags are loose fitting in the leg, constructed with a waistband and belt loops. Waistband pattern includes front extension.

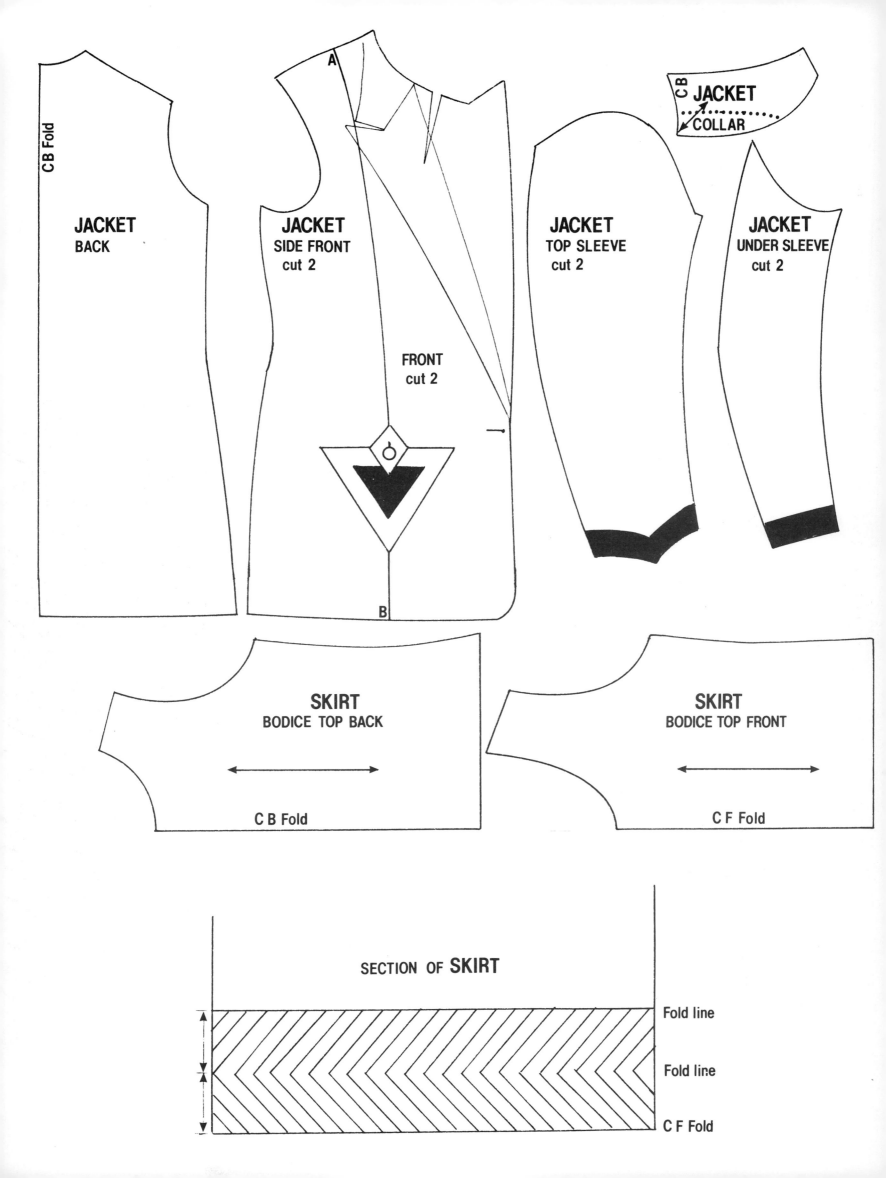

JACKET
BACK

CB Fold

JACKET
SIDE FRONT
cut 2

A

FRONT
cut 2

B

JACKET
TOP SLEEVE
cut 2

JACKET
UNDER SLEEVE
cut 2

CB

JACKET
COLLAR

SKIRT
BODICE TOP BACK

C B Fold

SKIRT
BODICE TOP FRONT

C F Fold

SECTION OF **SKIRT**

Fold line

Fold line

C F Fold

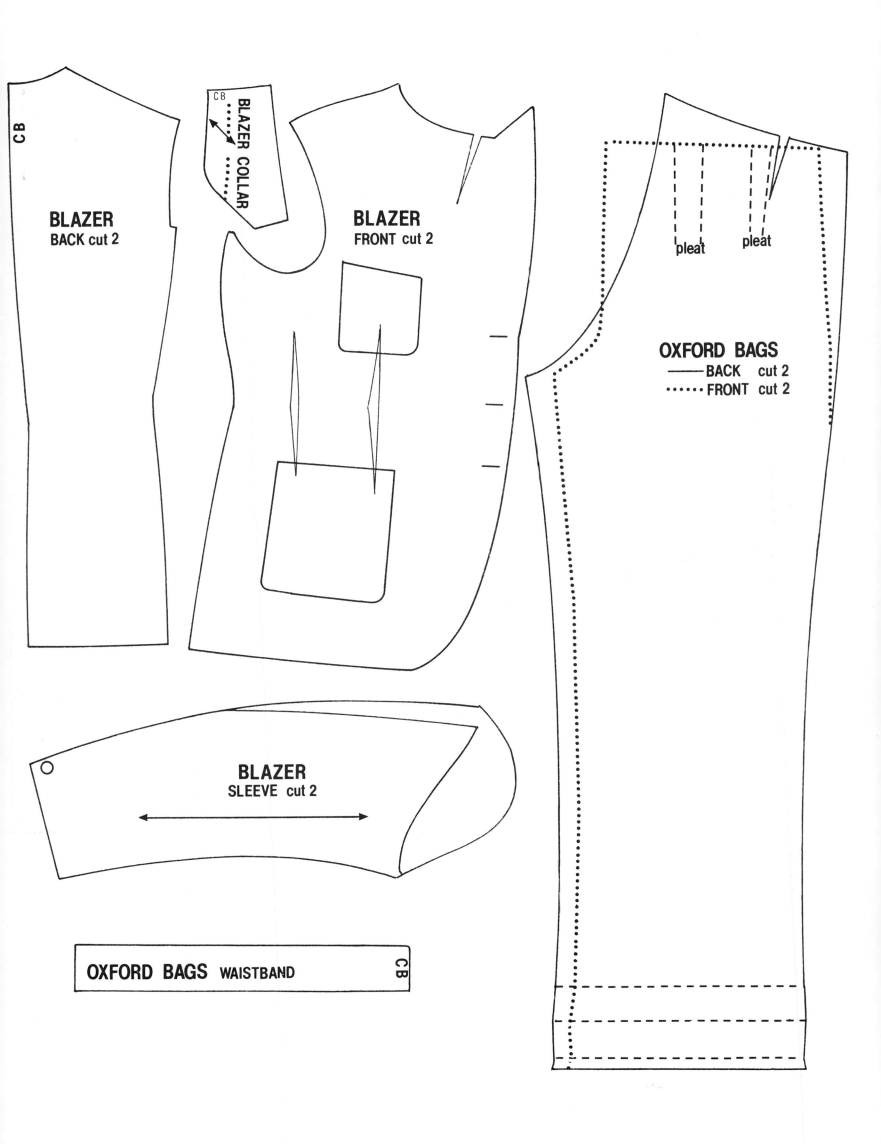

BLAZER
BACK cut 2

CB

BLAZER COLLAR
CB

BLAZER
FRONT cut 2

OXFORD BAGS
—— BACK   cut 2
······ FRONT   cut 2

pleat   pleat

BLAZER
SLEEVE cut 2

OXFORD BAGS WAISTBAND
CB

1929

Predominant fashion features

Women

Designers endeavour to lengthen the skirt by means of transparent or false hems and trains. Day wear follows suit, with dipping or pointed hems and a general lengthening of skirt, but the trend is more extreme in evening fashions.

Tweed coats and skirts worn with jumper. Blouses are tucked into the skirts at the waist. Dresses and skirts flare low, moulding closer to the figure around the hips.

Evening wear – sleeveless with back *décolletage* more pronounced, dipping with the hem and reaching half-way down the back. All dresses fit closely over the hips, flaring to the hemline. Higher 'waist', with drapery effects from the shoulders and hips, sometimes trailing the ground.

Fabrics: Lighter weight woollen fabrics, firm silks and satins, tweeds, cashmere, shantung, wool crêpes.

For evening: satin, chiffon, voile, moiré, georgette, tulle, metallic brocades – patterned and plain fabrics combined.

Colours: Day – beige, brown, navy, black and white. For summer and evening wear, brighter colours – blue, yellow, rose pink, pale green, black and white.

Decoration: Scarves, jabot collars and frills. Geometric patterns. Chiffon flowers worn on one shoulder or one side of 'waist'.

Undergarments: Foundation garments cease to achieve the straight-line effect. 'Corselettes' mould rather than constrict the figure, and include two breast pockets.

Camisole almost obsolete as separate garment.

Footwear: Frequently employing two colours and materials, e.g. white and tan, suede and snakeskin. Cuban and louis heels.

Stockings: Coloured stockings and 'flesh' tones in silk or artificial silk.

Hats: Brim of cloche hat becomes larger and softer, tilted back at the front to reveal more of the face.

Hair: Worn longer, with rolls of curls at the nape of the neck. For women growing their hair, a small slide is worn to keep straggling ends in place.

Accessories: Gauntlet-style gloves in dyed leather. Envelope handbags often co-ordinate with shoes. Large evening wraps, chiffon squares; plaid or striped scarves for day wear, wrapped tightly around the throat with tails hanging behind. Jabot collars. Strings of pearls shorter than previous fashion. Costume jewellery.

Make-up: Vaseline and kohl on eyelids. Black mascara, rouge and darker lipsticks.

Movement: Similar to previous fashion, although shoulders less hunched.

Men

Day wear styles remain similar to previous fashions, with trend for wider, more pointed lapels and increased shoulder width. Double- or single-breasted. Lounge suit waistcoat fronts more usually match the rest of the suit. Trousers with permanently pressed turn-ups.

Overcoats: 'Breadth of shoulder and a short, broad lapel is the most predominating feature of this season's styles' (*Tailor and Cutter*, September 1929)

Chesterfield for more formal wear, double or single-breasted, the latter usually with fly front. This style ceases to feature a velvet collar. Ulster – looser-fitting style, belted, with patch pockets. Raglan – usually single-breasted, belted, with patch pockets. Raincoats of proofed tweed or gabardine.

Fabrics: Flannel suiting, tweeds and checks, worsteds, cashmere. Raincoats of proofed tweed or gabardine.

Colours: Black and white for evening. Shades of grey for day wear. Dark grey or black for formal lounge suits. Putty, camel, for less formal overcoats.

Undergarments: Soft-fronted shirt with turn-down collar worn with double-breasted dinner jacket. Stiff shirt front remains correct with formal lounge suit and other evening styles.

Singlet and trunks or combinations in knitted wool, aertex or artificial silk.

Footwear: Oxford-type laced shoe, plain black calf or brogued, black for town, brown for sports or country. Co-respondent leather shoes in two colours, e.g. white buckskin with brown toe-caps.

Socks: Coloured or striped ribbed socks, reaching to mid-calf and secured with garters.

Hats: Trilby remains most popular style, available in soft felts, straw and tweeds. Bowler hat for business.

Hair: Centre-parting with hair slightly raised at the hairline and brushed back, short-back-and-sides.

Accessories: Gloves fasten at the wrist in chamois, kid, buckskin or cloth in pale colours, grey or white. Rolled umbrellas, wrist watches.

Details of illustrated patterns

Woman

Bias-cut evening dress with draped cowl from lowered neckline, bloused bodice and dropped waist. The shaped skirt falls from fitted hip yoke with draped inserts at side fronts and back. Set-in bishop sleeves fasten at deep pointed cuffs with rouleau loops and covered contrast buttons. Contrast bands at shoulder and hip yokes harmonize with matching binding at dress edges, emphasizing design features. The dress remains loose-fitting over the natural waistline. Displaying characteristics of the twenties, the style is indicative of a more feminine trend in ladies' fashions, and lengthening skirt hem.

Fabrics and colours: Pale peach crêpe de Chine, brown satin contrast binding.

Footwear: Evening shoes of gold kid with single strap fastening and high curved heels.

Accessories: Clasp fastening, beaded clutch handbag, with metal frame.

Man

Dinner jacket worn with black waistcoat and dress trousers. The waist is not close-fitting but shape is suggested by giving breadth and squareness of shoulders and ease at the chest; the waist is defined without the more abrupt shaping of earlier styles.

Pointed lapels are bold in proportion, faced with silk and rolling to a one-button fastening. Outside breast pocket and jetted hip-pockets preserve the slim, smoother appearance of the skirt, the length just covering the seat of the trousers. The back is cut with moderate drape and centre back seam and vent. Two-piece, set-in sleeves finish with slit cuffs and single button to harmonize with front.

A black waistcoat or vest is more usual with dinner jackets, although white or delicately coloured versions may be worn. Low V-shaped opening with lapels, fastens with four small buttons.

Trousers are generally slimmer than for day-wear, without pleats or turn-ups.

Fabrics and colours: Jacket and trousers in black wool worsted; black silk for waistcoat and tie.

Undergarments: White dress shirt with starched front and single-stud fastening, separate starched wing collar and cuffs.

Footwear: Black patent leather Oxfords; black lisle socks.

Accessories: Shirt studs, waistcoat buttons and cuff links to match in onyx, jade, smoked mother-of-pearl, pearl. White handkerchief worn in outside breast pocket, for decoration only.

Notes on construction of garments

Woman

Bias cut requires more careful handling of the fabric. Additional length is allowed in the dress bodice for blousing at lowered waistline.

Skirt drape is stitched in at side front and back seams between **A** and **B**. There are no side seams in the skirt.

1.5 cm (5/8 in.) bias-cut strips are applied at shoulder and hip yoke edges; cuff, hemline and drape edges are finished with 1 cm (3/8 in.) binding. Cut all strips on true bias of fabric (measurements indicate finished widths). Position of binding is indicated by heavier black areas on pattern.

Sleeve cuffs are finished with rouleau loops and covered buttons, also in contrast fabric.

Undergarments: Use knee-length, princess petticoat and closely fitted, elasticated corset – the bust remains unaccentuated.

Man

Expert cutting and tailoring skills are required to achieve the correct balance and proportion. The back shoulder seam requires easing on 1.3 cm (1/2 in.); the back scye held in and the front scye worked up to form a breast shape.

Trousers may be finished with two rows of braid at side seams; if two, they are placed approximately 6 mm (1/4 in.) apart. The latter is more usual when worn with a dress coat; one row with dinner jacket.

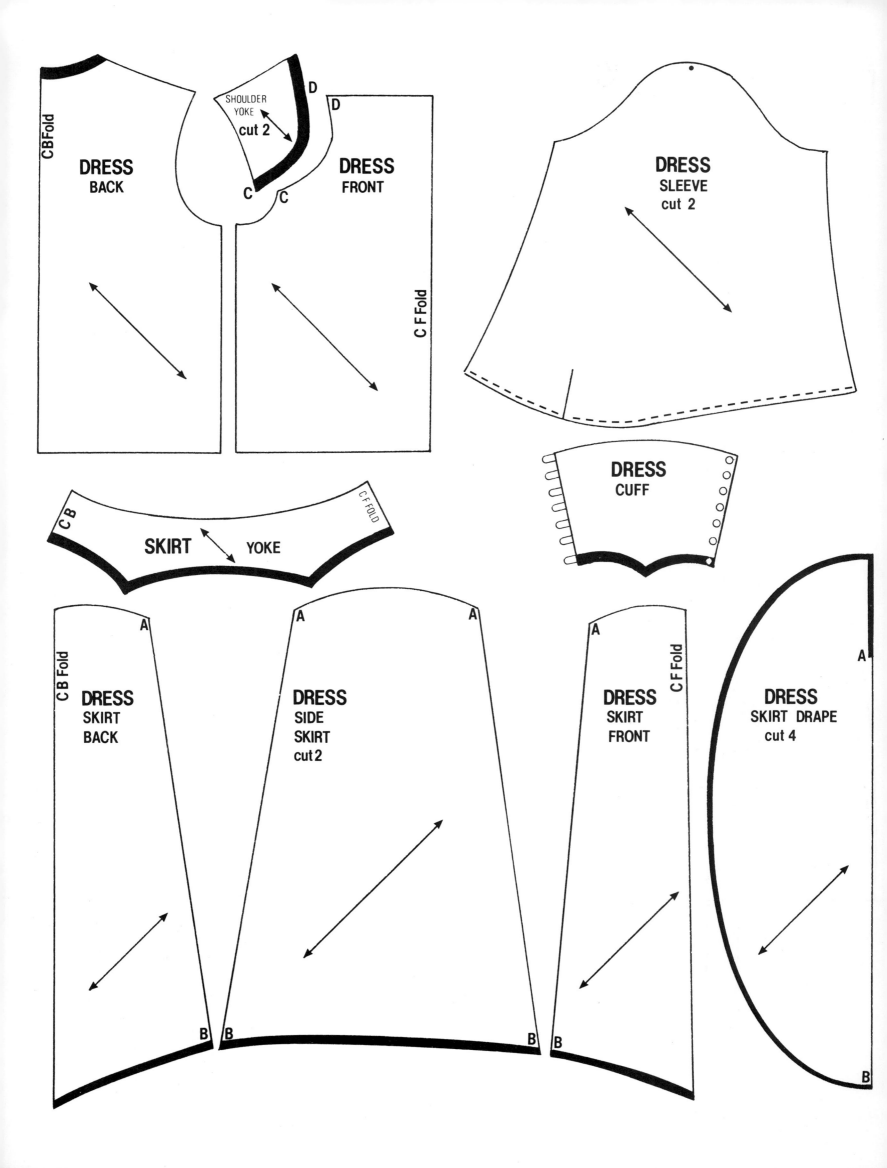

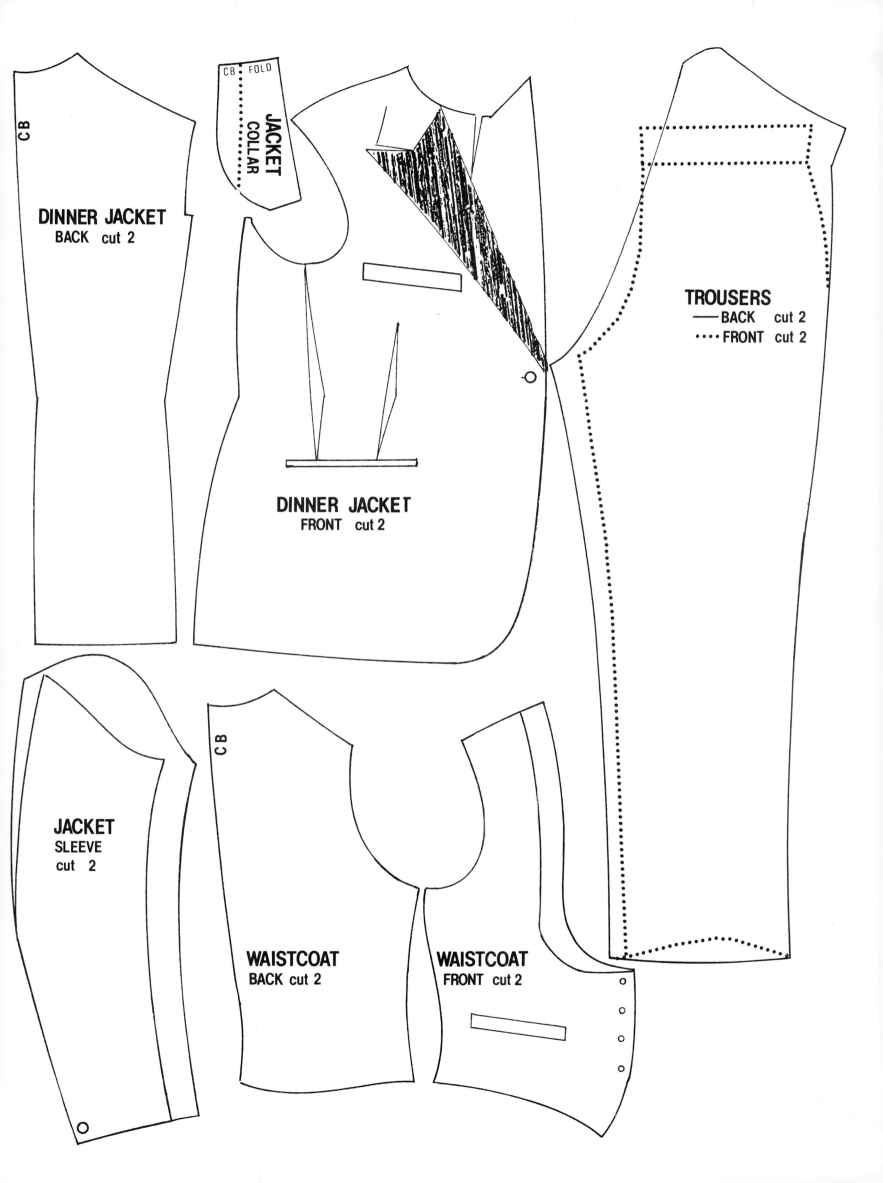

DINNER JACKET
BACK cut 2

CB

CB FOLD

**JACKET
COLLAR**

DINNER JACKET
FRONT cut 2

TROUSERS
— BACK cut 2
···· FRONT cut 2

JACKET
SLEEVE
cut 2

CB

WAISTCOAT
BACK cut 2

WAISTCOAT
FRONT cut 2

The Thirties

By the opening of the decade the waist had resumed its normal position, and throughout the 1930s emphasis was on the shoulders and hips. Hair was worn longer and with more waves, all contributing to a more feminine, mature emphasis on dress, in contrast to the boyish, youthful line of the nineteen-twenties.

By the mid-thirties the all-in-one corset and brassière was the most popular advertised garment, and the word 'uplift' entered the fashion vocabulary. Before the advent of the Second World War the bosom was well re-established, along with the hips and the pinched-in waist. Vionnet introduced the bias cut in 1930, and dresses grew more clinging and complex in cut, perhaps as a reaction to previous simplicity and the growth of the ready-to-wear industry. The new cut necessitated careful handling of the fabric and there was thus a more observable distinction between those who could afford the work of expensive couturiers and those who had to buy imitations in the cheaper shops.

The standardization of male costume in the twentieth century continued, as did the trend of informality and ease in men's dress witnessed during the previous decade. By 1939 dark-coloured shirts appeared in navy, wine, red or brown with light-toned coat and trousers for informal wear, and striped fabrics became an acceptable alternative to the white business shirt. The popularity of summer resorts in the Mediterranean, Florida and the Bahamas and the vogue for sunbathing inspired the introduction of summer evening jackets and light-coloured suits. Lower and middle classes, too, enjoyed more leisure; in the early twenties only about one-and-a-half million people had paid holidays, whereas by 1939 the figure was over eleven million. To capitalize on the holiday boom, the first all-in holiday camps on the American model appeared; Billy Butlin opened his first camp in Skegness in 1937.

A rising standard of living, paid holidays and public transport put holidays and day-trips within the reach of a wider section of the population than ever before. With the increased popularity of seaside resorts the bathing-costume inevitably assumed greater importance.

The 'bare-back' craze, with emphasis on the rear of the female dress, can be partly attributed to the backless swimsuit and sunbathing craze. Evening and summer wear throughout the period often gave the impression, from the back, of the wearer being 'stripped to the waist', and decoration and embellishments were often reserved for the back view. It is for this reason that the decade has acquired the name 'the Dorsal Period'.

The ready-to-wear market, in its infancy during the 1920s, was now being more firmly established as fashion became available to a larger proportion of the population. The salaried middle class, civil servants and clerks, were able to enjoy new luxuries. As prices fell they found they could buy houses, small cars, household gadgets and furniture as never before. A small car – an Austin 7 or a Ford 8 – cost £105 by 1932, a third of a year's salary. With the rise of the mass market Britain increasingly became a consumer society, and with the introduction of hire purchase a man without capital could for the first time equip himself on credit, although this was much frowned upon at the time. In the field of entertainment the cinema

provided a cheap means of escapism; half the population went to the pictures at least once a week. The period between the wars was one of technical revolution, with change and improvement accelerated at a pace far beyond that achieved in similar time spans in previous centuries. It is significant that in a time of mass unemployment the one industry which steadily increased its labour force was the service industry, providing comforts and entertainments.

The development of man-made fibres also accelerated at this time, and further discoveries in the production of artificial silk, in its early stages in the 1920s, overcame many of the initial problems. Rayon, as it became known from 1927, was greatly improved in quality, one advance being the discovery of how to dull the metallic gleam of the early product, making possible the production of fine, flesh-coloured yarns suitable for knitting into women's stockings. The sum total of all these changes was a gigantic increase in the output of rayon; moreover, as competition grew fiercer and as costs of production were cut, prices fell sharply – much more than those of silk, cotton or wool. Cheap woven or knitted fabrics and hosiery in rayon or rayon mixtures tapped new levels of demand in all classes.

Research into new fibres continued in Britain and abroad, and in 1938, in the USA and the UK (jointly by ICI and Courtaulds) the first fully synthetic fibre was produced; this was the polyamide Nylon 66. Innovations to improve the properties of natural fibres were also introduced: 'zingale' (uncrushable) and 'sanforized' (pre-shrunk) finishes for cotton fabrics. Stiffening methods such as 'Trubenizing' were used for men's shirt collars, which required no further starching. Separate collars also ceased to be the norm, and ready-to-wear shirts were made with collars attached.

Improvements in mass-production techniques had in themselves simultaneously raised standards and lowered costs. Combined with the wider availability and variety of cheap fabrics, the growth of factory-produced clothes forged ahead particularly rapidly. Because of the growing sophistication of clothes in the early thirties, as we have seen, home dressmaking became less viable for the amateur, and the factories were able to take over a large share of the market with passable imitations of *haute couture*. Many of the clothes produced for the retail trade were very shoddily made; the financial depression seems to have provided an excuse for a general lowering of standards. Despite the enormous improvements which had been made in the production of rayon since its inception, it is not naturally a durable fibre, and mass-production techniques generally tended to lower standards in garment construction. These two factors, both of which reduce the life of garments, served to accelerate the pace of fashion. Thus this period witnessed a basic change in attitude towards clothes, from those which had been made to last a lifetime to the new mass-produced, short-lived garment. Other inventions, such as simplification of dress fastenings, facilitated both wear and mass-production. Elastic replaced laces in underwear, and the press stud the hook and eye. Press studs often lay concealed beneath a row of decorative but useless buttons. The metal zip fastener, at first limited in use to heavier and stronger materials, proved indispensable in sports and leisure wear, and buttons were replaced by zip

fly fronts on men's trousers. Refinements, including attaching the zip to a band of stronger material, extended its use in connection with lighter fabrics employed in evening wear.

Advertising, too, continued to stimulate the fashion industry. Mass-circulation of the women's press did not really take place until *Woman* was launched by Odham's in 1937. This was the first magazine to be printed by the colour-gravure process, and offered readers and advertisers plenty of high-quality pictures much cheaper than the upper-class 'glossies'. It had a readership of half a million by the end of the year. Such developments in communication placed increasing demands on the retailer to produce new and exciting trends to attract customers. Competition between rival firms increased with the growth of advertising, which was not without its advantages for the consumer. Reduced prices and improved standards were one method of capturing the market.

The monopoly of Paris designers and couturiers on fashion was not only threatened by ready-to-wear and the rise of the department store, for now fresh influences came into play. The cinema was unparalleled in the influence it exerted on fashion. With the massive expansion of the cinema after the advent of the 'talkies' in 1927, it became a leading force in promoting new modes and methods of attraction. By 1939 the cinema was easily the most important and persuasive form of mass entertainment. It was vitally important for a number of reasons, but mostly because its influence was unambiguous and direct. There was an obvious link between fashion and the screen – the vogue for wide shoulders, slim hips and a flat chest was unmistakably popularized by the silhouette of Greta Garbo, one of the most influential stars of the period. This trend also affected the male silhouette, and by the end of the decade men's jackets were well padded and featured broader shoulders and chests. Lapels, too, became wider and more pronounced, and the vogue for turn-ups continued on the wide trouser leg.

The romance and glamour of the cinema was readily exploited by the women's journals at all levels. *Vogue* continued to emphasize Paris, the theatre, and society as the main trend-setters, and gave little recognition to the cinema until the early thirties. Yet the growing sophistication of the film and the widespread building of new super-cinemas at this time made it a respectable form of entertainment for the middle and upper middle classes at least. By 1934 *Vogue* talked of 'clothes to wear to the cinema', and fashion models were now photographed in cinematographic style. The feminine reaction in dress was no doubt heightened by the romance of Hollywood. The term 'sex appeal' entered the fashion vocabulary, and inevitably led to emphasis on the more obvious womanly attributes. The influence of the cinema was much more marked on 'glamour' dress than on practical day costume. However, more important than the dress itself was the total impact or 'look' to which every important film star made some individual contribution. The actual costume thus became representative, its aim being to create an impression of the glamour of the film world. The majority of women achieved this idea by imitating the make-up and hairstyles of their favourite film star. Naturally, this gave an overwhelming stimulus to the cosmetic and beauty industry. It is a vivid commentary on the changes that had taken place that a woman's journal advertised in 1919 a lipstick which was 'imperceptible when properly applied', while another in 1935 claimed that 'the alluring note of scarlet will stay on your lips for hours'.

Popular imitation of the stars is a fundamental consideration in understanding the fashions of the thirties. Their essentially escapist character is perhaps symbolic of the uneasiness of the decade, for it is important to remember that despite the steady rise in living standards, the period was characterized by depression and unemployment. The decade began with financial crisis in 1931, and unemployment remained at a high level throughout the thirties, reaching a peak of 3,750,000 in September 1932. Although the slump did not dramatically affect fashion, an ever-present, underlying insecurity was felt by everyone, employed or unemployed. This, plus the concern from the mid-thirties onwards about the possibility of a second world war, undoubtedly affected attitudes.

Concurrent with escapism was the amusing note which entered many fashions as the thirties continued. Hats became smaller and madder, often tilted to a degree which now seems purely ridiculous; they were a popular topic of many cartoons. Frills and decorations were often exaggerated. In 1933 the fashion emphasis fell still more heavily on the shoulders; evening gowns and summer frocks had frills arranged in tiers which jutted out over the sleevehead. Shops were full of bows, ruffles and frills, all meant to accentuate the shoulder width. Women were able to appear more feminine without sacrificing any of their new-won liberties in dress or life.

The influence of the sports world also continued to be felt throughout the 1930s, seen mostly in the more casual approach adopted by both men and women in dress. Tennis clothes had, however, followed the influence of the day dress with the reversion to a longer skirt, and by 1931 had already returned to half-way down the calf. Men's plus fours, too, became longer. Despite the evident reluctance to return to the short skirt in sport, it was inconceivable that women should return to the disadvantages of dress endured earlier in the century. Another solution was thus found which led to the wearing of shorts. This began in 1931 with the 'short sports dress', consisting of a trouser skirt reaching well below the knee, with inverted pleats. Shorts grew in popularity, and in 1935 a new kind of pleated shorts was introduced, with a double advantage: 'while the trousers allow plenty of freedom of action, you cannot tell it from a flared skirt when you stand at ease'. As the thirties drew to a close, sports clothes became increasingly functional, and complete physical freedom was established. The stylization of sports clothes, their development and tendency to become uniform, robbed them of any chance of influencing fashion. Sports clothes were now dominated by separate rules which stressed practicality and freedom of movement, regardless of contemporary fashion trends.

The same trend is apparent in day wear during this decade, which in many ways also came to be influenced by separate rules. In the mid-thirties particularly, when industry was reviving after the depression, the number of women in paid employment was expanding. During the entire span of the war, the number of women employed in commerce and its associated occupations doubled. It is in such statistics that we encounter a central phenomenon in the sociology of women's employment in the twentieth century – the rise of the business girl. The development of large-scale industry and bureaucracy would undoubtedly have brought this development in time, but it was the war, by simultaneously creating an abundance of government committees and departments, and a shortage of men, which brought an instantaneous and permanent step forward in the economic and social power of women. During the 1920s both day and evening wear, although different in many respects, followed essentially the same lines, both keeping to the straight silhouette and short skirt. However, in 1928, when designers endeavoured to lengthen the skirt by means of transparent or false hems and trains, the movement was on the whole confined to evening wear. To a limited extent day wear did follow suit, with dipping or pointed hems and a general lengthening of the skirt, but it remained essentially practical. This gap continued to widen as the thirties progressed, until there were almost two separate fashions. Comparing the elaborate fantasy evening wear with the jumpers, skirts and dresses of the business girl, it is difficult to realize that they were contemporary. Day wear was, in effect, becoming an occupational costume, designed primarily for that purpose. Evening dress no longer shared the same demands or influences.

The thirties, then, a decade of technical innovation and change, developed a characteristic approach to fashion. The period significantly marked the end of the pre-mass-production era, and the beginning of ready-to-wear clothes with the consequent wider availability of fashion. Perhaps there was a certain quietening down after the 'roaring twenties' in fashion and social life; certainly much of the outrage died away. Many phenomena persisted however: high heels and the use of make-up; and *décolletage* in evening wear, continuing to expose a large portion of the female body. The thirties, then, were not a period of startling innovation, but more a period of consolidation of many of the movements which had begun in previous years.

Female fashions, in particular, reached extravagant heights during the latter part of the decade, but this reaction was curtailed by the probability of war in 1939. The Second World War broke out on 3 September 1939.

1931

Predominant fashion features

Women

'There is more than emphasis placed on natural feminine lines, there is exaggeration.' (*Vogue*, 14 October 1931)

The waist has resumed its normal position, and emphasis falls on the shoulders and hips. Dresses grow more clinging and complex in cut, constructed largely on the bias of the fabric to achieve the necessary smooth lines and flowing hems.

The day costume evolves along practical lines, cut with long, shaped panels, fitting at the hips, flaring low and continuing to dip at the sides. Skirts 30.5 – 33.5 cm (12 – 14 in.) and dresses approximately 30.5 cm (12 in.) from the ground. Shorter blouses are often worn over the skirt.

For evening, sheath-like, slinky dresses swathe the figure, tightly moulding the hips and flaring from the knees, ankle or full-length. Low back to the evening dress – sometimes as low as the waist.

Some collarless coats, some with shorter, broader lapels. All with broad shoulders, belted to nip in the waist. Patch pockets.

Fabrics: Luxurious, heavier, clinging fabrics – satin, crêpe (rayon, silk), chiffon, shantung for evening. Softer for day – wool, rayon or silk jersey or crêpe, satin; tweeds and firm woollens for suits. Undergarments – tricot, washing satin, crêpe de Chine, Celanese.

Colours: Evening – black and white, pinks, blues, cyclamen, mauve. Day – black and white, navy, beige.

Decoration: Intricate seaming often cut diagonally across the figure. Small prints, diagonal lines and stripes. Scalloped edges. Drapery at neckline and on bodice.

Undergarments: Princess slips with attached brassière, shaped closely at the waist. With the close-fitting evening gown and heavier fabrics the slip is sometimes discarded. Corsets mould the figure to achieve the desired slimness of hips and waist. Cami-knickers and cami-bockers.

Shoes: Low-cut, court style with higher, straighter heels. Frequently in two colours and materials; pointed toes.

Stockings: Darker shades following vogue for sun-tanned skin.

Hat: Shallow crowns with upturned brim worn tilted forward over one eye.

Hair: Worn longer with more waves, side-parting.

Accessories: Gloves tighter fitting in darker shades, matching the handbag. Scarves fill in low V-necklines.

Make-up: More natural-looking than mask-like face of the twenties.

Men

'The emphasis in tailoring is on the chest, and the main object is to imply breadth and fullness in that region.' (*Tailor and Cutter*)

The waistline is above the natural hollow; buttons and pockets are higher. Lapels have diminished in length and increased in width. The double-breasted reefer jacket is a very popular style, with two rows of buttons and wider front. Jetted pockets remain the vogue because they help to suggest narrow flanks.

Trousers are of medium width, cut rather long in the leg, with turn-ups. Pleats and a top welt or waistband persist. For business and formal wear black jacket with striped trousers continues, and a dark lounge suit is frequently worn. Two-piece suits often worn, with the waistcoat replaced by a pullover or sleeveless slipover.

For sports – flannel trousers and sports jacket or tweed lounge suit.

Overcoats feature squareness and breadth of shoulder.

Fabrics: Fine woollen suiting, serge, worsted, in dark colours, grey or navy for business attire. Striped flannel, herringbones and checks. Large checks or patterned tweeds for sports jackets and suits or overcoats.

Colours: Browns and blues in forefront as suitings, grey and fawn for summer. Subdued colours with brighter overcheck or woven flecks.

Decoration: Hand-stitched edge of collar and lapels of informal suits is a new feature during 1930s. Racoon fur collars for winter overcoats.

Undergarments: Similar to previous fashion.

Socks: Plain or ribbed, silk or lisle, black or dark blue. Half-hose to tone with suits, white and cream half-hose for sports.

Shoes: Lower in heel than previous decade. Spats continue to be used with low shoes or Oxfords. Summer and sports shoes of white buckskin. Generally, shoes tend to be heavy to balance the wide trouser leg, as in the twenties.

Hair: Short hair remains fashionable for men, although fuller and with more waves than the former flattened style.

Hats: Trilby for day wear. Bowler hat for more formal and business attire.

Accessories: As previous fashion.

Details of illustrated patterns

Woman

Wedding dress cut in similar style to contemporary evening wear. Diagonal-cut bias panels ensure the bodice drapes the figure closely. The bodice continues through defined waistline, giving essential slimness of hip. The full-length skirt is also cut on the bias, flaring from hip yoke to full hemline. The centre back panel is cut entirely in one – extended to form a sweeping train. Moderate V-neckline faced in satin, and wrist-length slim-fitting sleeves.

A simple headdress of orange blossom and small pearls secures the full-length veil; the proportion of the head must always remain small.

Fabrics and colour: White crêpe de Chine with white satin contrast fabric at neckline; white tulle for veil.

Footwear: White satin slippers – frequently made in the same fabric as the dress.

Accessories: Mid-length white suede gloves, worn wrinkled over wrists; large bouquet.

Man

Formal wedding outfit consisting of morning coat, waistcoat and trousers. The coat fits closely over the hips, with cutaway fronts, and length of skirt reaching to around the bend of the knee. Pointed lapels roll low from single-link fastening at high waistline. Other variations of the morning coat include one or two bone or silk-covered buttons and right-angle step collar. There is an outside breast pocket and dart taken out of the forepart, defining the waist and giving breadth and ease over the chest; squareness of shoulders also imparts size to the chest. Two-piece set-in sleeves finish with slit cuff and four-button fastening. The jacket back is cut with centre back seam, vent and side pleats in the skirt, ending with two covered buttons at waist seam. Light-coloured double-breasted waistcoat, cut low in fronts, and just visible both above and below the buttoning of the coat. The Ascot cravat is more usual, since it balances the large expanse of shirt, although a narrow knot or bow tie may also be worn. The trousers are cut on the same lines as day wear, and always without turn-ups.

Note: Younger men often wear a black lounge jacket waistcoat and striped trousers.

Fabrics and colours: Black or grey woollen worsted suiting; black-and-white striped cashmere for trousers.

Undergarments: White linen shirt with starched wing collar and cuffs.

Footwear: Plain laced shoe in black patent leather with white spats.

Hat: Silk top hat.

Accessories: White kid gloves; walking stick; white flower in left lapel; white handkerchief for decoration only; tie pin, cuff links.

Notes on construction of garments

Woman

Bias cut requires careful handling of the fabric – the dress should mould the upper figure and hips, with easing allowed at the waistline. Lower part of dress back is illustrated by broken lines on pattern. The pattern pieces should be joined at 1 and 2 *before* cutting; back and extended train are then cut in one panel.

Separate back neckband from dress back by cutting pattern piece along dotted line. Adjust the pattern pieces as necessary to achieve required slimness of hips and fullness of skirt in proportion to the figure.

The veil is gathered on to the narrow headdress and secured to the head with hair combs. It may be cut from one length of wide tulle and rounded at corners. Sufficient length should be allowed to cover the train at the back and form a short face veil.

Undergarments: Use full-length, princess-style petticoat and close-fitting, ready-made corset. The bustline must not be emphasized.

Man

Tailoring skills are required to achieve the correct balance and proportion. Additional ease is allowed in the back shoulder seam and over front scye to provide fullness over the chest.

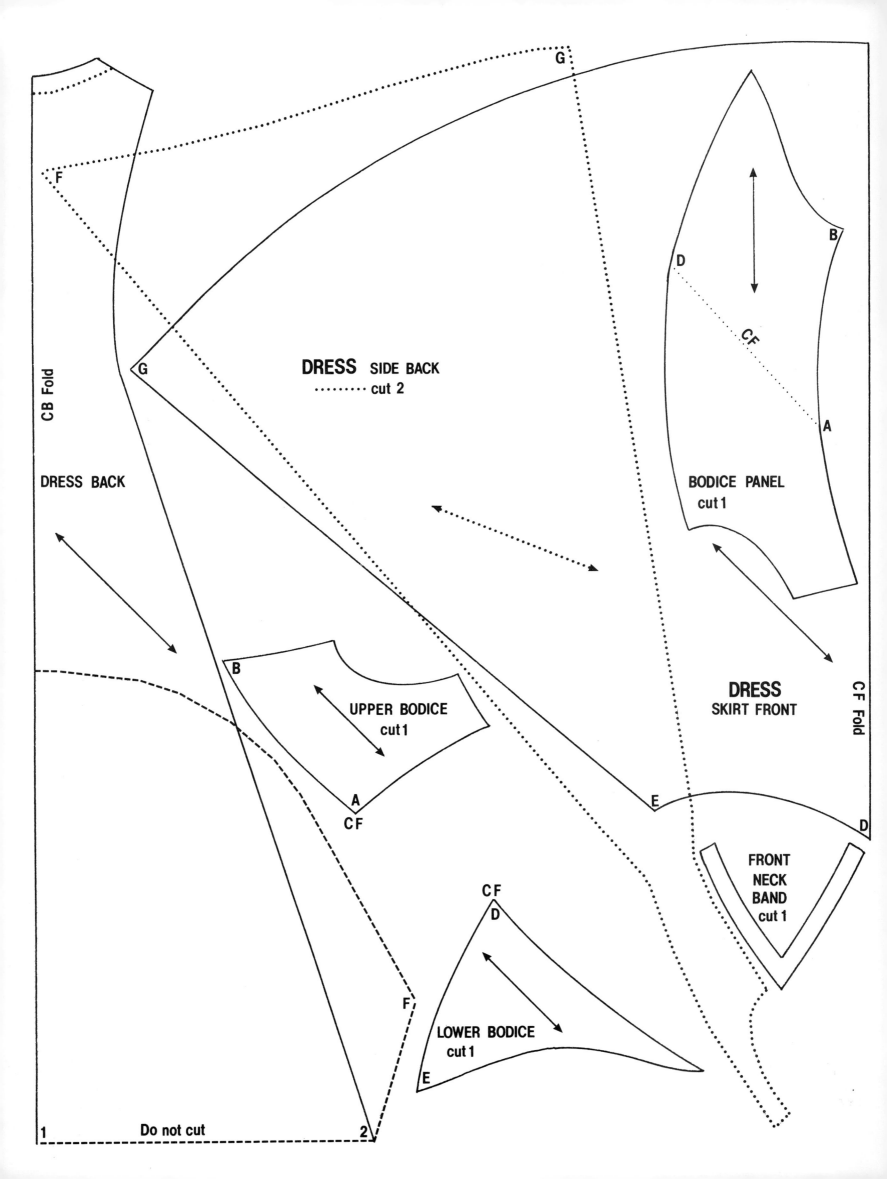

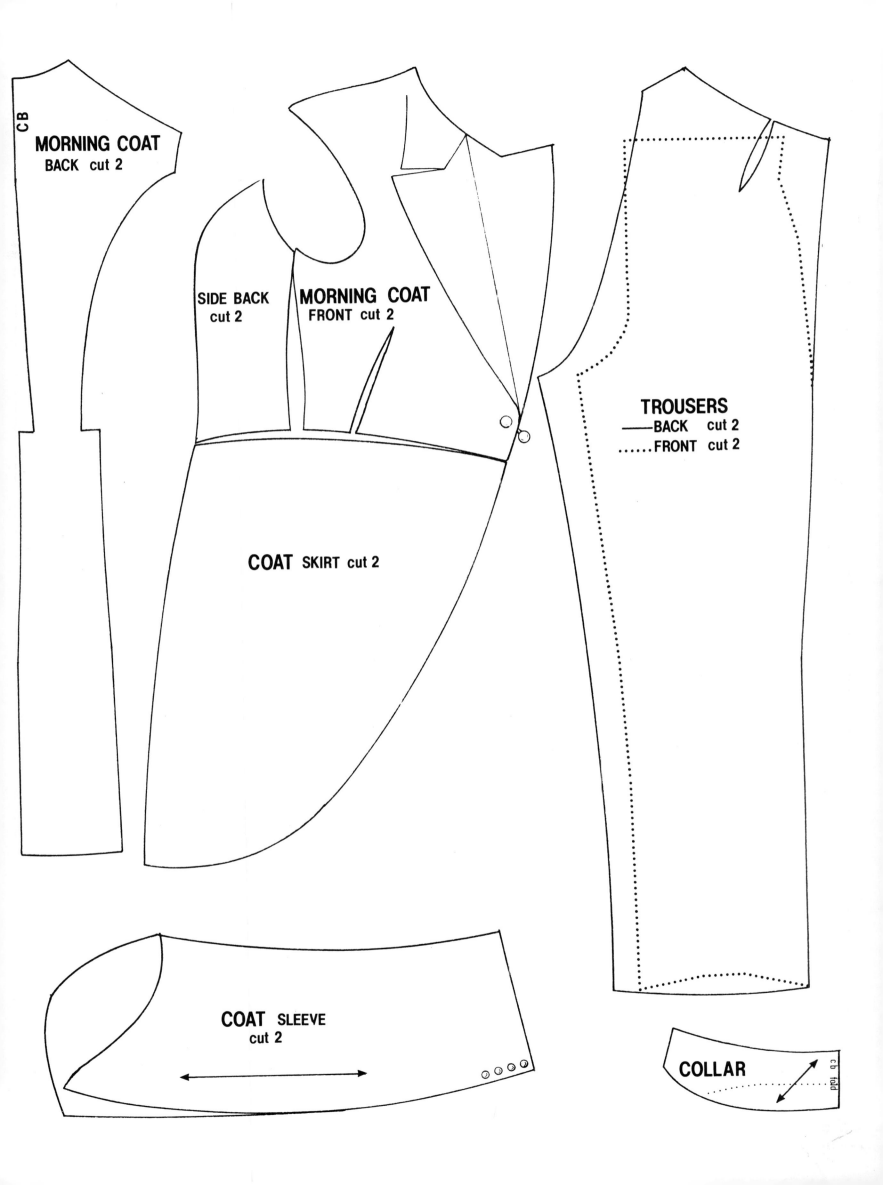

CB

MORNING COAT
BACK cut 2

SIDE BACK
cut 2

MORNING COAT
FRONT cut 2

TROUSERS
——— BACK cut 2
······ FRONT cut 2

COAT SKIRT cut 2

COAT SLEEVE
cut 2

COLLAR

cb fold

1934

Predominant fashion features

Women

Fashion emphasis falls more heavily on the shoulders. Long coats are longer than the dresses they are worn with, 117 cm (46 in.) from nape of neck. Coats belonging to costumes are rather short, all heavily padded. Lapels are broad and pointed, tailored along masculine lines, waists fit closely and appear very small in comparison to the broad shoulders. Capes are a popular feature, especially with single-breasted styles.

Three-quarter-length swagger and jigger coats create a triangle over slim skirt, cut with additional fullness at the back.

Skirts for morning and afternoon take rather a straight, tight line, with fullness below the knee. Short inverted pleats, box and knife pleats, are placed at the sides and back to give freedom of movement. Diagonal seams are frequently used. Short overblouse often worn belted over the skirt.

Evening gowns and summer frocks have frills arranged in tiers which jut out over the shoulders. Bows, ruffles and frills all accentuate the shoulder width. Decoration and low necklines confined mostly to the back of the dress. Fullness is low, close-fitting over the hips and flaring from the knee, with long trains.

Summer dresses in softer fabrics follow the contour of the figure. Cowl necklines and sleeves popular. Dresses approximately 30.5 cm (12 in.) from the ground.

Short vogue for Tudor-look fashion with slashed and padded sleeves. Sports clothes become briefer.

Fabrics: Fine dress woollens, jersey, crêpe.

Luxurious evening fabrics – velvet, reversible satin, taffeta, moiré, crêpe de Chine, crinkle rayons.

Heavily flecked angora and Scotch tweeds for coats, suits and sportswear; diagonal and honeycomb weaves, checks, tartans, plaids and stripes.

Colours: Black and white, browns, dark chocolate, navy, grey. Other favoured colours – Persian red, raspberry red, royal and midnight blue, terracotta, mulberry. Plain and figured fabrics are frequently combined; a plain dress may have a figured coat, or the dress may be figured while the coat is plain.

Decoration: Diagonally striped fabrics; large bows in bold checks or stripes with tailored suits; brighter trimmings and scarves in orange, turquoise, pink, emerald, purples.

Furs – silver and blue fox, grey astrakhan, seal, skunk, used wherever possible, especially for collars and cuffs. Large, square wooden buttons, brass buttons.

Top-stitching detail on plain fabrics.

Undergarments: Brassières begin to separate and support. Lightweight bras of bias fabric cut low for evening wear. Backless evening slips and princess petticoats, moulding the figure closely.

Lastex yarn effects revolution in undergarments, providing two-way stretch, support without stiffening. Step-in hip belts and 'roll-ons', entirely composed of lastex yarn. Singlettes – brassière, vest, girdle and pantie combined.

Footwear: Dyed leathers to co-ordinate with the costume.

Stockings: Medium or subdued tints, 'skin tones'.

Hats: To match the outfit, tricornes, berets, worn well tilted over one eye or at the back of the head. Tudor fashions – velvet Tudor halos, juliet caps.

Hair: Side-parting with flat crown and curls at the side and back of the head, swept back from the face.

Accessories: Long gauntlet-style gloves. Bags co-ordinate with shoes, gloves and stockings – brown and grey leathers, pochettes and clutch handbags.

Large box-calf belts.

Fur capes.

Make-up: Imitation of favourite cinema stars. Eyebrows plucked into thin, arched line and reshaped with eyebrow-pencil. Make-up dark, following craze for suntans. Red lipstick.

Men

Jackets continue popular trend with fullness over the chest, square cut shoulders and closer-fitting over the hips. Lapels slightly rolled, wide and pointed.

Thick overcoats in fleecy woollen fabrics – 'teddy bear' coats. Raincoats and mackintoshes, loose-fitting, trench styles with belts popular.

Evening – dinner jackets and dress coats cut with wide, pointed lapels with wide-chested effects. Link-fastening and jetted pockets popular. Backless waistcoats of white piqué, joined at the back of the collar and with a strap and buttons or buckle at waist-level. Black waistcoats with dinner jackets.

Fabrics: Similar to previous fashion.

Colours: Similar to previous fashion. Midnight blue an acceptable alternative to black for evening wear.

Undergarments: Many shirts with attached collars, celluloid stiffeners inserted between a double piece of fabric in the undercollar. Short-sleeved sports shirt with polo collar, the sleeves reaching to just above the elbow. Plain fronts for dress shirts and decline in use of fancy fabrics. Shorts and trunks with lastex waistbands.

Footwear: Similar to previous fashion.

Socks: Similar to previous fashion.

Hats: Similar to previous fashion; crowns generally higher and brims broader.

Hair: Similar to previous fashion.

Accessories: Gloves essential item of male dress; short gauntlet style. Ties – spotted, striped, or small figured silks. Tie-clips used when no waistcoat is worn .

Details of illustrated patterns

Woman

Double-breasted collarless coat, with shoulder cape cut in one with back panel. The cape is edged with a separate band of self fabric and top-stitching detail. The coat is slim-fitting over natural waistline, accentuated by quarter-belt at the front and two-button fastening. It is calf-length, fitting slimly over the hips and with only moderate flare in the skirt. Plain, two-piece, set-in sleeves are narrow throughout. It is worn longer than the skirt or dress.

Fabrics: Fine woollen facecloth or twill weave.

Colours: Brown, beige or cream.

Shoes: Leather court shoes with high slim heel, dyed to match the outfit.

Hat: Felt hat with narrow brim and grosgrain ribbon trim on shallow crown, worn tilted.

Accessories: Gauntlet-style gloves to match outfit, worn over coat sleeve; cream suede, leather and patent clutch bag with clasp fastening and metal frame; a silk scarf fills in the low neckline.

Man

Lounge suit consisting of jacket, waistcoat and trousers. Single-breasted lounge jacket with two-button fastening is cut with square shoulders and wide back stretch. There is a dart taken out of the foreparts, an angled welt pocket on the chest and flap pockets at hip-level. The roll is cut moderately low with wide, notched collar and foreparts rounded at lower edges. Two-piece set-in sleeves with slit button cuffs, and centre back seam with no vent.

The single-breasted waistcoat is just visible between jacket lapels, fastening with five buttons.

Trousers are generously cut with pleats into waistband at fronts, and side seam pockets. Permanent turn-ups at lower edge are 4.5cm (1¾in) in depth.

Fabrics and colours: Fine, striped worsted suiting of grey or blue.

Undergarments: Plain white shirt with attached collar.

Footwear: Laced Oxford-style shoes.

Hat: Bowler hat with curled brim.

Accessories: Grey leather gloves; bold striped tie with pointed ends; handkerchief in breast pocket for decoration only.

Notes on construction of garments

Woman

Coat back panel is underlined with firm linen or cotton fabric and joined to main fabric from **A** to **B**. The underlining is therefore left free below top caped section. Join back to side back from **A** to **B**; break the stitching at point **B** and continue to stitch side back to underlining only as far as **C**. The lower band of the cape may then be attached, and is caught into front neckline dart only after shoulders, side seams and sleeves are complete. Position of coat back underlining is indicated by broken lines on pattern.

Separate band from cape pattern along dotted lines *before* cutting in fabric. Seam allowance will be required on both edges for joining, and at lower edges of band. Seam allowance must also be added to outer edges of front belt pattern.

A 1cm seam allowance is given on all remaining edges. Hem allowances are not included.

Top-stitch cape and front belt as illustrated.

Man

Ease back to front at shoulder seams of jacket. Padding is required to achieve fashionable squared shoulders and wide-chested effect.

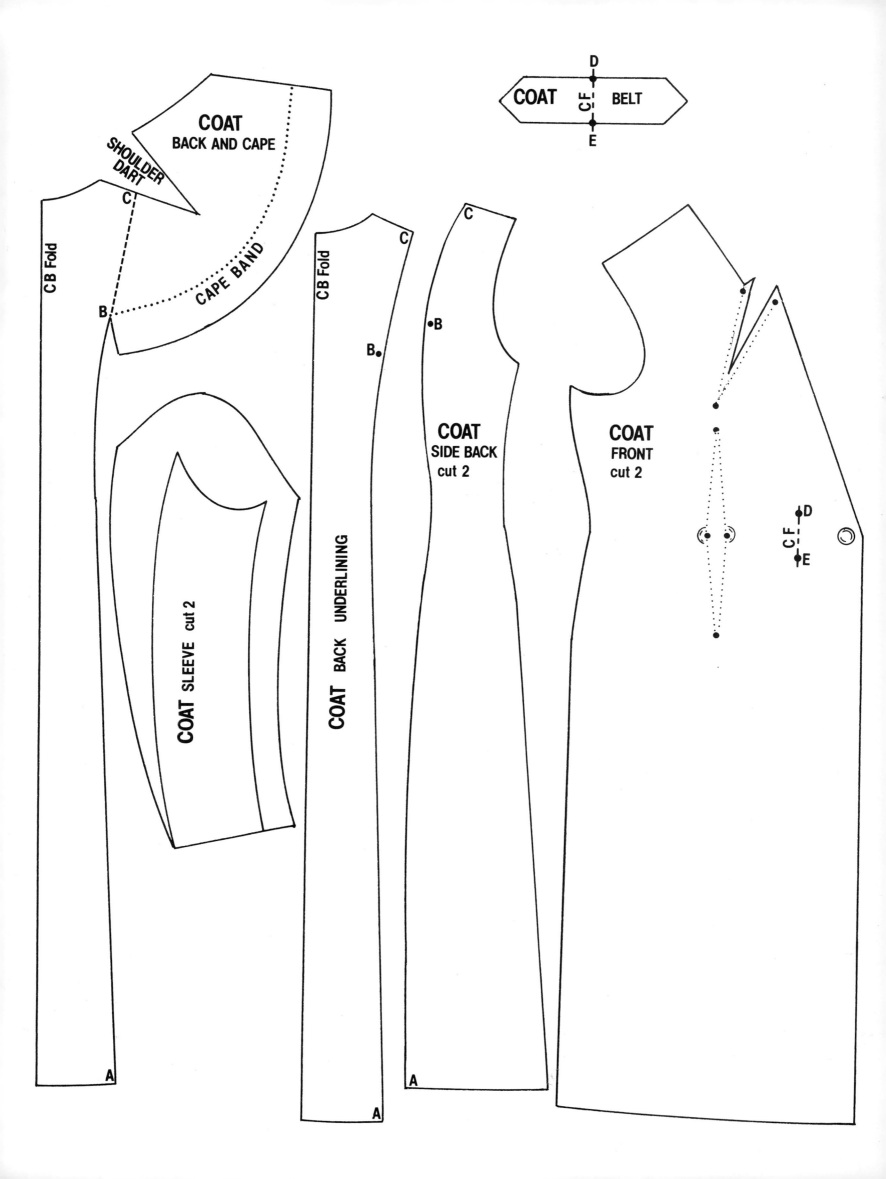

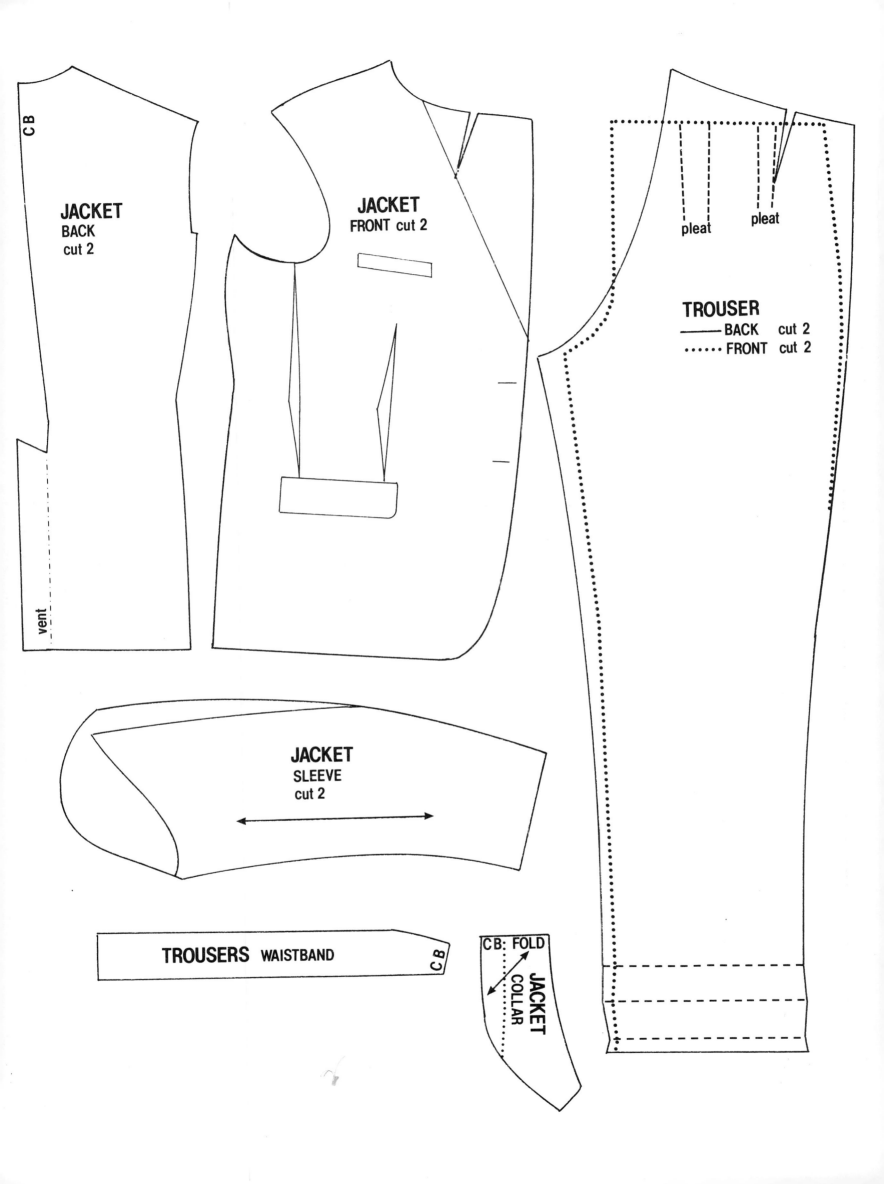

JACKET
BACK
cut 2

CB

vent

JACKET
FRONT cut 2

JACKET
SLEEVE
cut 2

TROUSER
—— BACK   cut 2
······ FRONT   cut 2

pleat   pleat

TROUSERS WAISTBAND

CB

CB: FOLD

JACKET
COLLAR

1935

Predominant fashion features

Women

Similar to previous fashion, with less severe emphasis on the shoulders; sleeves, belts and necklines important. Softness at neckline achieved with scarves and cowl necks; ruffles, collars, jabots, frills, exaggerated bows on blouses, and loose, full bishop sleeves.

In contrast, severe military daytime look with square epauletted shoulders, frogging and regimental-style buttons.

'Women have set themselves the rather difficult task of producing the military silhouette during the day, and an alluringly feminine silhouette for evening wear.' (*Daily Express*, 24 October 1932)

Short bolero jackets over wool dresses. Panel skirts, fitting slim from waist to hips with hip basques, pleats, intricate seaming, flaring low.

Coats — loose three-quarter-length with large collars, bold revers, dropped shoulder lines. Swagger coats with bias cut, swing back, creating a triangle over close-fitting skirts. Capes for day and evening in every length, caped coats and evening dresses.

For evening — greater emphasis is given to the bust, with pleated fullness, shirring between and under the breasts; unbelted dresses are cut up in a triangle with the bodice gathered to it. Necklines less low-cut than in previous year. Interest, fullness and low neckline continue at the back.

Fabrics: Textured fabrics — crêpe (silk, wool, rayon), crinkle silks and rayons, soft woollen dress fabrics, small checks, diagonal stripes. Tweeds, checks, fancy worsteds, Bedford cords.

Evening - velvets, satin, chiffon, artificial silk, ninon, lamé.

Colours: Black and white predominant. Navy and white for town and business. Day — red, orange, yellow, green, purple, plum. Evening — black, white, gold, silver, dark blue. Pastel shades for day and evening — soft and subtle smoky greys, pinks.

Decoration: Predominant use of contrasts — matt and satin textures, plain suits with striped, checked or spotted bows, prints with reversed backgrounds. Embroidery, scallop edgings, top-stitching detail. Fur on collars and sleeves.

Undergarments: Seamless, roll-on hip belts in lastex, zip fastenings. Lastex yarn and lace brassières. Corsets with new 'uplift' brassière and insets of lastex for diaphragm control. Open-mesh elastic for sports and summer. Backless bras and corselettes cut on true bias.

Footwear: As 1936.

Stockings: As 1936.

Hats: Hats are getting smaller and smaller — 'little nothings perched at precarious angles on your head'. Matching the outfit, sometimes made in the same fabric as the coat.

'Veils will be more important than hats' (*Vogue*, December 1935)

Large-brimmed hats with tiny, shallow crowns in straw or taffeta for summer, trimmed with fabric bows, bindings and tulle.

Hair: Mass of curls high on the head for evening, all hair swept back from the face and curled.

Accessories: As 1936.

Make-up: Similar to previous fashion. Bright red lipstick. Blue eyeshadow, black mascara; eyelash dye and false eyelashes. Make-up more pronounced for evening.

Men

Similar to previous fashion.

Overcoats shorter in length, just covering the knee. Shorter pullovers and knitted slipovers for sport. Knitted cardigans in plain colours with overworked check in self shades.

Fabrics: Fancy tweeds, whipcords and worsted suitings. Sports tweeds, flannels and serges.

Colours: Similar to previous fashion. Midnight blue is acceptable alternative to black for evening tail coats and dinner jackets.

Undergarments: Shirts — coloured grounds with coloured stripes. Semi-stiff collars for shirts, white or to match the shirt. Striped shirts predominate.

Footwear: As previous fashion.

Socks: Short length socks for summer sports — flannel greys, oatmeals, and white being prominent. Also darker suiting shades for everyday wear. 'Lastex' yarn in the top holds it firmly in position, below the calf of the leg. Suspenders or garters are unnecessary.

Hats: As 1936.

Hair: As previous fashion.

Accessories: Silk ties in two-colour stripe effect, e.g. brown and white, black and grey. Handkerchiefs with borders of a similar stripe arrangement.

Other accessories as previous fashion.

Details of illustrated patterns

Woman

Norfolk-style jacket, panelled at front and back. Wide revers are cut moderately high with wide notched collar and lapels, faced in contrasting check fabric, and single-breasted four-button fastening. Four patch pockets trimmed with check material and buttons match collar and revers. The natural waistline is emphasized by wide insertion of check fabric, forming a mock belt. Narrow two-piece sleeves are set into broad shoulder line.

A divided sports skirt completes the costume. It carries a single knife pleat at each side front, also a small strapping with three imitation holes and buttons. The skirt is cut with hip basque and continuation waistband.

The outfit is worn with masculine collar and striped tie.

Fabrics: Fine tweed or worsted.

Colours: Tan, brown or blue with toning overcheck for contrast.

Shoes: Low-heeled, brown or black leather brogue lace-ups.

Hat: Small felt hat with shallow, flattened crown and narrow, curled brim, turned up at sides. Narrow grosgrain ribbon trim.

Accessories: Gauntlet-style, wrist-length suede gloves to match the outfit.

Man

Golfing costume consisting of single-breasted, lounge jacket and long striped plus fours. The jacket is cut on contemporary lines, with fullness over the chest, square-cut shoulders, and closely fitting over the hips. Pockets with flaps at hip level and a breast pocket showing a handkerchief. Step collar and three buttons on front, but with only the middle one fastened, throwing additional ease over the chest by making the waistline appear smaller. The jacket back is cut with centre back seam and vent. Two-piece, set-in sleeves finish with slit cuff and three-button fastening.

Long plus fours are made wide at the knee, pleated into wide bands at lower edges, fastening with buckle and strap. Two pleats are put in the front waist on each side, and pockets are inserted in side seams.

The outfit is worn with a sleeveless vest-pullover of tweed with linen trim, replacing the traditional waistcoat. The garment buttons on left side seam with fly and four buttons; waistband buttons through with two holes.

Fabrics: Flannel or serge for jacket, striped flannel for plus fours.

Colours: Muted shades of grey, brown or tan.

Footwear: Brown leather shoes with fringed over-tongue to cover laces. Ribbed golf hose, toning with the suit.

Accessories: Tie with cream background and overcheck to match the suit; suede or leather gloves; handkerchief in breast pocket for decoration only.

Notes on construction of garments

Woman

Jacket — cut belt, pocket decoration and collar and lapel facings in check fabric. Position of pockets is indicated on pattern.

Cut jacket front and side front pattern pieces along lines **A** to **B** and **C** to **D**. The belt is cut as a separate section and constructed with jacket front. The same applies at jacket back with panel seam stitched through belt. Padding is required over the shoulders to give squared appearance. Allow for all seams except the scye.

Skirt — the waistband is split for the side seam and placket each side.

Man

Padding is required over the shoulders of jacket to indicate broad chest and wide shoulders.

Pleat plus fours into waistband and knee straps. Fly front opening may fasten with zip or buttons. Pockets may be inserted at side seams.

Add overlap of 1.9 cm (¾ in.) to left side of vest-pullover for button opening. V-neckline and armholes are bound with bias linen tape, with waistband also of linen fabric. The vest-pullover should fit the figure closely and is especially trim at the waist.

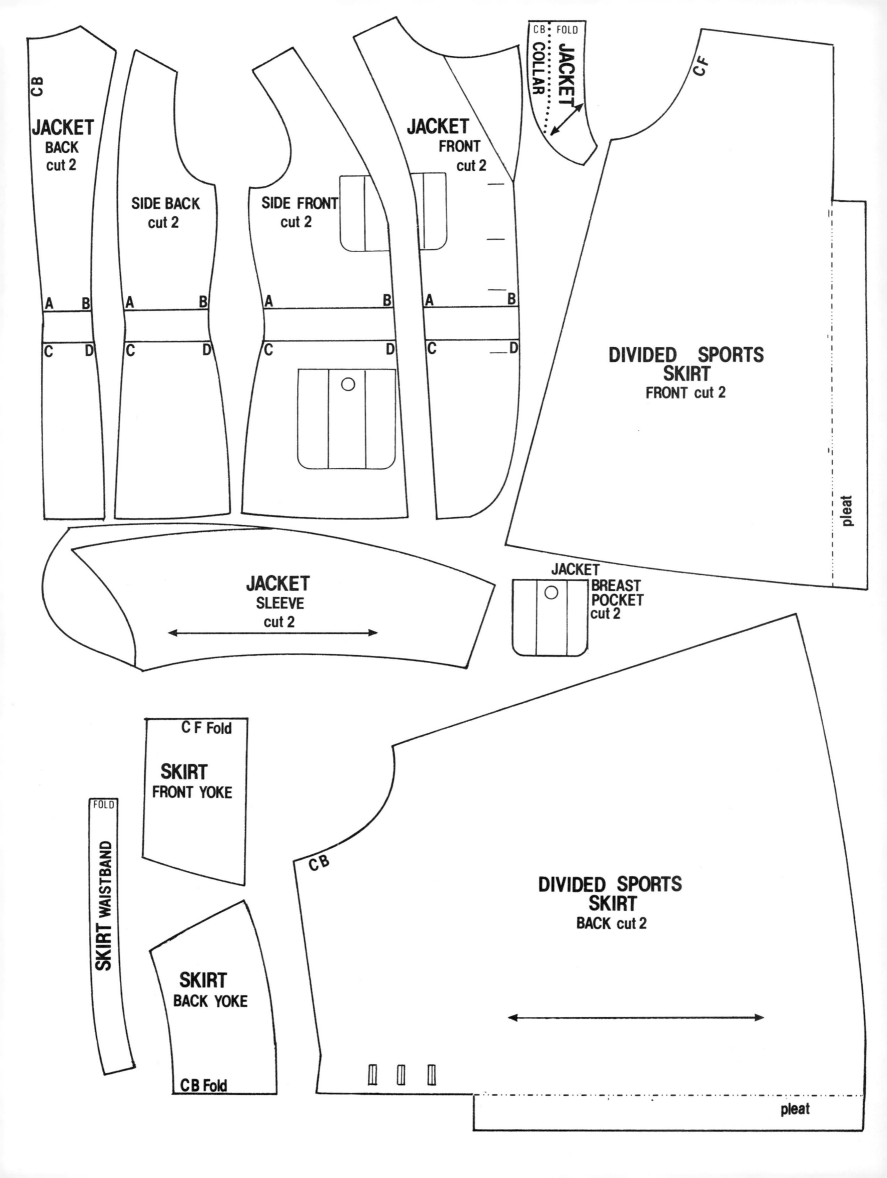

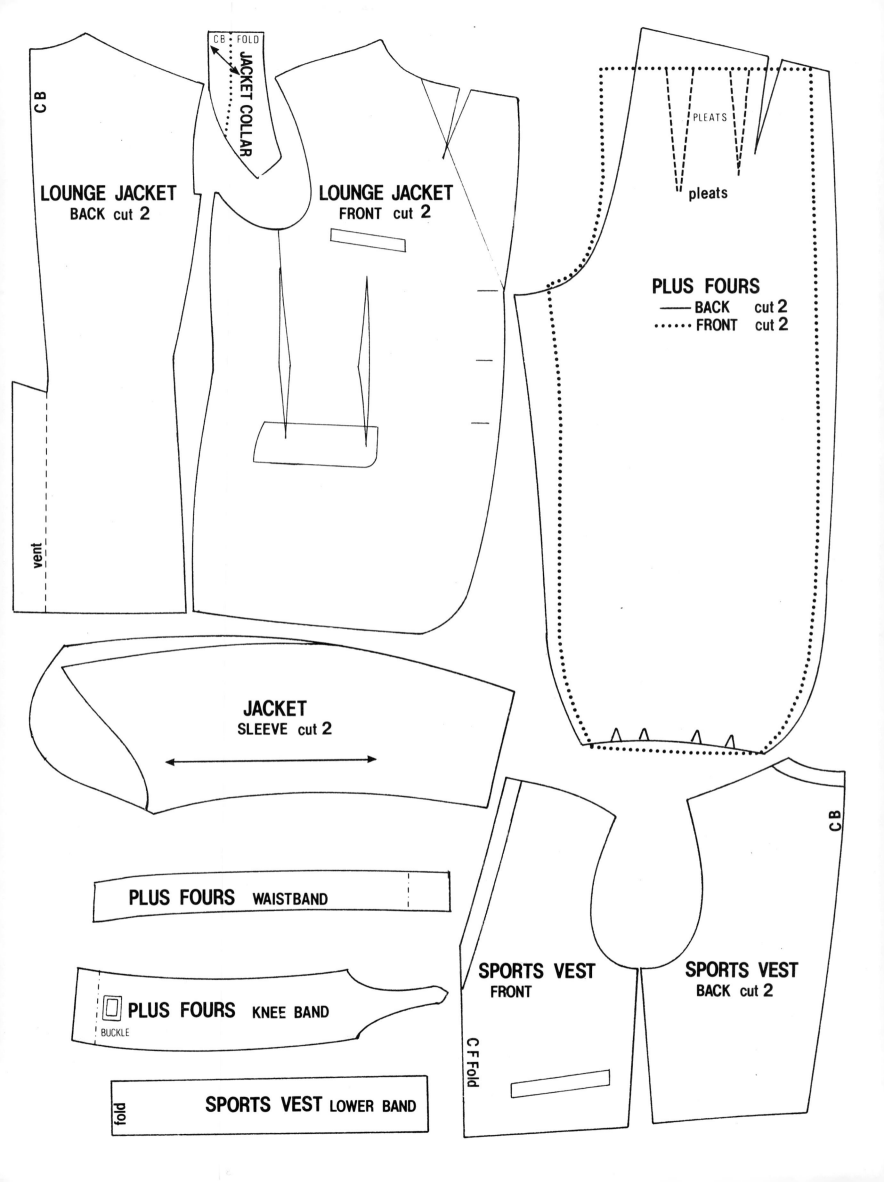

1936

Predominant fashion features

Women

The fashion lines of the previous year continue, with prevalent use of contrasts in fabric and colours. Jackets and coats are lined with shirt or dress fabrics, with padded shoulders — less accentuated shoulder width than first half of the decade; large collars and rounded lapels.

Tunic-styles predominate — peplum jackets, flaring from the waist to finger tip length over bias-cut skirts. Tunic coats or loose swagger or jigger coats flaring from the shoulders.

Blouses high-necked with short, puffed sleeves. Matching knitted jumpers, short-waisted cardigans and skirts.

Sports and informal wear — dull tweeds, boxy or swagger coats over slim skirts; divided sports skirts or flannel trousers. For tennis, shorts or very short sports dress well above the knee, evolved from shirts and shorts outfit.

Evening fashions show a change in emphasis to more romantic, feminine appeal. Some Empire line, bustle effects with large bows and drapery. Back remains low. Fullness swings to the back of the dress, remaining straight at the front and slim on hips. Short boleros cover evening gowns.

Dinner suits with long slim skirt, flaring from the knees with jacket and closely fitting blouse, in luxurious fabrics — velvets and satins.

Fabrics: Tweeds, alpaca, fine dress woollens, crêpe, taffeta. Flannel and tweeds for sports and informal wear.

Wide range of crease-resistant fabrics. 'Lystav' — new linen-look, rayon fabric; 'Tootal Linen' — a pure dress linen.

Satin, velvet, crêpe, taffeta for evening.

Colours: Black and white, navy and white, royal blue, turquoise. Pastel shades for evening.

Decoration: Contrast effects using reverse grounds of prints, and contrast textures. Black and white novelty prints — newsprint, handwriting, pins, pigs, matches.

Drapery from shoulders or hips, sunburst pleats of chiffon; shirring and cording under the bust for emphasis.

Flower worn on bosom, belt, or as hair and hat decoration — 'real or artificial — it doesn't matter — but somewhere, somehow, you must have a flower'. (*Vogue*, 1936) Flowers embroidered on corsage; bead embroidery. Novelty buttons — birds, flowers, bows, geometric shapes.

Undergarments: Tailored, bias-cut slips fit smoothly over the hips, swinging at the hemline towards the back. Brightly coloured taffeta petticoats. Bias-cut hip belts, seamless roll-ons or with zip fastening. Uplift brassières. Panties and girdles in one for under trousers.

Peach, candy and shell-pink fashionable colours, edged with écru or coffee lace.

Footwear: Open-toed sandals — leather for day, gold and silver kid, satins and brocades for evening. Shoes frequently made in two materials and colours to co-ordinate with contrasts in dress — white and navy, white and brown, white buckskin and black patent popular. Higher heels 6.35 cm (2½ in.). Lower-heeled shoes for sport 3 cm (1⅛ in.). Overshoes worn over the ordinary shoe for protection in wet weather.

Stockings: Darker shades for day wear; ladderproof stockings constructed with lastex. Ribbed lisle stockings or knee-high stockings with lastex supports for sports.

Socks: As previous fashion. Ankle-length socks for tennis, supported with lastex yarn.

Hats: Slightly shallower crowns and narrow brims, Bretons, pill-box and panama styles, turbans and toques. Fabric, flower and veil trimmings all popular.

Hair: Upward curls frame the face, flat on sides and back.

Accessories: Suede gloves to match the outfit, gauntlet-style, long or short; short gloves for evening in satin, organdie, taffeta. Belts — wide at the front, sloping to narrow width at the back: 'so wide that they come up and support the bust'. Pochettes — large clutch bags. Spanish shawls, velvet and fur evening wraps and capes. Revival of small muffs. Jewellery — earclips, wrist bangles, strings of pearls worn high at neck. Brooches on wide revers.

Make-up: Matching rouge, lipstick and nail enamel. 'Bright red', 'gay red', 'poppy', 'geranium', 'rich raspberry', 'terracotta'. Run-proof mascara.

Men

Style of the early thirties, with wide-pointed lapels and broad shoulders, continues. Trousers remain moderately wide in the leg with turn-ups.

Sports jackets might be worn with open-neck shirt or pullover, longer plus fours or flannel trousers.

Waist-length golf jackets of suede or proofed gabardine, with knitted welts at waist and wrists. Fastening to one side with zips or buttons.

Overcoats follow loose, square-cut trend, with patch pockets.

Fabrics and colours: Similar to previous fashion. Striped flannels and worsted suitings predominant. Tweeds and checks for sports in brighter colours, greens and tan.

Undergarments: Coat-style shirts (button-through), easily available ready-made.

Sports shirt with attached polo collar; the sleeves reach to elbow-length while the body part is cut more fitting than the day shirt. Singlets sleeveless with jersey or low round necks. Trunks and shorts with lastex waistbands.

Footwear: Oxford laced shoe most popular style, brogued for sports with fringed tongue protecting the laces. Monk shoes with side buckle fastening.

Socks: Golf hose in ribbed styles, plain fawns, browns and greys, toning with the suit. Lastex tops support socks below the knee. Golf hose to match pullover.

Hats: Trilby with snap brim which can be turned up or down, according to taste. Pork pie hat, flatter than the trilby with rounded dent in crown. Loose-fitting tweed peaked caps for sports and country.

Accessories: Similar to previous fashion. Gloves — coarser leather and knitted for sports and country. Smoother leather and kid, light for summer. Light-coloured gloves with formal evening dress. Brief- and attaché-cases with business suits.

Details of illustrated patterns

Woman

Swagger coat and skirt featuring slightly dropped shoulder line with a front and back yoke into a narrow panel. Pin-tucks are arranged to give a wider appearance to the upper section. The cross-fastening tabs which are cut on at the neck are high, but low enough to wear a decorative scarf in a large bow if desired. The coat is cut on straight lines and can be made either in three-quarter or seven-eighth length. The sleeves are two-piece, slit through the centre and finished with two buttons and tabs at wrist. Two roomy outside patch pockets with a cut-on strap and button are placed fairly high on the foreparts. The skirt is cut with a front yoke and panel with an inverted pleat in the centre and a knife pleat either side. The centre pleat is 28 cm (11 in.) long, and the knife pleats 20.25 cm (8 in.) long, providing ample ease for movement. It is cut on modest lines, and only widened by pleats below the knees.

Fabrics: Medium-weight flannel, tweed, alpaca.

Colour: Beige.

Footwear: Two-tone court shoes of white buckskin and brown leather.

Hat: Flat-brimmed felt hat with rounded crown and cream and brown striped ribbon trim, worn tilted over one eye.

Accessories: Silk cream-and-brown-striped scarf worn in large bow at neckline; suede gauntlet-style gloves to match outfit; brown leather clutch bag with strap buckle fastening.

Man

Single-breasted, knee-length raglan overcoat fastening high at the neckline; roomy patch pockets with flaps at hip-level and split sleeves with stitched double cuffs. The style retains fullness across the chest and broad shoulders characteristic of the period. The top button may be worn unfastened with collar turned up. The coat is easy-fitting throughout, with centre back seam and vent.

Bold checked trousers are cut wide in the leg, pleated into waistband at fronts, and have turn-ups at lower edge.

Fabrics: Proofed gabardine or Melton cloth.

Colours: Dark tan or beige.

Hat: Felt trilby.

Notes on construction of garments

Woman

Make pin-tucks along broken lines indicated on front coat pattern.

Padding is required at shoulders, extending to outer yoke line. A 1 cm (⅜ in.) seam allowance is included in the pattern, except at front edges.

Man

Split, raglan sleeves are top-stitched 1 cm (⅜ in.) from centre seam line. Padding is required at shoulders. Use trouser pattern from 1934.

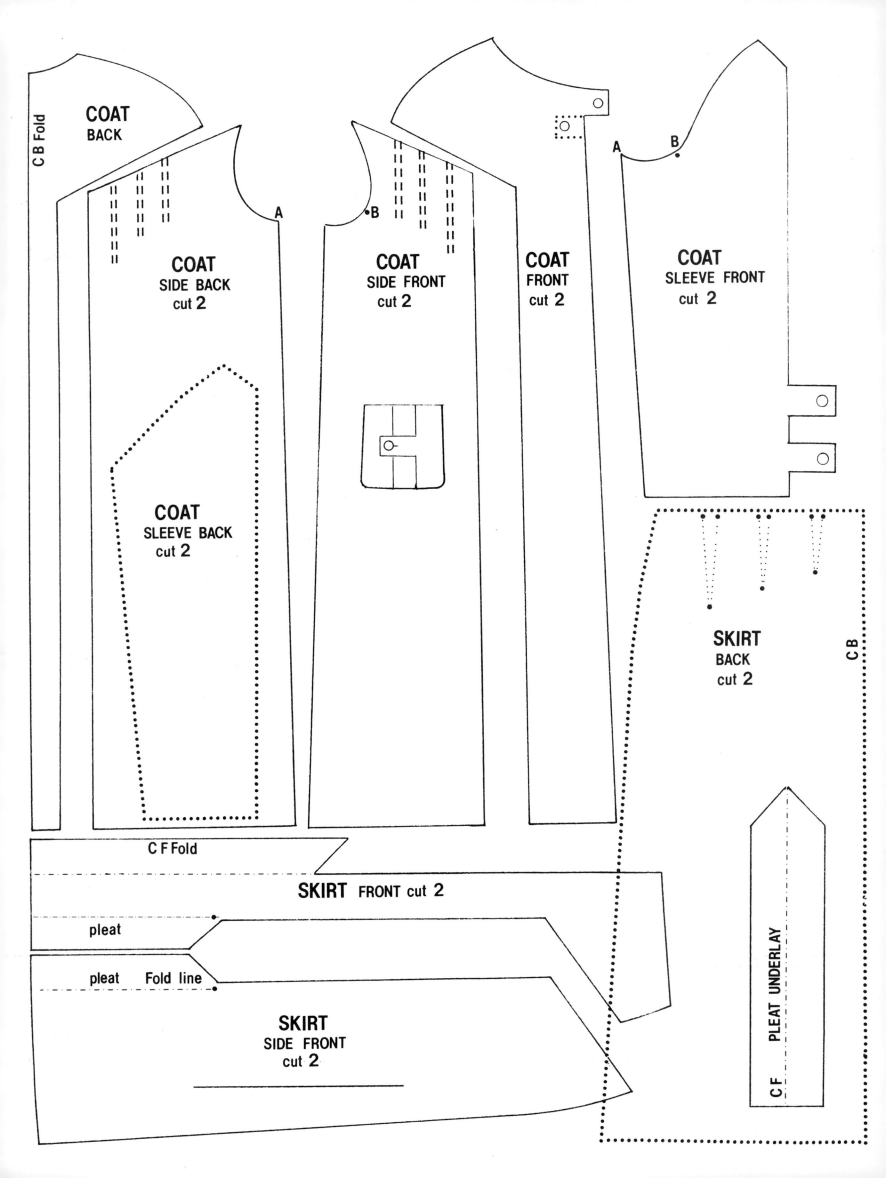

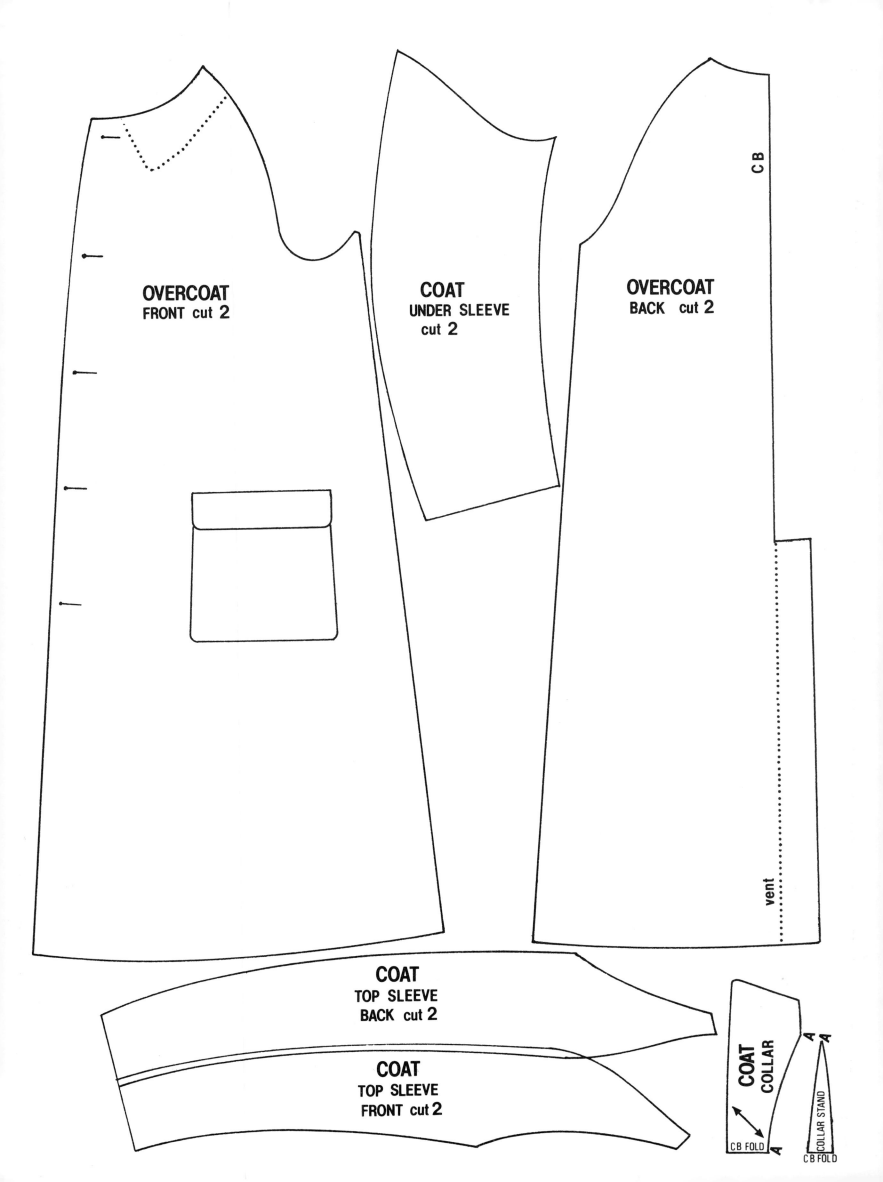

OVERCOAT
FRONT cut 2

COAT
UNDER SLEEVE
cut 2

OVERCOAT
BACK cut 2

CB

vent

COAT
TOP SLEEVE
BACK cut 2

COAT
TOP SLEEVE
FRONT cut 2

COAT
COLLAR

CB FOLD

A
A
A

COLLAR STAND

CB FOLD

1938

Predominant fashion features

Women

Broad-shouldered look continues, although the effect is softer and less square. Romanticism continues in evening wear with full-flowing or circular skirts and frills and flounces; full-length, touching the ground, but rarely seen with trains. Crinoline dresses of diaphanous and transparent materials over stiffened slip.

Low and scooped *décolletage* at the front and back remain important features of the evening dress, with draped interest at shoulders; often worn with a short box jacket or small, tightly fitted bolero.

The day skirt is shorter and fuller with draped, gathered and tucked bodice and fuller sleeves, tightening towards the wrist.

Popular fabrics: Evening – organza, voile, coloured tulle, crêpe and taffeta (printed or plain), slipper satin, chiffon, crêpe de Chine.

Day – crease-resistant and textured cotton and linen fabrics, crêpe, Celanese (rayon), jersey.

Colours: Bright colours for evening wear. White popular background for boldly coloured or black prints. Large floral designs for summer and evening dresses.

Decoration: Evening – bold flowers, applied or printed, ribbons, sequins and gold embroidery. Garlands of flowers or coloured feathers worn around waist, on bodice or to accentuate neckline.

Day – tucks and pleats to decorate bodice and emphasize the bust; feathers at waist and lace trimming. Ribbons everywhere, trimming dresses, hats, gloves, shoes and bags. 'Ribbon is young and gay and decorative and belongs to this era of feminine clothes'. (*Vogue*, December)

Undergarments: Uplift brassières become known as bras; feminine curves are enhanced although the hips remain slim. Wasp waist is essential, held in by lightweight, boned corset. Brightly coloured stiff taffeta petticoats with full skirts.

Shoes: Elegant slim heel and rounded toes, leather often perforated and combined with mesh fabrics, suede or two-tone. First cork or wooden wedge soles for day and evening. The 'hooded heel' – a seamless heel covering all in one with the back of the shoe. Open-toed sandals with 6.35 cm (2½ in.) heels.

Hats: Generally smaller than previous fashions, achieving more height, often more elaborate, and worn tilted; also becoming essential feature in evening wear. Berets decline in popularity.

Hair: Worn 'off the ears' – well off forehead and temples to show nape of the neck; swept on to the top or back of the head in curls or waves, braided or in a figure-of-eight chignon. Fastened with tortoiseshell hairpins or held by combs.

Accessories: Costume jewellery as previous fashion. Jewelled wrist bracelets with bare arms for evening. Bags – small with clip fastening or satchel style with long handles; evening bags embroidered or sequined. Dorothy bags.

Ostrich feather or fur stoles. Bright handkerchief or scarf worn with plain coloured day suit and brighter belts.

Make-up: Continued use of false eyelashes; blue, green or blonde mascara sometimes used instead of black. Lips full and deep red, sucked-in cheeks; eyebrows are plucked and arched.

Men

Follows trend of menswear throughout 1930s, although a less exaggerated cut is noted in men's suits, which are straighter, with well-padded square shoulders and wider lapels. Trousers are narrower in the leg, with zip-front fly fastening replacing buttons.

Waistcoats discarded for informal wear with lounge suits. Trousers frequently of a different shade to jackets.

Fabrics and colours: Wool worsted or flannel, or light-coloured linen for summer suits.

Undergarments: As previous fashions. Rayon shirts for men. Jockey shorts, briefer than trunks.

Shoes: Popularity of Oxford-style shoe continues, fully laced or with two eyelets for less formal wear. Two-tone, white and tan or white and black for informal occasions, or 'monk' shoes with side buckle fastening. Chukka or desert boots with two-tie fastening introduced for sports and casual wear, and sandals, sometimes with crêpe sole, for summer.

Socks: As previous fashions.

Hats: As previous fashions, although crowns are generally higher and brims broader to balance squarer shoulders.

Hair: Often worn without a parting, brushed back and slightly raised at the sides. Small, clipped moustaches.

Accessories: Tie pins, clips and collar bars (to hold points of collar beneath the tie) continue in use.

Details of illustrated patterns

Woman

Floor-length evening dress with full skirt gathered into bodice at front, with applied ribbon rosettes. Fitted bodice, tightly ruched at the front and supported with fabric stay and boning, emphasizes the bust and a narrow waist; wide tucked shoulder straps serve to accentuate the shoulder width. The dress is worn with separate, matching cummerbund, tucked in the same manner as shoulder straps. Light zip fastener and hook-and-eye closure at side seam.

Fabrics: Taffeta or heavyweight satin, with tulle overskirt.

Colours: Powder blue with deep blue ribbon decoration and accessories.

Shoes: Satin or gold kid open-toed, sling-back evening shoe with slim, high heel.

Hair: Hair is swept up with curls towards the back of the head; just one wave in front.

Headdress: Consists of a cluster of three ostrich feathers in shades to tone with dress, mounted on composition tortoiseshell comb, finished with fancy-edged circular veil.

Accessories: Small pearl earclips; gold-plated jewelled vanity case holding cigarettes, lighter and make-up. Long, white or pale-coloured kid gloves decorated with ribbon bows.

Man

Informal evening dress consisting of dinner jacket, waistcoat and dress trousers. The single-breasted jacket fastens with single link button, throwing ease over the chest and making the waistline appear smaller; fashionable broad-chested and wide-shouldered effects are indicated. Wide pointed lapels, faced in silk satin, have buttonhole at left. Welt pockets retain slimness over the hips. Slanted welt pocket on the breast displays handkerchief with double points. Two-piece, set-in sleeves finish with slit cuff and single-button fastening.

Double-breasted dinner jackets are also popular, regarded as slightly less formal.

Dress trousers are cut on similar lines to day wear trends, pleated into the waistbands at fronts, with ample ease over the seat and wide in the leg, but without turn-ups. A single row of silk braid may be present at outer leg seams.

The waistcoat is single-breasted, fastening with five buttons, and with welt pockets at waist-level and on left breast. A silk cummerbund may replace the waistcoat.

Fabric: Wool worsted.

Colours: Deep midnight blue is an acceptable alternative to black, the latter remaining popular. Waistcoat of white piqué or marcella, or black silk.

Undergarments: Stiff-fronted shirt and wing collar are considered correct, although soft-fronted styles with turn-down collar are frequently worn for less formal wear.

Shoes: Patent leather Oxford-style, fully laced.

Socks: Plain blue or black silk.

Hair: As previous fashion.

Accessories: Black silk tie correct with dinner jacket. Gloves – light-coloured kid. White linen handkerchief in top jacket pocket and a second, for use, tucked in sleeve. Boutonnière – dark red carnation, either fresh or artificial; white worn with tails. Gold cuff links, signet ring.

Notes on construction of garments

Woman

Undergarments – use a ready-made, tightly fitting, backless corset. Layers of silk and organdie, or tulle petticoats are cut on similar lines to the dress skirt to support the bouffant style. Cut two layers of tulle for the overskirt and one layer of firm silk fabric for foundation.

Bodice sections are boned to the waist at front, back and side seams. The bodice is underlined with firmer silk fabric. To join bodice to skirt, cut a piece of tape to waist measurement; gather skirt and front bodice to fit.

For the cummerbund cut a piece of fabric 66 cm (26 in.) x 28 cm (11 in.) as shoulder strap. Belt is attached to the dress at side seam opening and meets edge to edge. Add seam allowance to all belt edges. Leave opening at left side seam of dress for fastening.

Man

Use waistcoat pattern from 1939.

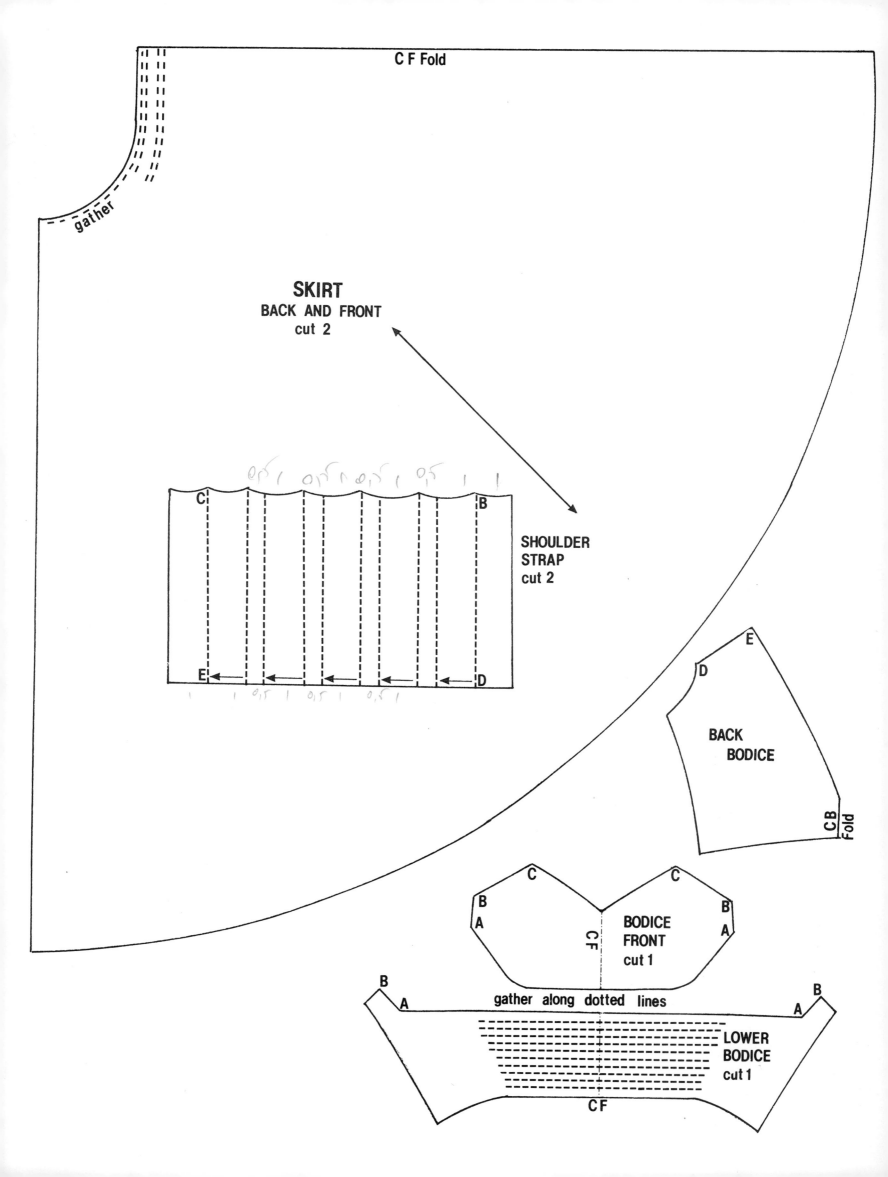

CF Fold

gather

SKIRT
BACK AND FRONT
cut 2

C   B

SHOULDER
STRAP
cut 2

E   D

E

D

BACK
BODICE

CB
Fold

C   C

B   B

A   A

BODICE
FRONT
cut 1

CF

B   B

A   gather along dotted lines   A

LOWER
BODICE
cut 1

CF

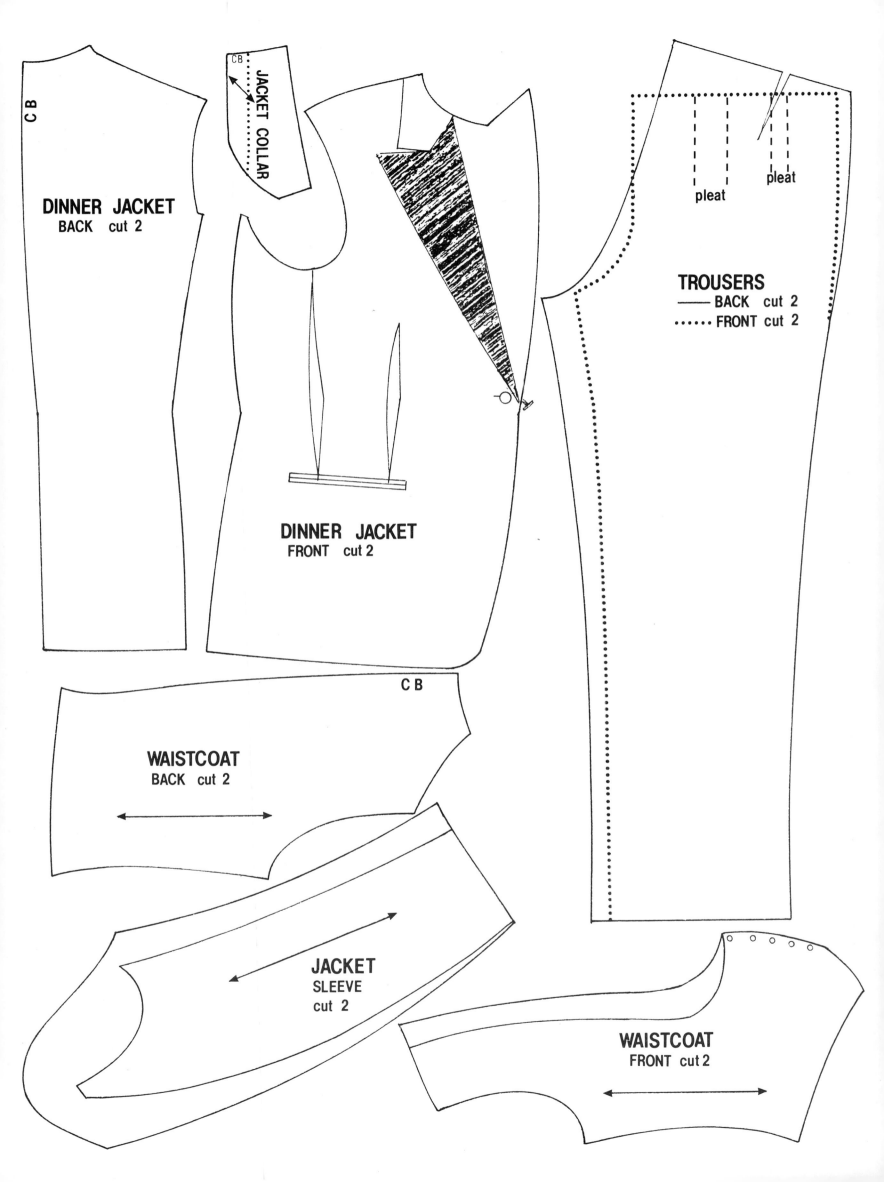

DINNER JACKET
BACK cut 2

C B

C B
JACKET COLLAR

DINNER JACKET
FRONT cut 2

TROUSERS
—— BACK cut 2
····· FRONT cut 2

pleat

pleat

C B

WAISTCOAT
BACK cut 2

JACKET
SLEEVE
cut 2

WAISTCOAT
FRONT cut 2

1939

Predominant fashion features

Women

Before the outbreak of war fashion looked set towards wasp waists and fragility. 'Now with the brilliance of an acrobatic somersault, it turns a new fashion face towards a new future' (*Vogue*, November). Two contrasting fashion trends are thus observable.

The military look of the early and mid-thirties is revived: severer suits, epaulettes, wide shoulders and revers. Skirts are shortened dramatically.

Coats fuller with loose sleeves and backs, not nipped in at the waist.

Trousers – flannels, slacks, in grey, stripes and checks. 'Your wardrobe is not complete without a pair or two of the superbly tailored slacks of 1939.' (*Vogue*, November) These were sharply creased, with turn-ups, fitted waistbands. Worn with sweaters and cardigans.

War has its impact – 'If we dress at night we dress down.' (*Vogue*, November) 'Afternoon dresses will often function as dinner dresses now.'

The main trends observable in the fashions of 1939 – wide shoulders, small waists and shorter skirts – continue as the main trend of the war years.

Fabrics: As previous fashion. Tweeds, twills, worsted, pin-stripes, checks, herringbones, 'zingal' – new uncrushable fabric.

Slacks – flannel, serge, heavy linens, tweeds, corduroy, velvet. Jersey suits, firmer silks.

Colours: Navy and white fashion favourites; also beige and brown, camel, fawn. Raspberry, prune, cocoa, sage.

Decoration: Bold top-stitching. Navy and white polka dot, stripe and check prints; use of contrast continues.

Undergarments: Similar to previous year – shaped princess petticoats. Brightly coloured taffeta underslips with fuller skirts. Pantie-girdles for wearing under slacks.

The foundation of the mode – uplift and small waist. 'The nipped-in waist, dresses demand it – corsets contrive it.' (*Vogue,* January)

Footwear: The accent is on heels – wedge, high, Dutch boy, solid, square-heeled shoes and platform soles. 'In this war we walk tirelessly in our chunky shoes.' (*Vogue*, November)

Hats: Hoods and snoods, knitted caps.

Hair: Longer and drawn back from the face and above the ears, curled.

Accessories: 'Elizabeth Arden's fitted handbag-cum-gasmask case.' Large boxy handbags. Brightly coloured contrast belts and scarves.

Make-up: 'Burnt Sugar' rouge and lipstick for khaki shades. 'Stop red' ideal with navy blue uniforms, as well as dark town clothes. Helena Rubenstein 'regimental red' lipstick and nail groom.

Men

Three-buttoned lounge jacket with pointed revers; usually it fastens only at the centre, throwing ease at the chest and making the waist look smaller. Waistcoats not always worn with summer suits.

Sports jackets with yoke at back and front, knife pleats to waist, patch pockets with pleats, belt reaching front of pleats; worn with pullover and flannel trousers.

Evening – double-breasted dinner jacket with wide, pointed lapels, worn with soft double collar and shirt. Narrow turn-back cuffs and lapels faced in silk. Single-breasted dinner jackets regarded as slightly more formal; wing collar and stiff shirt are considered correct. The dress coat worn for most formal occasions, short in the waist, with long tails, broad lapels and moulded chest.

Overcoats – double-breasted ulsters for travelling, motoring or informal wear. Lapels may be buttoned across the chest and collar fastened to the throat; ticket pocket on left sleeve. Often lined with checked woollen material, with silk for sleeves and around shoulders. Large patch pockets and split sleeves are other features. Single- and double-breasted chesterfields.

Fabrics: Similar to previous fashion – pin-stripes, checks, plaids all popular.

Colours: Similar to previous fashion.

Decoration: Top-stitching detail on overcoats and sports wear.

Undergarments: Striped shirts for business. Rayon used increasingly for men's undergarments.

Dark-coloured shirts in navy, wine, red or brown with light-toned coat and trousers for informal wear.

Shoes: Similar to previous fashion.

Socks: Similar to previous fashion.

Hats: Similar to previous fashion.

Hair: Similar to previous fashion.

Accessories: Similar to previous fashion. Coloured handkerchiefs, striped or plaid in rich colours, used only for informal wear. White linen or batiste correct for evening.

Spotted, striped or small-figured silk ties.

Details of illustrated patterns

Woman

Day dress with yoke effect cut in one with front and back panels extending over squared shoulders; shoulder width further emphasized by gathered sleevehead and band of contrast fabric. Saddle stitching on front bodice continues around raised scallop neckline and is repeated on front skirt panel. The natural waistline is well defined by contrast fabric belt and panelled skirt fits slimly over the hips, flaring softly towards the hemline, with single knife pleats at side fronts for ease of movement. Long sleeves fit tightly from elbow to wrist.

Fabric: Wool or rayon crêpe.

Colours: Sage green with medium brown contrast.

Footwear: Pre-war brown leather court shoes with high slim heels and rounded points.

Hat: Brown felt hat with shaped brim and dented crown perched forward on head. Grosgrain ribbon trim.

Man

Double-breasted reefer jacket with wide, pointed lapels rolling from waistline, giving fullness over the chest and emphasizing broad, square shoulders.

Fronts with four buttons and squared lower edges have straight flap pockets at hip-level and slanted welt pocket on left breast. The back is cut wide across the shoulder blades with shaped centre back seam and moderate flare at skirt. Two-piece set-in sleeves finish with slit cuff and two buttons and holes. The jacket is cut squarer than previous styles, with less definition at waistline.

Trousers are cut generously over the seat with pleats into front waistband. Legs are wide with sharp centre crease, and permanent turn-ups a common feature.

Fabrics and colours: Blue woollen suiting fabric with bold overcheck.

Undergarments: Pale-coloured shirt with attached, turn-down soft collar.

Footwear: Black leather Oxford shoes, fully laced.

Hat: Felt trilby.

Accessories: Spotted tie with pointed ends, grey leather gloves, handkerchief worn in breast pocket for decoration only, tightly furled umbrella.

Notes on construction of garments

Woman

Leave centre front open above small triangle. Cut dress bodice band and belt in contrast fabric. Padding is required over the shoulders to give essential squareness and broad-shouldered effect. Leave opening in left side seam for zip fastener. The dress should fit closely over the waist and hips. Secure tops of pleats with hand-worked arrowhead.

Man

This style of jacket is designed for tall, slim and shapely men as it is apt to pull at the front if not properly fitted and adjusted.

Additional ease is required at sleevehead, which must be carefully manipulated to achieve smooth finish at armhole.

Dotted lines show extension for left waistband.

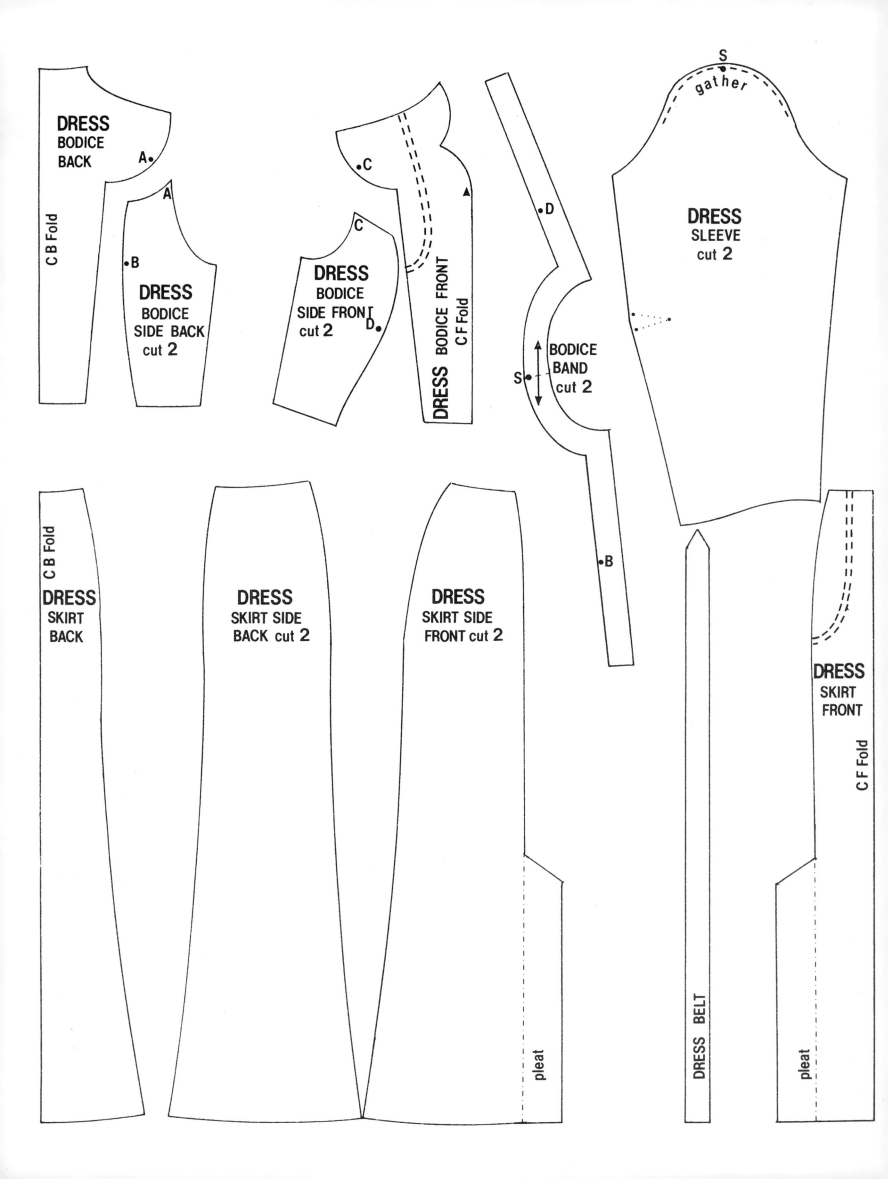

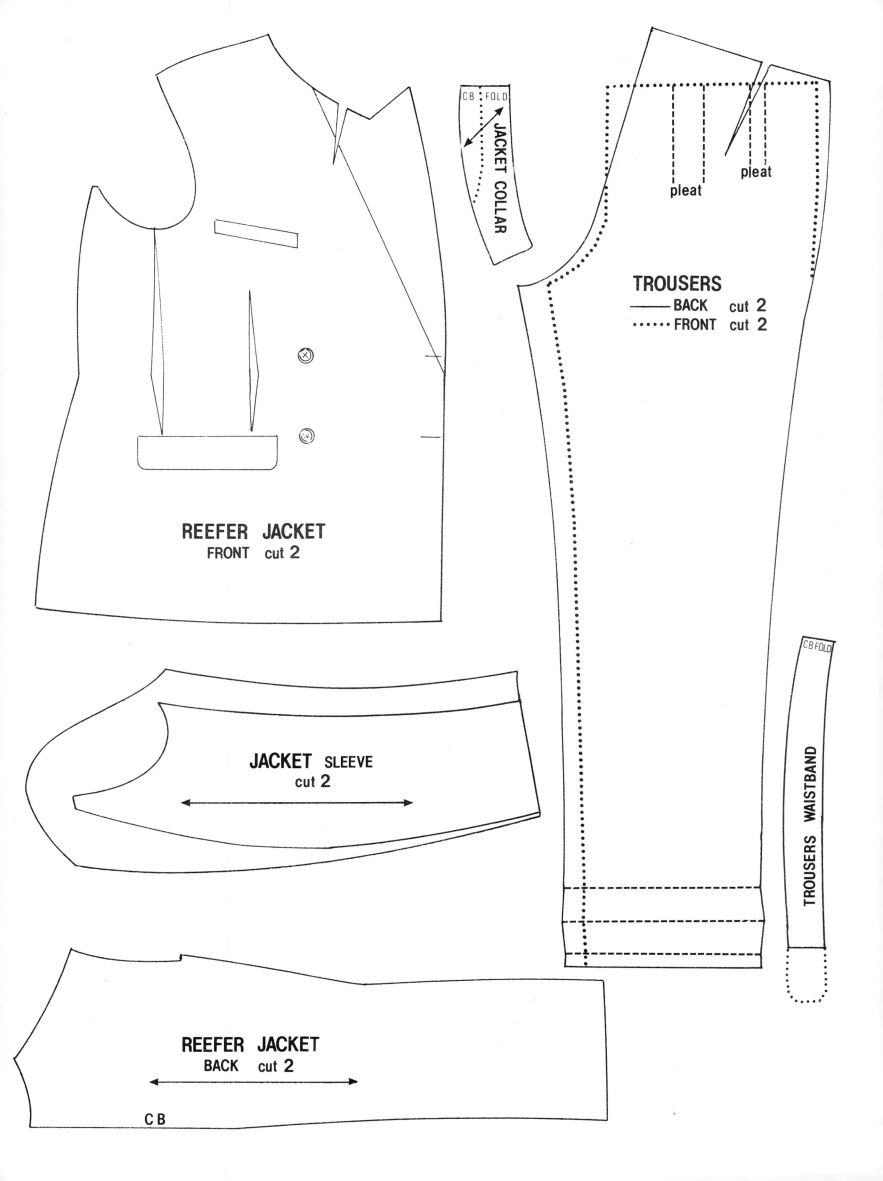

REEFER JACKET
FRONT cut 2

JACKET SLEEVE
cut 2

REEFER JACKET
BACK cut 2

C B

CB FOLD
JACKET COLLAR

TROUSERS
—— BACK cut 2
······· FRONT cut 2

pleat

pleat

CB FOLD
TROUSERS WAISTBAND

The Forties

A bare month before war broke out . . . we were all set to lace in our waists to suit the new waspish lines . . . Yet though the fashion tide was running at its strongest, at the first impact of war the designers and the public swung round instantly, instinctively and went full-steam ahead for fashions with a new feeling – fashions that fitted both the practical needs and atmosphere of war. (*Vogue*, January 1940)

It is evident that in the late 1930s a new style in women's fashions was emerging which looked set to revive the more feminine silhouette and tight-waisting of an earlier era. 'Fashion was as fantastic, as mad as world affairs' – a conspicuous comment on the uncertainty felt throughout Europe. With the outbreak of war fashion became attuned to that purpose, and women's dress evolved a definite military flavour, with large patch pockets, braiding and epaulettes; 'military braiding' also featured in hairstyles, with the hair plaited and knotted at the back of the head. A shorter skirt, up to 48 cm (19 in.) from the ground, and an exaggerated shoulder line, initiated in the late thirties by the Italian designer Schiaparelli, formed the most distinctive style features of the war period. The fashion, once set, continued without conspicuous change until late in the decade, the severe military cut softening gradually with the progress of the war.

The cut of men's clothes also remained virtually at a standstill, with suits following the line set in 1939. With the majority of the male population in uniform, the main focus, for the present, was on female fashion. Uniforms are examined in greater depth in the information accompanying the patterns.

A considerable proportion of younger females also adopted a uniform and, as in the First World War, women were to play a fundamental role in the war effort. From 1938 women could enlist in the Auxiliary Territorial Service (ATS), which formed part of the Territorial Army. Then in 1941 the War Office announced the National Service Act, involving the unprecedented conscription of women into the armed services. This initially 'called up' all unmarried women and childless widows between the ages of 20 and 25, the age limit later being extended from 19 to 30 years. In the Defence Regulations of the same year the ATS were given equal status with men, initiating another vital step in the direction of emancipation. For the first time, too, women were involved in active service, and were used in operational duties from mid-1942. Soon the majority of women, apart from mothers of children under the age of 14, had enlisted, with each employed woman required to work a stipulated number of hours per week. In 1943 came the 'grannies' call-up' requiring women between 46 and 50 to register for war work.

Once again the manner in which women tackled new jobs brought about changes in attitude to the working woman.

For the lady in civilian dress, shortages in cloth and labour, and the directing of the clothing industry towards the war effort, necessitated government intervention and began a period which Cunnington describes as 'dictated fashion'. In 1941, when the war-time clothing situation became critical, the Board of Trade introduced the Utility scheme, which regulated the quality and price of manufactured cloth. The leaders of London's couture banded themselves together to co-operate with the government on a practical clothing policy. They formed the Incorporated Society of London Fashion Designers, under chairman Edward Molyneux.

Upon the introduction of the Civilian Clothing Order in 1942, which reinforced the Utility scheme, the Society produced for the Board of Trade utility designs which proved to the world that shortage of labour and material need not mean restriction of elegance and taste. Utility designs followed the prevailing taste of square shoulders and straight lines, but adhered to set regulations as to the amount of cloth, incorporated trimming and standards of workmanship. In September 1942 *Vogue* noted, 'Your Autumn suit will be devoid of trimming, tailored on austerity lines,' and Cunnington remarked in an article in 1941, 'Your wardrobe, instead of being a three-volume novel will now be a short story in which each line will count.'

Men's Utility suits likewise followed a slimming and simplification, using a lower-grade quality wool, usually mixed with other fibres and available in three major colours – brown, grey and navy. As with women's clothes, all additional features such as fastenings were reduced to a minimum. The single-breasted jacket had no drape or shoulder pads, trousers were devoid of turn-ups, back pockets and pleats, and the waistcoat disappeared completely.

Vogue and *Harper's Bazaar* ran a series of articles on making every coupon count, and offered ideas for renovating and updating an existing wardrobe. Clothes rationing was to continue well after the war ended; the Utility scheme was maintained until 1952 and clothing coupons to 1949.

Clothes rationing represented but one of the many shortages of the period. As shipping was disrupted food-stuffs began to be in short supply. With food rationing introduced in 1940 'lemons and oranges became as exotic and rare as caviare', and women learnt to introduce dried eggs, evaporated milk and tinned meats and fish into trusted recipes. The nation was encouraged to 'dig for victory', to turn lawns and any available open space into vegetable gardens, while parsley, herbs and small vegetables decorated window boxes. In every way people tried to avoid waste; all edible scraps were collected and used for pig and poultry food, and transport was restricted to war supplies and the constant movement of troops and evacuees.

Rescheduling of production lines for the national effort caused the scarcity of a number of fashion accessories such as cosmetics and stockings. After the ban on silk stockings in 1941 women went bare-legged throughout the summer months, from necessity. Coloured creams were often applied to give a meagre form of coverage, but proved unsuccessful, often causing indelible stains on precious clothing. Some swimming pools banned bathers 'bronzed by art' and the Board of Trade published 'Rules for Rayons' to ensure longer life for an essentially weak fibre. For factory work women adopted slacks, while short-sleeved shirts saved fabric, and hats were generally replaced by headscarves.

Shortages, too, encouraged the use of unconventional materials such as raffia and straw for hats and bags. Leather, as a munition of war, was in short supply for civilian shoes and other goods, and clumpy wooden soles and cork wedge heels came into use. With cotton, rubber and steel on the priority list, underwear factories were converted to produce kites, balloons, sails and flags. Alongside this, though, production of underwear for the women's forces still continued. Make-up was cherished – a last desperately defended luxury – and hair, remarkably, defied the First World War trend of a short bob, and hung in bleached curls to the shoulders.

Restrictions did not end with the war, and a period of 'silence' was observed in the fashion world. The British fashion industry actually emerged from the war in a stronger position than it had enjoyed during the 1930s. The designers of Utility wear concentrated their efforts in establishing the prestige of British fashion abroad. Collections were designed for export to South Africa, South America and Canada, and to the women at home appeared like forbidden fruit among the pages of the glossy magazines. In the field of mass-production, the lack of outside competition, the experience gained in the mass-production of uniforms, and government regulations which stipulated quality and sizing standards as well as quantity of cloth, led to improved methods and provided the essential impetus of stability and prosperity necessary to organize the clothing industry. Better wages and set profit margins enabled women to enjoy far higher standards in mass-production techniques than in the pre-war years.

New technology, too, had been developed for the war effort, with the production of nylon as a strong and lightweight fabric refined and concentrated in the manufacture of parachutes and other war accessories. Resins developed to stabilize mosquito nets in the Pacific held the promise of permanently starched, water-repellent, crease- and stain-resistant finished fabrics. Resins could be further used in binding seams without stitches in the way that army tents had been constructed, and further developments were promised in the development of vinyl plastics for lightweight raincoats, and costume jewellery in electro-polished steel. The role of television, too, as a major force in the promotion of fashion was established, although it was more importantly an asset of the fifties. In January 1947 *Vogue* was the first magazine asked to televise a Basic Wardrobe in the BBC's programme 'Editor's Choice'.

Two years after victory there was still no end to drabness in fashion and food, and it was in such a climate that Dior presented his 'New Look' in 1947. This represented the ultimate in femininity, with a neat waistline, accentuated by a rounded hip-line, natural sloping shoulders and long, swirling skirts. Dereta was the first British ready-to-wear firm to capture the Paris look, and had sold its first designs in a West End store within the first day. Not all were so ready to welcome the New Look. The Board of Trade criticized its extravagant use of fabric, for with Britain still under the restrictions of the Utility scheme, production was restricted and delayed, and the New Look could only develop along non-Utility lines. However, despite opposition, the New Look was to dominate the fashion scene until the end of the 1940s. Dior presented an alternative, equally elegant, straight and slender silhouette with the brief jacket worn over a long, straight skirt. Such designs used 'reasonable' quantities of fabric. As skirt hems lengthened to 30.25 cm–33.5 cm (12 in.–14 in.) from the ground, *décolletage* in evening and cocktail dresses became very wide and deep, revealing a large expanse of bosom seldom seen since the eighteenth century. Underwear took on a new importance with the introduction of the strapless wired bra and the return of the corset as an essential foundation of the mode, producing a small, tight, boned waist, trim above and rounding below. The petticoat also added to the line; stiffened and flounced and worn in two or three layers, the swirling skirt stood away from the figure. Hip pads provided roundness of hip for the slimmer woman.

A 'New Look' in men's clothing was to lag behind women's fashions, but post-war styles did lose the exaggerated shoulder line. More relaxed clothing became common for day wear in preference to the ill-fitting Utility suits. Sports clothes included the short battle dress bought from army surplus, often worn with the new 'Daks' – trousers made with pleats at the front and a waistband which required no belt. The duffle coat, also sold as government surplus at the end of the war, attained a new popularity for males and females, sometimes dyed blue. It was not until 1949 that a large range of clothing became coupon-free.

With the end of the forties some form of recovery was apparent and Britain looked to re-establishing itself. The new Labour government, elected by a landslide victory immediately after the war, had made important inroads in the field of social welfare. The National Health Service established free health care for all, and nationalization of the Coal Board and British Rail looked set to provide a country for the people. The outlook was one of hope – a 'New Look' for fashion and a new look for the country.

1942

Note: Imperial measurements precede metric equivalents in the case of war uniforms as they relate to exact specifications laid down by the War Office. Utility regulations are also given in imperial measurements, as set out by the Board of Trade (from the *Tailor and Cutter*).

Civilian clothing – Utility scheme from 1941

The schedule as laid down by the Board of Trade.

Women

- The simplification of jackets means the elimination of double-breasted styles, vents and slits, pleats and belts. Jackets are not to exceed 28 in. (71 cm) in length and not to have: more than two pockets; more than four buttons and buttonholes; open cuffs or imitation open cuffs. Hems are not to be more than 2 in. (5 cm) deep.
- No cloth or fabric waistcoats are to be made.
- Skirts are not to have: more than three buttons, six seams, one pocket; two inverted or box pleats or four knife pleats; flares; accordion or all-round pleating. Hems not to be more than 3 in. (7.5 cm) deep.
- The maximum width of women's slacks is 21 in. (53.25 cm) and permanent turn-ups, raised seams, elastic in waistbands, straps or buckles, slant pockets, pocket flaps and loose belts are forbidden. Trousers are not to have: more than six buttons and six buttonholes; more than two pockets; rubber or fabric device (other than belt loops) for maintaining slacks in position.
- Overcoats not to have: more than two pockets; more than five buttons and buttonholes; more than one inverted or box pleat or two knife pleats; more than one vent; external epaulettes; turn-back cuffs, tabs, buttons or buttonholes on sleeves; belts other than of self cloth. Sleeves are not to measure more than 14 in. (33.5 cm) at the wrist. Width of collar not to measure more than 6 in. (15.25 cm). Hem not to be more than 2 in. (5 cm) deep.
- Slide fasteners on any of these garments and bib-and-brace suspension for both skirts and slacks are prohibited.

Men

- Simplified suits for men are not allowed to have turn-ups to trousers. Pleats at waist are not permitted. Only three pockets may be put in trousers. The usual plan is two side pockets and either one hip pocket or one cash pocket in front.
- These plain trouser bottoms may have a maximum width (circumference) of 19 in. (45.25 cm) at hem. In addition there must be no pocket flaps, or leather trouser bottoms. Side straps and back-straps are barred. No self belt, extension waistband or elastic in waistband.
- Rubber or fabric devices (other than belt loops) in trousers for maintaining them in position must not be used.
- Waistcoats must have no more than five buttons and no long points in front. Pockets are cut down to two. They must not be double-breasted, must be minus a collar, backstrap, raised seams or slide fasteners.
- Jackets must not be double-breasted, are limited to three pockets. Buttons are confined to three on the front. Metal or leather buttons are not permissible.
- Men's overcoats may have width of skirt not to exceed chest measurement by more than 14 in. (33.5 cm) (both measurements to be taken from edge to edge). An overcoat must not have more than three pockets or more than six buttons – which indicates that overcoats may be double-breasted. Neither may it have such things as slits, cuffs, tabs, or buttons on the sleeves.

Note: For further details of civilian clothing see 1942-1943.

Details of illustrated patterns

Woman

Pattern of uniform approved for wear by officers of the ATS (Auxiliary Territorial Service – formed 1938) and the WAAF (Women's Auxiliary Air Force – reformed 1938), the material for the latter being blue.

Fitted-style jacket with step-collar front fastening and four 1 in. (2.5 cm) gilt buttons. Jacket buttons to the right, worn with self-material belt with two-prong gilt buckle. Buttons and buckle of approved pattern. ATS insignia in gilt metal to be worn on the collar of jacket 1 in. (2.5 cm) above the inner end of the step, mid-way between the outer edge and inner (rolled) edge. Two breast cross patch pockets 4½ in. (11.5 cm) wide, 5½ in. (14 cm) deep to top of flap; 2½ in. (6.25 cm) deep pointed flap to fasten with small button. Bound pocket below waist with 5½ in. (14 cm) opening concealed by flap 2½ in. (6.25 cm) deep and 7 in. (17.75 cm) at top edge. Shoulder straps of matching fabric to carry badges of rank, fasten in scye at shoulder and button at neck edge. Centre back vent 7¼ in. (18.5 cm) in length.

Four-piece skirt with plain seams, panel back and front with 8 in. (20.25 cm) placket or zip opening on the left, 4½ in. (11.5 cm) bound pocket on left back across panel seam. Skirt to hang 16 in. (40.5 cm) from ground.

Fabric: Jacket and skirt – khaki (drab) wool barathea, serge, drill or wool mixture of approved shade according to regiment. Shirt and tie – khaki Viyella. Lining to match colour of cloth.

Undergarments: Forces issued with vests with built-up shoulder, long woollen pants for under slacks and *Directoire* knickers ('passion killers') in khaki shade rayon lock-knit. Lastex step-in corsets.

Shirt: Button-through shirt fastens to left with shoulder yoke, matching shoulder straps and detachable collar.

Cap: Of soft fabric in approved shade, made with plain seams with self material strap and bronze buttons, back curtain, 2½ in. (6.25 cm) peak slightly stiffened and starched.

Belt: A leather Sam Brown belt and strap may be worn as an alternative to cloth belt.

Shoes and stockings: Brown or black leather lace-ups, 1 in. (2.5 cm) heel, flesh-coloured stockings.

Gloves: Brown or black leather.

Man

Garment worn by all officers of the British Army and Royal Air Force, the material for the latter being blue.

Length of jacket skirt 13 in. (33 cm) for size given, varies in proportion to height. Step-collar front with four buttons of regimental pattern; the depth of opening being about 3 in. (7.5 cm) from the throat. Two breast cross patch pockets, 6½ in. (16.5 cm) wide and 7½ in. (19 cm) deep to top of flap. Box pleat in centre 2¼ in. (5.75 cm) wide, and 2¼ in. (5.75 cm) three-pointed flap to fasten with small button. Two expanding pockets below the waist 9¼ in. (23.5 cm) wide at the top and 10¼ in. (26 cm) at the bottom, 8 in. (20.25 cm) to top of pocket under flap, and fastened with a small button. Shoulder straps on shoulder seam to carry badges of rank. The formed cuffs are pointed in centre, the point being 6 in. (15.25 cm) high and tapering down to 2¾ in. (7 cm) on either side. Centre back vent.

Trousers – cut moderately wide in leg with 19 in. (48.25 cm) plain bottoms. Ordinary side seam pockets, two pleats at front edge and five-button concealed fly.

Fabric: Jacket and trousers: – khaki wool mixture, trousers usually of lighter weight. Lining to match colour of cloth. Shirt and tie – khaki Viyella or heavy cotton.

Undergarments: Khaki Viyella shirt with long sleeves, front fastening and separate, matching soft collar. Vest, long pants or trunks, in wool and cotton lock-knit.

Belt: 2 in. (5 cm) cloth belt with two-prong gilt buckle or Sam Brown leather belt.

Cap: Stiffened 2¼ in. (5.75 cm) peak with soft top 9¾ in. (24.75 cm) in diameter and 2 in. (5 cm) stand. Metal badge worn at front.

Shoes: Brown or black leather lace-ups, 1 in. (2.5 cm) heel. Black ankle boots.

Gloves: Brown or black leather.

Notes on construction of garments

Woman

Construct with plain seams throughout.

Inside waistband of skirt to be of 1½ – 2½ in. (3.75 – 6.25 cm) boned petersham. Hem of 2½ in. (6.25 cm) finished with prussian binding.

Man

Pattern shows original form of the coat, that is, with a separate front skirt, the waist seam coming under the belt. The forepart may, however, be cut in one, continuing the two breast cuts into the pocket over the hip.

JOIN THE ATS

CARELESS TALK COSTS LIVES

"..... but for Heaven's sake don't say I told you!"

...o through ...our wardrobe

Make-do and Mend

WOMEN OF B...
COME I...
THE FACT...

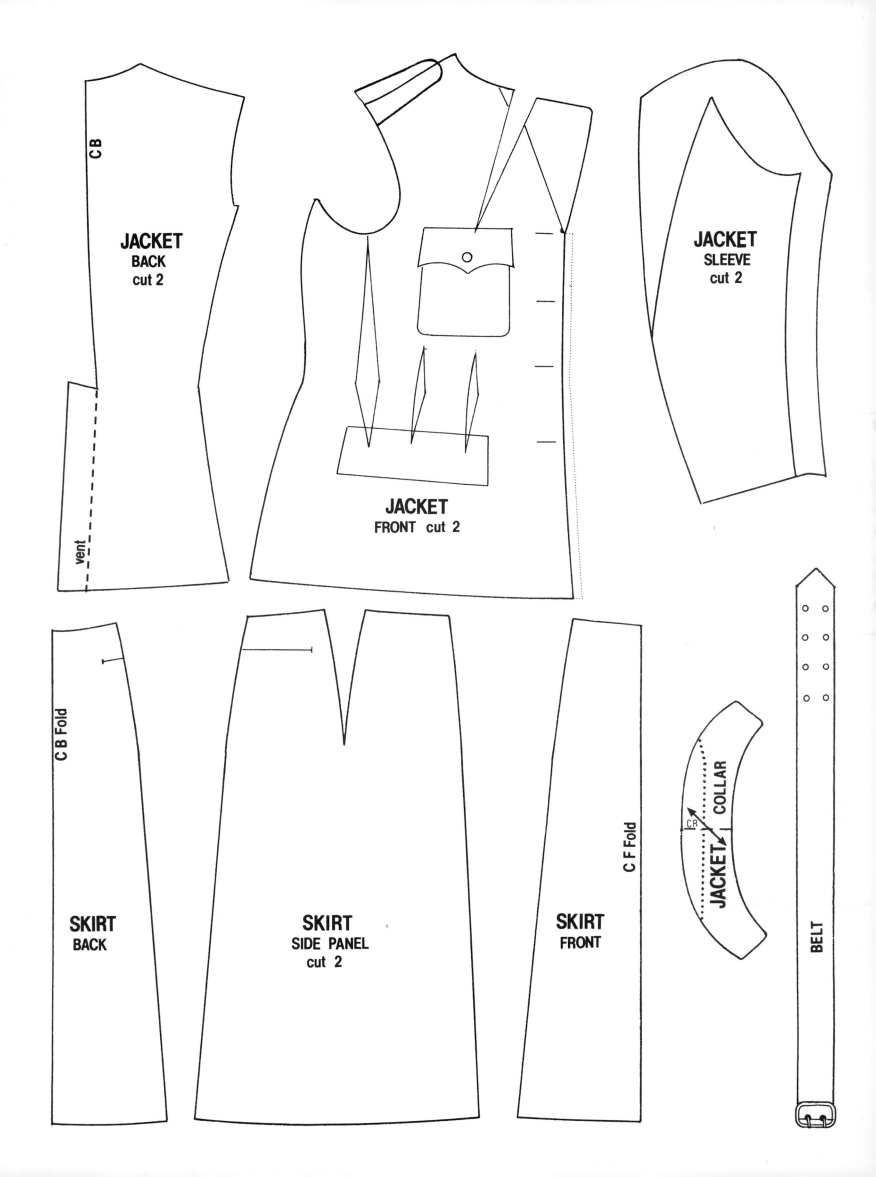

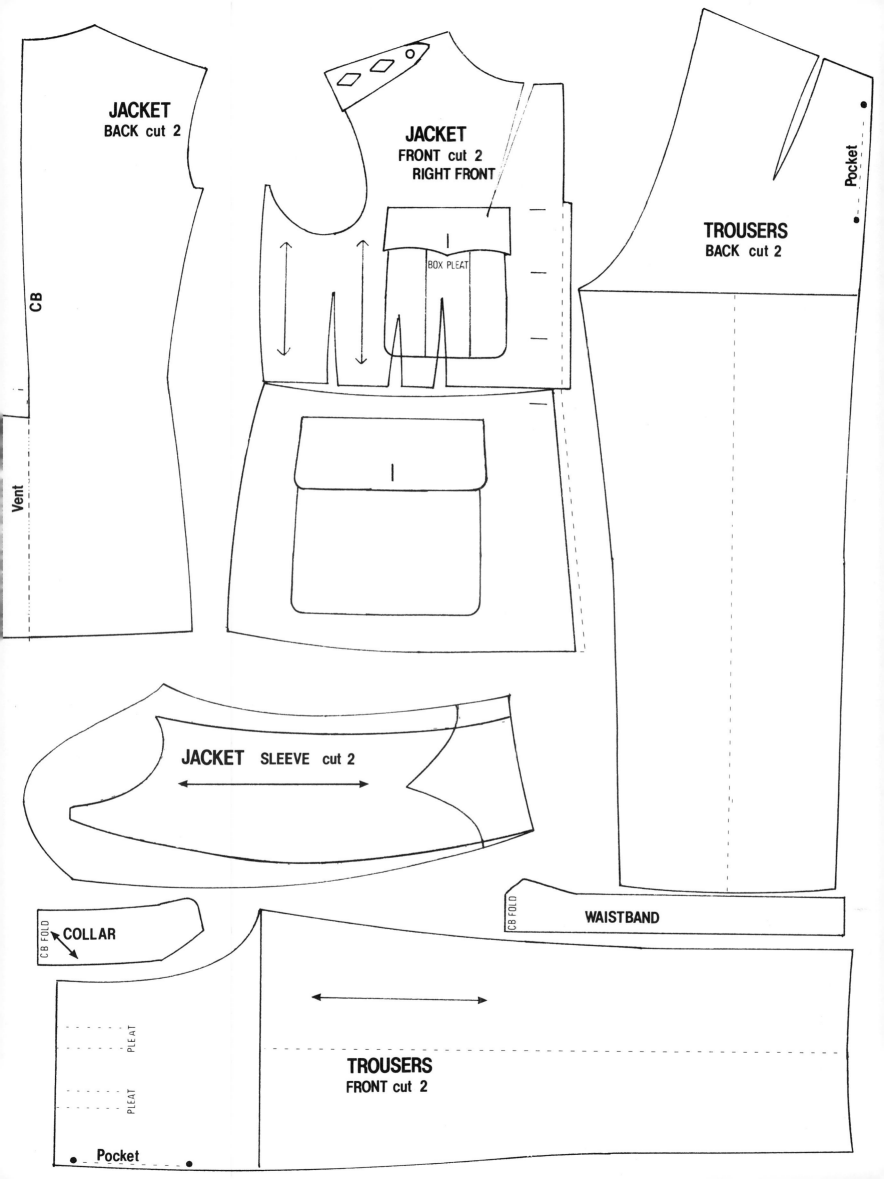

JACKET
BACK cut 2

CB

Vent

JACKET
FRONT cut 2
RIGHT FRONT

BOX PLEAT

TROUSERS
BACK cut 2

Pocket

JACKET   SLEEVE cut 2

CB FOLD

CB FOLD   COLLAR

CB FOLD

WAISTBAND

PLEAT

PLEAT

TROUSERS
FRONT cut 2

Pocket

1942~1943

Predominant fashion features

Women
There are no major changes in fashion throughout the war years – shoulders remain square, waists small and skirts knee-length. The exaggerated military cut of 1939 gradually softens.

'The progress of war has made it necessary to prohibit all superfluous material and superfluous labour ... Fashion is undergoing a compulsory course of slimming and simplification.' (*Vogue*, 1942)

1941 – Civilian Clothing Order. Utility scheme introduced, controlling quality and price of at first 50% and later 85% of all cloth manufactured, reinforced by the Making of Clothes (Restrictions) Order in 1942.

The schedule as laid down by the Board of Trade is given under 1942.

Daywear – standard tailored Utility suits with four buttons, large hip pockets with knee-length skirt, two pleats front and back. For variety, costumes use cross-cut pockets and skirts in contrast fabrics, e.g. checks or stripes and plain colours. Collarless costume coats also popular.

Trench-style coats and raincoats.

Increasing popularity of blouse and skirt, or jumper and skirt. Slacks frequently worn with blouse or jumper.

Fabrics: Checked and striped tweeds, herringbones for coats and suits with plain skirts. Lower grade wool for Utility, sometimes mixed with other fibres.

Colours: Blue, black, navy, brown, and brighter, clear colours – coral red, milky chocolate brown, terracotta, rust, mushroom, pink.

Decoration: Top-stitching never less than 19 mm (¾ in.) in width, sometimes a full 2.5 cm (1 in.) from the edge.

'Your autumn suit will be devoid of trimming, tailored on austerity lines. Your hat will follow suit, relying on line rather than trimming for its effect.' (*Vogue*, September 1942)

Utility regulations – flares, capes, braid, embroidery, appliqué, ornamental quilting, pin- or other ornamental tucking prohibited. No fur, fur fabric, velvet, silk, rayon or leather trimmings may be used, and buttons, buttonholes, and imitation pockets for purely decorative purposes are not allowed. Ruching, gauging and shirring prohibited, as is ornamental stitching, except on collars, revers, front edges, pockets, or at waist and hem (such ornamental stitching in each case not to exceed four rows).

Undergarments: Princess and waist petticoats continue in use, shortened to correspond with skirt. Brassière (bra) now universally worn, circular stitched for uplift.

Pantie-girdles increase in popularity, without suspenders, especially for under slacks.

Vests with built-up shoulders and long woollen pants (for under trousers) for warmth – rayon, Celanese lock-knit. Man-made fabrics used increasingly for undergarments.

Shoes: Leather, as munition of war, in short supply for civilian shoes and other goods. Wooden and crêpe-soled shoes. Cork and wedge heels, rounded or squared toes. Sandals with open toes and wedge heels for summer.

Stockings: 1941 – ban on silk stockings. 'Non-existent nylon and pure silk stockings are replaced by heavy brown or navy rayon' (*Harper's Bazaar*, December 1942).

Bare legs in summer, ankle and knee-length socks.

Hats: Sparse trimming – rolled or dipping brims, berets, back-of-the-head hats, high crowns. Pill-box hats with headscarf tied under the chin – in straw and raffia, felts rare and expensive. Snoods, crochet and knitted caps, turbans, headscarves.

Hair: Piled on top of the head in curls, worn longer at the back. Veronica Lake style – hanging loosely to the shoulders and curled under, side-parting, hair brushed back from the face. Permed and bleached hair.

Accessories: Raffia popular for hats and bags. Larger handbags with long shoulder straps. Bright scarves and belts. Hand-knitted gloves and mittens.

Make-up: With austerity in fashion, make-up assumes greater importance – a last desperately defended luxury. Red rouge and lipstick, blue-green eye-shadow, mascara, eyebrow pencils. Clear red nail varnish also used on toe-nails with open-toed sandals. Bare legs darkened with leg make-up, seam-line carefully drawn at the back with eyebrow-pencil.

Men
Utility regulations also affect male civilian clothing. Double-breasted jackets, so popular in the late 1930s, replaced by single-breasted styles. Utility suits retain squareness of shoulders.

Fabrics: Utility suits in lower grade wool, sometimes mixed with other fibres. No fancy weaves.

Colours: Utility – brown, grey or navy.

Decoration: Belts and half-belts are not permitted. Pleats at centre or side of back are not allowed. Fancy backs are eliminated. One-piece raglan sleeves are restricted, and no patch pockets, fly fronts, or leather or metal buttons. Raised seams are restricted. Slide fasteners are banned and slides or buckles. No embroidery or braid, velvet, velveteen, silk, or rayon trimmings, except on the collar, may be used.

Undergarments: Stiff, detachable collars less common, soft shirt collars in the same fabric as the shirt, with removable celluloid stiffeners. Utility shirts – tails reduced and double cuffs prohibited. Lock-knit vests with long and short sleeves; short trunks.

Shoes: Brown or black laced leather shoes and brogues continue to be worn. Boots and shoes with rounded toes.

Socks: Shorter during the war, wool and rayon, lisle, elasticated tops.

Hats: Many men go hatless. Soft felt hats, fabric caps.

Hair: Short-back-and-sides for forces.

Accessories: Knitted gloves replacing leather. Woollen ties.

Details of illustrated patterns

Woman
Collarless costume jacket with four-button fastening, conforming to Utility regulations. The jacket is cut with panel and yoke effect at back and front. Jetted breast pockets are set into front yoke seams.

Foreparts are cut away below bottom button. Sleeves are plain in austerity fashion and shoulders built up to give broad, square appearance.

Short four-gored skirt with panel front and plain back.

The blouse is yoked with gathers or pleats for fullness across the bust, and the waist reduced by means of darts to within 5–7.5 cm (2–3 in.) of the tight waist measurement. The darts are sewn to waist-level and then left loose to form unpressed pleats. Pointed collar, buttoned up to the neck, and a long full sleeve gathered into a cuff band and darted into the shoulder.

Fabric: Small checked tweed; plain cotton blouse.

Colour: Shades of brown on beige ground.

Footwear: Brown leather laced shoes with crêpe soles and squared toes.

Hat: Large brimmed hat worn on the back of the head with single-ribbon trim.

Man
Overcoat in line with Utility regulations laid down by the Board of Trade. It is cut with little shaping, single-breasted three-button fastening, and notched lapels; shoulders are fairly square and there are two cross pockets with flaps at hipline. It will be noted there is no cuff to the sleeve, although the stitching may give that impression. Flaps and edges are stitched to 1 cm (⅜ in.) to 1.3 cm (½ in.) wide. The jacket back is cut with centre back seam and no vent.

Trousers, having turn-ups, do not conform to austerity rules, but are frequently worn.

Fabrics and colours: Wool or wool mixture tweed in greys or brown.

Notes on construction of garments

Woman
Insert pockets in fronts at position indicated on pattern. Padding is required over the shoulders to give square appearance.

Leave 20.25 cm (8 in.) in left front side seam for placket or zip opening. Finish waistline with petersham.

Adapt blouse pattern from 1944.

Man
Padding is required over the shoulders. Sleeves are stitched above lower edge to give impression of cuffs.

Note: Vent not allowed under Utility regulations.

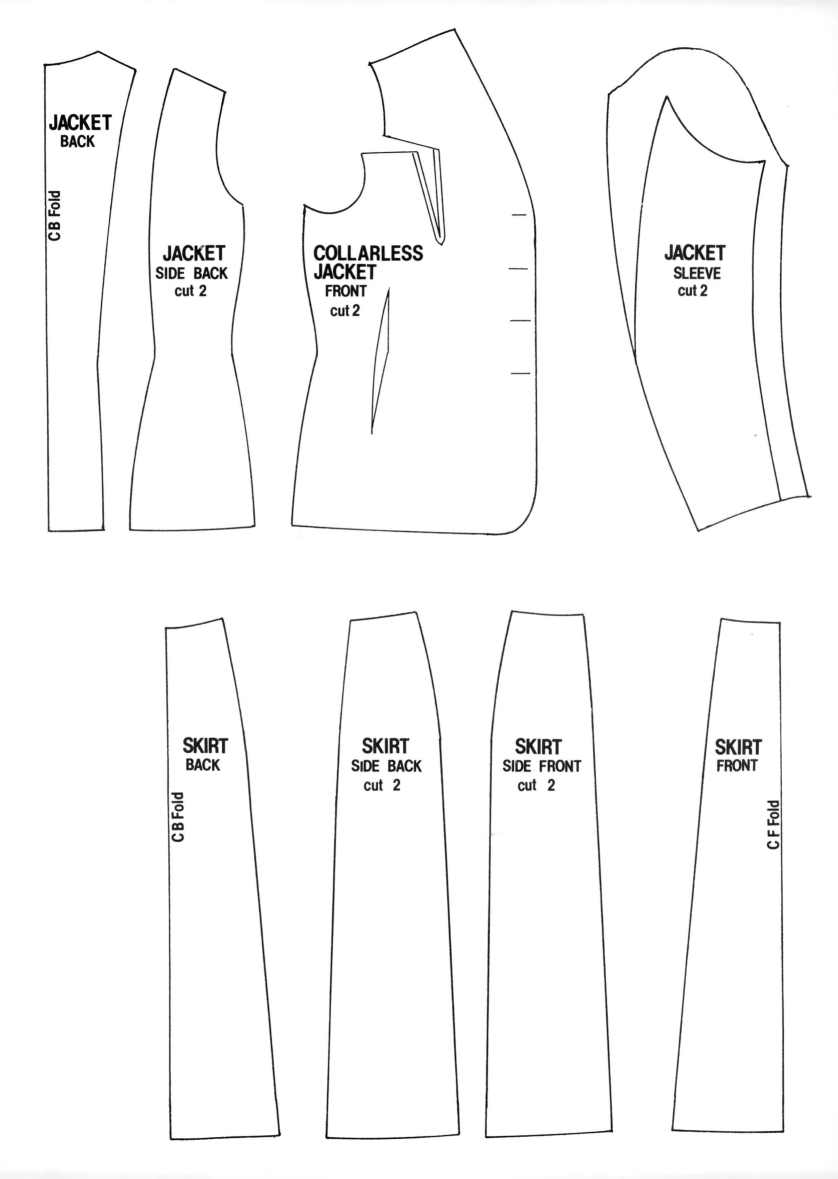

JACKET
BACK

CB Fold

JACKET
SIDE BACK
cut 2

COLLARLESS JACKET
FRONT
cut 2

JACKET
SLEEVE
cut 2

SKIRT
BACK

CB Fold

SKIRT
SIDE BACK
cut 2

SKIRT
SIDE FRONT
cut 2

SKIRT
FRONT

C F Fold

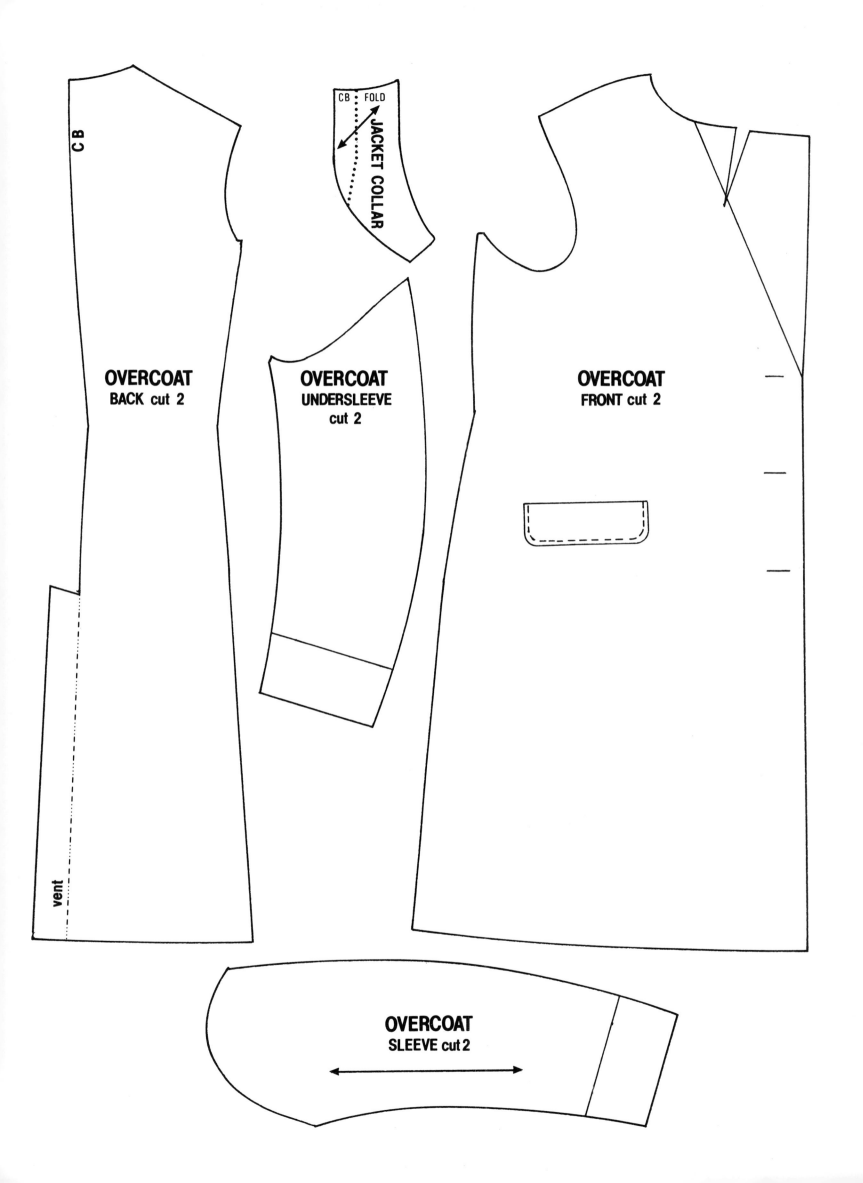

OVERCOAT
BACK cut 2

C B

vent

JACKET COLLAR

CB FOLD

OVERCOAT
UNDERSLEEVE
cut 2

OVERCOAT
FRONT cut 2

OVERCOAT
SLEEVE cut 2

1944

Predominant fashion features

Women

Styles change little from previous year – Utility regulations continue to dictate trends.

Blouses, jackets and coats with plain sleevehead, well-padded. Collarless jackets.

Pinafore dresses button to the neck over blouses and jumpers. Jigger coats or jeeps. Coats slightly shorter and belted, fuller in the skirt, large collars, yoked shoulders.

Slacks increasingly worn.

Afternoon dresses in softer fabrics – evidence of less austere silhouette with shoulders still squared, softness and drapery on bodice.

Fabrics: Similar to previous year. Men's suiting fabrics often used. 'Tebilized' cotton and rayon fabrics – crease-resistant finish.

Colours: Similar to previous year. Navy and white, black and white.

Decoration: Stripes and checks provide decoration without superfluous fabric. Boldly striped Utility dresses employ vertical, diagonal and horizontal lines.

Top-stitching detail – as 1943.

Undergarments: As 1943. Long bras and combined corsets, circular stitched inserts on bras.

Shoes: Clumpy wooden heels continue to save shoe leather. Low brogue-type shoes. Rounded and square toes.

Stockings: As previous year.

Hats: Generally replaced by headscarves, worn in variety of styles, e.g. tied under the chin, or on top of the head in turban style. Snoods and crochet caps.

Hair: Continues to be worn long at the back, drawn back from the face on to the crown.

Accessories: Shoulder bags. Collapsible umbrellas. Belts of elasticated fabrics in bright colours.

Make-up: As previous fashion. Tan make-up used on legs, seam drawn at the back with an eyebrow-pencil.

Men

Civilian clothes as 1943.

Details of illustrated patterns

Woman

Jigger coat with yokes at front and back, and wide collar and lapels, all serving to emphasize the broad, squared shoulderline. Fronts fasten with two buttons, and patch pockets are placed on hips; two-piece set-in sleeves are moderately wide with plain cuffs. The back is cut with inverted pleat from back yoke to hem. Top-stitching at panel seams, pockets and fronts is set well back from edges.

Knee-length four-gored skirt with panel front and plain back.

The blouse is yoked with ease allowed over the bust and the waist reduced by means of darts to within 5–7 cm (2–3 in.) of the tight waist measurement. The darts are sewn to waist-level and then left loose to form unpressed pleats. Long, full sleeve gathered into a cuff band and darted into

the shoulder. The narrow stand collar extends into tie ends at centre front, buttoned up to the neck.

Fabrics: Jacket – gabardine, Melton cloth. Skirt – herringbone tweed.

Colours: Greys, blues or browns.

Headwear: Plain headscarf worn in turban style.

Footwear: Brown leather lace-up shoes with wooden wedge heels and crêpe soles.

Man

Officer's greatcoat (Royal Air Force).

Note: Imperial measurements precede metric equivalents in the case of war uniforms, as they relate to exact specifications laid down by the War Office.

The coat is lined shoulders and sleeves only. The length reaches to within 14 in. (33.5 cm) of the ground. The centre back seam is finished with a deep slit to within 5 in. or 6 in. (12.75 – 15.25 cm) of the belt. The slit fastens with two holes and buttons in fly. The belt is 2½ in. (6.25 cm) wide and fastens with a gilt buckle and runner.

Slits are left in the side seam for the passing through of the belt when required. The belt is stitched down as far as the darts in the back waist. A sword slit is included at the left side as indicated at underarm seam on pattern 1 in. (2.5 cm) below top of belt and extending upward for 5 in. (12.75 cm). The pocket on the slant is 8 in. (20.25 cm) by 3¾ in. (9.5 cm). Jacket pocket inside right cross pocket and inside breast pocket on left side. There are five buttons, the lapel rolling to the third button; the coat can, however, be fastened up to the throat.

The lower buttons are 4½ in. (11.5 cm) apart and are opposite front end of pocket. The top buttons are 8 in. (20.25 cm) apart and then grade down as follows: 8¼ in. (21 cm), 7¼ in. (18.5 cm) and 5¾ in. (14.5 cm). The two top holes are worked on both sides.

Loops for the shoulder straps are fitted on body part as indicated on pattern. The straps are 2¼ in. (5.75 cm) at shoulder and 2 in. (5 cm) at top, and about 5 in. (12.75 cm) in length. They are lined black leather over bone foundation. Tabs which pass through the loops are fastened to button which has long shank and split pin.

The collar has a tab which is buttoned back inside when not in use.

Sleeve has open cuff with 4 in. (10.25 cm) opening and three holes and buttons.

Blue and black ranking braid.

Fabric: Blue-grey mixture cloth, twill weave, milled and proofed.

Notes on construction of garments

Woman

Jacket – a seam allowance of 6 mm (¼ in.) is included in the pattern at front panel seams; no provision has been made for the cross sections **A** to **B**. Therefore add as much as possible for this purpose when cutting the material.

Top-stitch 1.9 cm (¾ in.) from finished edge of fronts, pockets, yokes and panel seams.

Blouse – 1.3 cm (½ in.) seams are allowed on

the pattern round the scye and shoulders, and down the side seams and undersleeve seams. 1 cm (⅜ in.) seams are included round the collar, fronts and cuffs.

Pattern illustrates turn-down collar. For narrow stand collar with tie, cut a bias strip 5 cm × 100 cm (2 in. × 39 in.) plus seam allowances. Finished width is 2.5 cm (1 in.).

Waist darts are stitched to waist-level and then left loose to form unpressed pleats.

An alternative short sleeve is included, illustrated by dotted lines on pattern.

Soft pads are stitched to the edge of the sleeve seam at the top of the shoulder.

Skirt – use skirt pattern from 1942/1943.

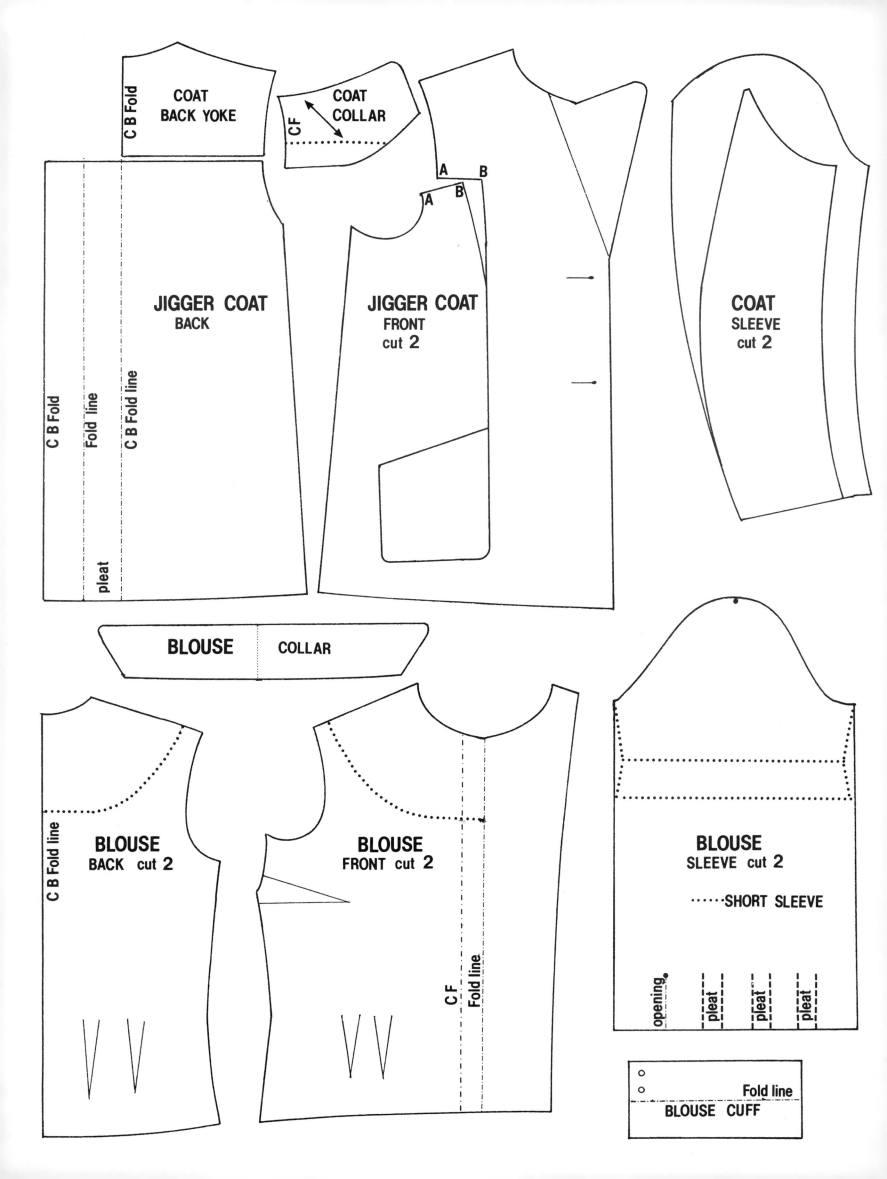

COAT
BACK YOKE

C B Fold

COAT
COLLAR

CF

A B
A B

JIGGER COAT
BACK

C B Fold

Fold line

C B Fold line

pleat

JIGGER COAT
FRONT
cut 2

COAT
SLEEVE
cut 2

BLOUSE   COLLAR

BLOUSE
BACK cut 2

C B Fold line

BLOUSE
FRONT cut 2

C F
Fold line

BLOUSE
SLEEVE cut 2

·····SHORT SLEEVE

opening   pleat   pleat   pleat

Fold line
BLOUSE CUFF

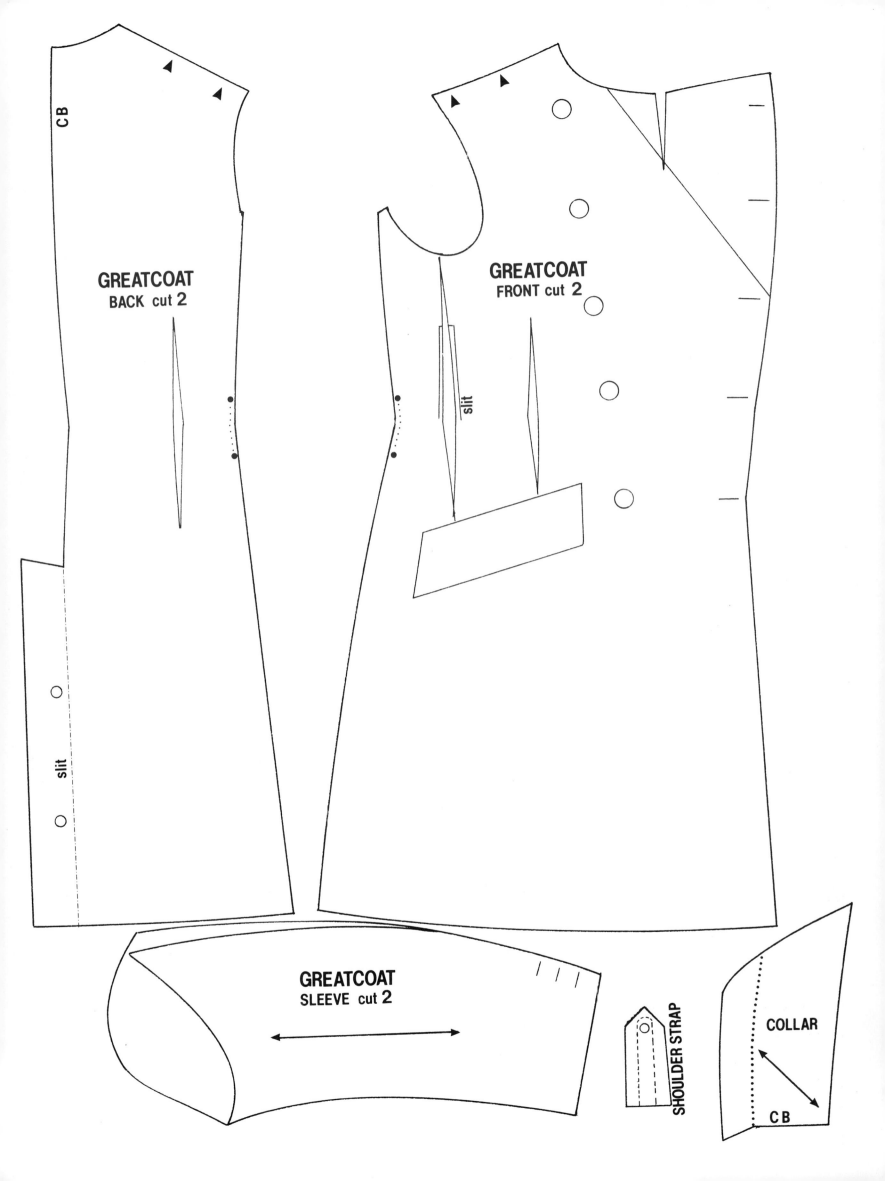

CB

GREATCOAT
BACK cut 2

GREATCOAT
FRONT cut 2

slit

slit

GREATCOAT
SLEEVE cut 2

SHOULDER STRAP

COLLAR

CB

1947~1948

Predominant fashion features

Women

'Feminine and ever more feminine is the way fashion is moving. Most is made of every curve and every hard line is softened . . . Squared-up looks are out; curved lines are here.' (*Vogue,* December 1947)

Dior's 'New Look' makes fashion headlines, but can only develop along non-Utility lines.

Natural shoulders – narrower and less padded, rounded with kimono or raglan sleeves. Neat waist-lines accentuated by rounded hipline. Hiplines made apparent by actual padding or pleats or patch pockets. Skirts perfectly straight or really wide. The width is gained by circular cut, gores, pleats, gathers. Hemlines longer – 33.5 cm (14 in.) from the ground, 12.75 cm (5 in.) below the knee.

Day version of the New Look is a suit with tiny, brief jacket with short, flared peplum over long, straight or full skirt.

Coats are either tiny-waisted or full and loose, with contrast linings of fur, plaid, satin.

Ankle-length cocktail or full-length evening dresses fasten demurely high at the neck or are cut very wide and very low, often strapless.

Fabrics: Tweeds, soft fine dress woollens, wool and rayon jersey, velvets.

Evening – failles, satin, tulle.

Small checks in contrast to bolder patterns. Closer-woven, higher quality fabrics.

Colours: Blended colours – grey-greens, grey-blues, aubergine, cactus, sage, olive, bay. Geranium red. Evening – browns and greys; soft, subdued greens.

Decoration: Knotted girdles, bows and cascading draperies concentrate interest at hip-level.

New interest at the neckline – frills, ruffles.

Undergarments: Dior's New Look necessitates return to the corset as the foundation of the mode, fashioned in lighter fabric. 'Waspies' – for nipped-in waist – 15.25 – 20.25 cm (6–8 in.) deep, rigid material, boned and laced at the back, worn on top of the roll-on. These are a luxury item.

Circular stitched bra cups for emphasis; evening wear brings about the strapless wired bra.

The petticoat takes on a new importance; two or three worn, flounced and gathered in taffeta or tulle, stiffened with horsehair braid or feather boning. Lace, denied during the war, begins to return in non-Utility.

Synthetic fabrics, nylon, used increasingly for undergarments. Parachute nylon and silk are sold for this purpose.

Shoes: Less clumpy, higher, slim heels, up to 10.25 cm (4 in.) in 1948.

Stockings: Rayon Utility. Sheer nylon stockings.

Hats: Hats worn 'off the brow'. With New Look small half-hats generally smaller and neater.

Summer straw hats with wide brims and shallower crowns.

'As skirts swirl wider, as coats get bulkier, so must the hat get neater, smaller to balance your outline.' (*Harper's Bazaar*, October 1947)

Hair: Cut short again. Urchin cut, following the line of the head.

Accessories: Long evening gloves with sleeveless dresses.

Make-up: Bright red lipstick, bluish and tawny shades, and rouge; eyebrows plucked into natural arched line, blue-green eye-shadow, black mascara.

Men

Utility regulations still apply. No significant changes in men's dress in the late forties.

Two-piece lounge suits without waistcoats continue to be worn. Lounge-suits now worn for all occasions except the most formal. Black lounge suits with white carnation and handkerchief in breast pocket acceptable wear for weddings, whereas morning coat always required previously.

Summer suits, made less skimpy, closely fitting over the chest, less squared shoulderline and lower waist than the war years, made unlined by ready-to-wear firms in lightweight fabrics.

Trouser legs are wider again, pleated into the waistband and longer over the instep. Flannel trousers, requiring no belt.

Lounge and sports jackets influenced by American service styles are adapted for the British market – wide shoulders and double-breasted styles.

From Army Surplus, short battle-dress for casual wear; a loose, blouson-style jacket.

Duffle coat – unlined loose-fitting coat with yoked back, raglan sleeves, large patch pockets, attached hood, toggle fastening. Worn by men and women.

Fabrics : Man-made, synthetic and mixture fabrics enable lighter-weight suiting fabrics.

Flannel, gabardine, corduroy, cavalry twill, tweeds.

Colours: Navy, maroon, beige for duffle coats.

Deep navy, midnight blue in preference to black for dinner jackets and dress coats.

Shirts in pastel shades with bold stripes.

Undergarments: Shirts with longer points on collars from American influence. Soft shirt collars with dinner jackets. Sports shirts with attached collars in flannel, cotton and rayon, sometimes worn open-necked.

American-style beach shirts in spun rayon, plain colours with white collar.

Underpants in cellular cotton fabric with no front yoke and straight fly front.

Shoes: Chukka boot of brown or black leather based on army officer's boot. Elasticated side gussets eliminate fastenings. Crêpe-soled shoes, rounded toes.

Socks: Long again after the war, knee-length, with elasticated tops, often striped. Wool and nylon mixtures.

Hats: Less popular after the war. Trilby and snap-brim hats, pork pies, bowler hats (for business) all worn.

Hair: Remaining short-back-and-sides for business. American influence popularizes crew-cut – hair cut short all over.

Accessories: Gloves with string backs, leather palms for driving, strap fastening with gap at the back of the hand. Cigarette lighters.

Details of illustrated patterns

Woman

Close-fitting day dress with interest centred at hip-level. Wide bias girdle wraps round to tie in large bow at right hip. By contrast, the bodice is simple with high neckline and small Peter Pan collar, long, tight-fitting sleeves, and a softened, rounded shoulderline. The dress is characteristic of the gentler, more feminine vein which is replacing the mainly functional fashions of the past years.

Fabrics: Wool or rayon jersey.

Colours: Deep cherry red, amethyst.

Footwear: Court shoes with high slim heel, fine platform sole, and ribbon bow decoration.

Hat: Soft fabric hat with raised crown and drapery to match the outfit.

Accessories: Gauntlet-style suede gloves worn over dress sleeve; small pearl earclips.

Man

Three-button single-breasted summer jacket with notched lapels and rounded fronts. There are three patch pockets finished with stitching trim below upper edges. It is cut on easy-fitting lines at the waist with additional width at the chest and shoulders. Two-piece set-in sleeves finish with slit cuff and two-button fastening. The back is cut in one piece.

The trousers have bands and pleats at the waist and are finished with permanent turn-ups. They are of generous width throughout.

Fabrics and colours: Very fine worsted suiting fabric with smooth finish, or lightweight woollen mixture fabric, in several shades of grey, blue, brown or tan. The jacket may be worn with trousers of the same material or in combination with other shades as a sports coat, for street wear, business or social activities. Lightweight mixture fabrics also suitable.

Undergarments: Pastel-coloured shirt with soft attached collar, worn with spotted tie.

Footwear: Black leather laced shoes with rounded toes.

Notes on construction of garments

Woman

Sleeves should fit closely over the arm; adjust to fit as necessary. Wrist opening is finished with single covered button and loop. If woven fabric is used the dress and sleeve should be cut on the bias.

Insert 22.75 cm (9 in.) zip at left side seam.

Extend girdle pattern to 3 m (3¼ yds). Cut on the bias. Centre of girdle is caught into back of opening, along line **A** to **B**, thereby concealing the opening when tied.

Leave opening of 10.25 cm (4 in.) at centre back neckline for zip fastening.

Man

The edges, collar and welts are single-stitched 6 mm (¼ in.) from the edge.

Dotted lines on trouser waistband indicate extension for left side.

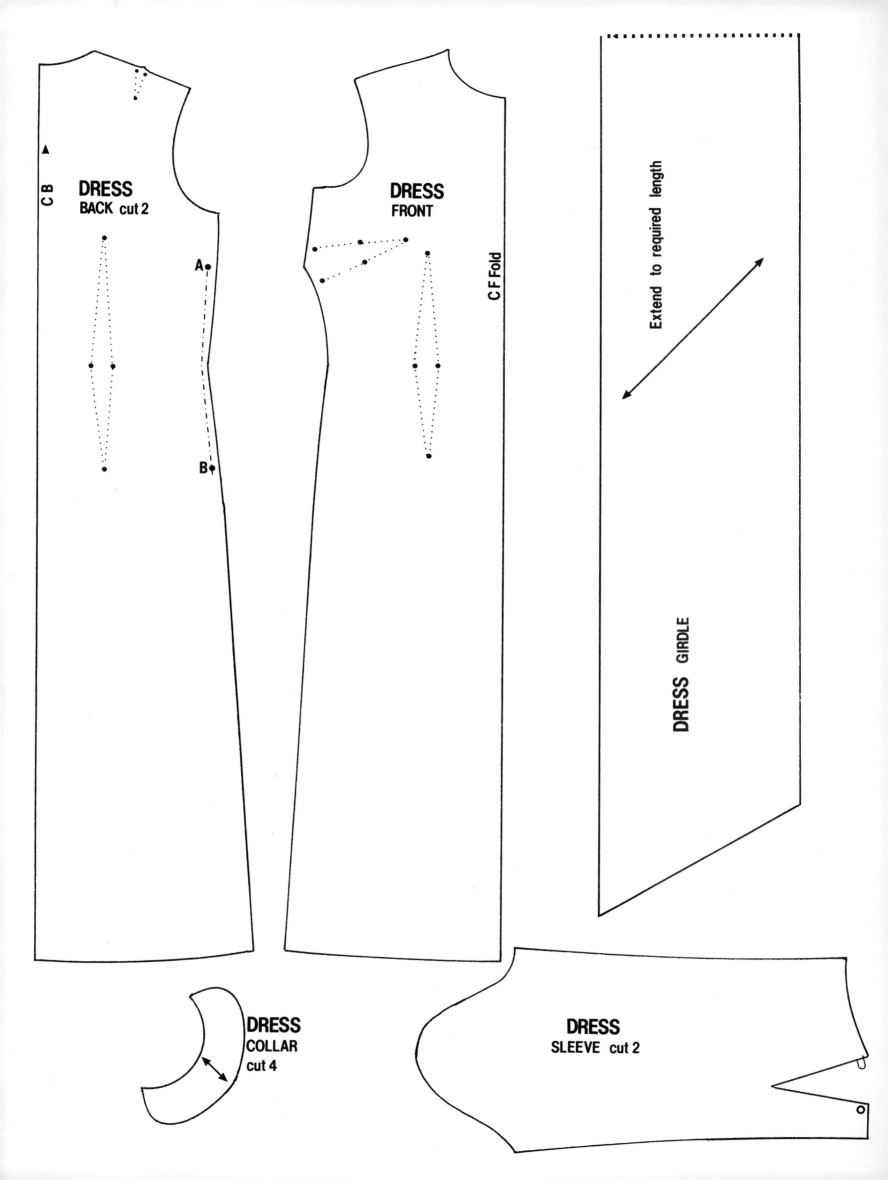

C B

DRESS
BACK cut 2

A

B

DRESS
FRONT

C F Fold

Extend to required length

DRESS GIRDLE

DRESS
COLLAR
cut 4

DRESS
SLEEVE cut 2

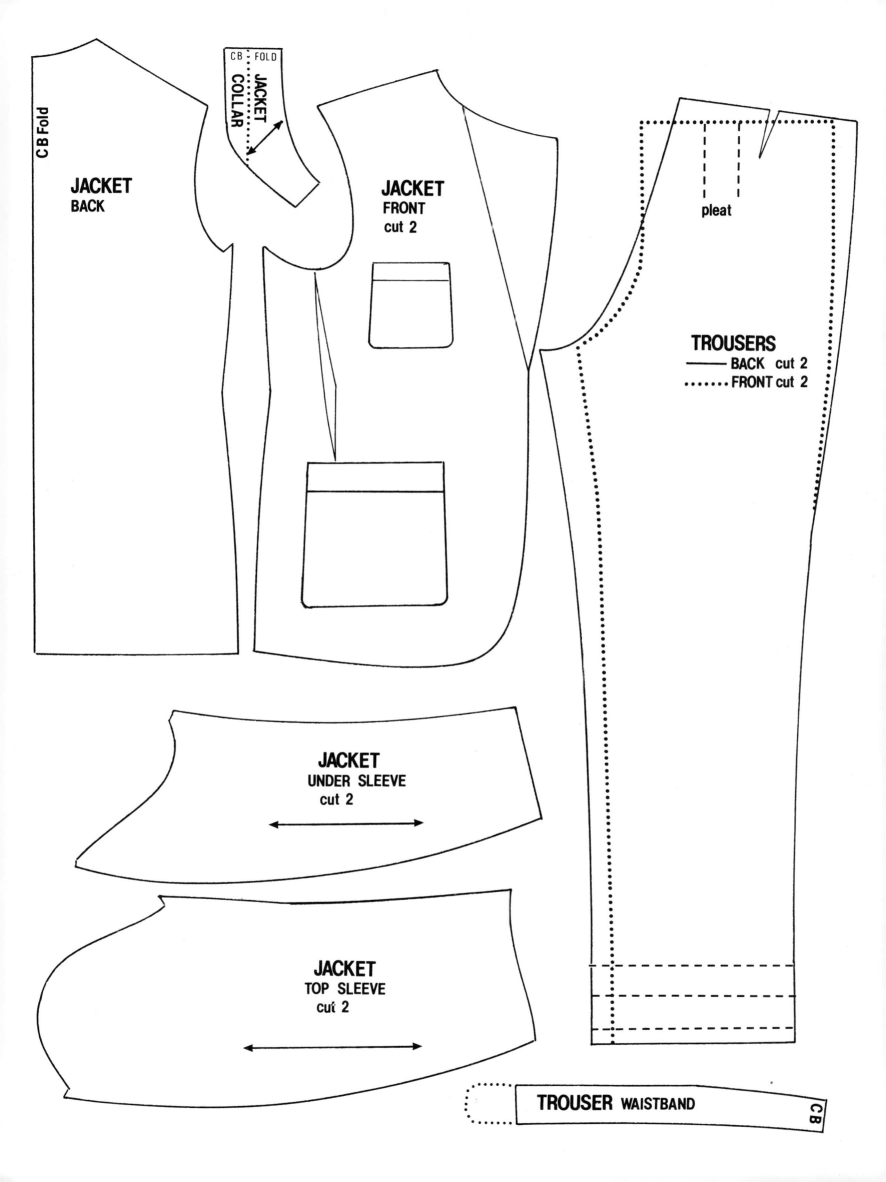

The Fifties

The fifties often seem to have passed unnoticed, an interim age between the turbulent forties and swinging sixties. By comparison, the fifties lack excitement and colour, but significant movements were developing which transformed Britain from the age of austerity to prosperity. Stability was essential to Britain's reconstruction programme, and fashion responded to this influence. Restrictions were still imposed, even after five years of peace: the Utility scheme continued until 1952, and petrol rationing continued well into the decade. In 1954 food rationing ended after fourteen and a half years, and coal rationing and price control only in 1958.

It was in such a climate that the government presented the 'Festival of Britain' in 1951, 'a year of fun, fantasy and colour, a year in which we can while soberly surveying our great past and our promising future, for once, let ourselves go'. Situated on the South Bank of the River Thames, the Festival set out to celebrate Britain's achievements in the introduction of the welfare state, new nationalized industries, our progress in the arts and sciences and design, free from Utility regulations. *Vogue* ran a feature on the 'Rise of Ready-to-Wear' to coincide – 'the most fastidious and fashion-conscious woman can dress in ready-to-wear clothes'. All seemed to signify that Britain was emerging from austerity into a new era.

The next event to brighten the lives of the British people was the coronation of Queen Elizabeth II in 1953, televised for the first time and seen by millions all over the country. The sale of television sets at this time rocketed, and television became firmly established; in 1959 the BBC had over 26 million viewers. Black and white sets usually had nine to ten inch screens at this time, housed in a wooden cabinet. Independent broadcasting from 1955 brought a wider range of viewing choice.

Despite Britain's floundering economy and recurrent financial crises throughout the fifties, for most people economic difficulties were less apparent than rising prosperity. The Festival of Britain was followed by the return of the Conservative government, which abandoned wage restraint, lifted much rationing and actively encouraged a consumer boom. Almost full employment and higher wages brought increased spending power and, as the government abolished systems of control, this stimulated business and industry, with consequential growth of manufactured goods. These were the years when the car, the television, the refrigerator, entered the average British household. With strict control on the number of cars manufactured for the home market, the expansion of the motor car industry was delayed. Nevertheless, car sales more than doubled and by 1959 it was estimated that one in every three families in Great Britain owned a car, compared with one in seven in 1950. 1959 was also the year of the Mini-car; relatively inexpensive at £497, it was an immediate success. The progress and expansion of the car industry was to provide the basis of prosperity in the sixties.

Nearly four million women, including a growing number of married women, were going out to work. This brought a second income into the home and contributed to rising living standards. Women provided a cheap labour source and were actively encouraged by the government to play their part in the country's recovery. However, advertising was still directed very firmly towards the housewife, and reinforced women's role in the home. It was in trying to fulfil these two roles that conflict arose in the following decades. Support for the family in various ways eased some of the financial pressure; the establishment of the welfare state provided benefits and relieved financial strain. The post-war 'housing drive' increased the rate at which families could be re-housed, ending much overcrowding. On cleared bomb-sites temporary dwellings, known as 'prefabs' (short for prefabricated), were set up to provide immediate accommodation. However, they continued in use well beyond the fifties and some are still in existence today. A more permanent planning measure was the 'new town' which was designed to relieve congestion in the cities by the setting up of housing estates and large shopping developments, with supermarkets and department stores in the country. The fifties also witnessed the first high-rise flats, extensively constructed throughout the sixties, and problem-creators of the seventies. The face of the environment was changing rapidly, the Clean Air Act of 1952 introducing the compulsory use of smokeless fuels such as coke, and thus ending smogs. The increase in sales of the domestic motor car brought a new form of pollution, and town planning now included essential roundabouts, traffic lights and car parks.

Fashion expanded alongside other British industry, as ready-to-wear, with improved standards and advanced technology, forged ahead. In very much the same way as war had provided the essential impetus to the expansion of commercialized fashion in the inter-war years, the Second World War, and in particular the Utility scheme, which had regulated quality of workmanship and cloth, helped to overcome many of the problems created by mass-production, and the industry emerged in a strong position. Conversely, in restricting clothes production for the home market, the Utility scheme delayed the availability of fashionable ready-to-wear. It was abolished in 1952, and was superseded by the more flexible 'D' scheme, in which garments below a certain price limit remained exempt from purchase tax, and above that level tax was graduated according to cost. The scheme was discontinued in 1955 and replaced by five per cent purchase tax on all clothes other than children's. Output of yarn and cloth increased, and ready-to-wear firms were thus able to develop their own materials and original styles of garments. Marks and Spencer were one of the most important firms of the period, rapidly establishing new stores and following a policy of value and quality. As Goronwy Rees, in his book on Marks and Spencer, states: 'Their prices after the war were not cheap. But given the quality which their merchandise embodied, it offered better value for money than anything else on the market.' Their share of national clothing sales more than doubled between 1950 and 1968, and was to increase to ten per cent of the total national consumer spending on clothing. In their centenary year, 1984, Marks and Spencer with its two hundred and sixty stores in the United Kingdom took one pound in every seven which was spent on clothes. Their large and powerful organization also played an important part in the textile revolution, initiating their own research from which many took a lead. The production of nylon, promoted after the war, effected its own revolution in underwear, and was followed by a succession of other new fibres: ICI introduced 'Terylene' in 1952; Du Pont were next on the scene with 'Dacron' and 'Orlon' in 1953; and in 1957 'Courtelle', the first British acrylic fibre, was produced commercially by Courtaulds. Most incredible was the speed at which the textiles, once discovered, were applied to industry. New fibres increased the range and variety of materials available to the textile industry enormously. Raw materials which were no longer artificial forms of existing fibres, but fibres in their own right, possessed properties quite distinct from those of natural fibres. Thermoplastic qualities enabled fibres to be bulked, and fabrics embossed and permanently pleated were light in weight, drip-dry and easy to iron. The fabrics themselves, then, influenced fashion, creating new styles and simultaneously lowering costs. Lightweight, easy-care clothes were appropriate to the needs of modern life.

Paris had, by the early fifties, with the import restrictions lifted and the overwhelming success of the New Look in 1947, re-established itself as the predominant fashion leader. Success in ready-to-wear was achieved by establishing close links with French couture, and designs were readily copied and adapted for the mass market. Until 1956 two silhouettes prevailed, with skirts either full or pencil-slim. For the most part the full bouffant skirts were retained for evening dresses, which could be floor- or cocktail-length. The ubiquitous strapless bodices of evening wear, heavily boned for support, relied on constructed foundations; numerous petticoats and weighted hems supported the skirt, where full.

The tailored suit was the basis of every woman's wardrobe, and usually consisted of a tight-fitting jacket, jutting out over a slim skirt. A scarf filled in the neckline, as the close fit often made a blouse superfluous, and tapes at the waistline heightened the fit at this point. Hemlines had risen slightly since the New Look, falling to the mid-calf and remained more or less stable until the late fifties, when skirts became significantly shorter. Fashion, and more importantly hemlines, made front page news, although this was usually only a matter of one- or two-inch variations introduced by individual designers. Christian Dior, Balenciaga and Chanel, who reopened in 1954, were the major designers of note. Dior introduced a succession of new fashions, based on letters, until his untimely death in 1957. Each gave a specific emphasis to the silhouette: the low-waisted, slim 'Ligne H' in autumn 1954 was closely followed by 'Ligne A', widening towards the hem, and 'Ligne Y' which expanded above the tapered skirt with dolman or full sleeves. His own version of Givenchy's sack dress, a waistless shift narrowing towards the hem, was his *coup de grâce,* but his fashion house continued to create new modes, with the young designer Yves St Laurent introducing the 'trapeze line' in 1958. The skirt was remarkably short, barely covering the knee, and flared from the shoulderline, creating a silhouette not dissimilar to the 'A line'. By 1959 the waist had returned.

Accessories were all-important; gloves and hats were always worn and could be large and flat or small and closely following the line of the head. Hair remained short with waves or bubble cut until the later years of the decade, when longer hair was brushed upwards, creating full-blown beehive effects. Shoes, round-toed and relatively clumpy in

1950 became shapelier and, as hemlines rose, heels became higher. From the mid-fifties toes became increasingly pointed and heels stiletto. Clothes were generally well-designed, elegant and feminine.

Much of the character of the constructed fashions of the fifties, with their boned bodices, built-in petticoats and weighted hems, looked back to an earlier page of history. Menswear, too, took a nostalgic influence from upper-class Edwardian fashion. The Neo-Edwardians wore long, tight-fitting, single-breasted jackets with velvet-faced lapels and cuffs, fancy waistcoats and narrow, fitted trousers. A bowler hat and winklepicker shoes, pointed well beyond the natural toeline, completed the look. The style was created by Savile Row and was adapted in a simpler form to the wider market. Men's clothes generally were slimmer fitting, losing much of their previous bulkiness and squareness of cut. Trousers were more shapely, with fitted waistbands, adjustable elastic inserts and zip fly fronts (now universal); turn-ups were phased out in the early fifties. They were also lighter in character, resulting partly from a more relaxed attitude towards dress, and increased use of man-made fibres meant trousers could be permanently creased. Shirts were often made of mixed fibres, incorporating a percentage of cotton for comfort, in bold colours and patterns, cut straight at the lower edge. These were sometimes worn outside the trousers and open at the neck, with either long or short sleeves.

Overcoats likewise became shorter and closer fitting, with single-breasted opening, and by the late fifties were knee-length. Motoring had ceased to be the dusty sport of its early days and no longer required protective clothing. The duffle coat, brought out by ready-to-wear after the war in heavy wool, also became popular. In the fifties the dress suit ceased to be worn for all formal occasions and the dinner jacket or dark lounge suit was favoured.

Young fashions began to take on fresh influences, distinct from those directing mature dress. Adolescence, to this date unacknowledged, was recognized as the important interim stage between child and adult. The needs of this younger set could not be met within the existing range of entertainments and fashions, and the 'teenage market' expanded at a phenomenal rate. Traditional family values declined and the idea of the 'generation gap' emerged, since parents often could not understand, nor participate in, the lives of their offspring. The young almost seemed to be hostile to their parents, and in dress, music and attitudes opposed the values of their parents' generation. The affluent society gave a new spending power to the young, and they found a world and culture of their own, different from, and often at odds with, those of their parents. American rock-and-roll idols, including Elvis Presley and Bill Hayley, and young film stars, like James Dean, a rebellious crazy mixed-up kid, became leaders, worshipped and imitated. The Teddy boys, or 'Teds', from 1953, were the first teenage sub-culture, and contributed to feelings of teenage anti-social behaviour. Their dress, not unlike that of the Neo-Edwardians, was inspired by the Edwardian age, with long jackets with narrow velvet lapels and cuffs worn over fancy waistcoats, white shirts with bootlace ties, crêpe-soled brothel-creeper shoes and winklepickers, and long hair slicked into quiffs and 'sideboards' with Brylcreem. Wimpys, youth clubs and coffee bars, with juke boxes sounding out the latest records, became new meeting grounds. Teenagers were to lead fashion in the sixties, but the seeds of the movement were sown in the previous decade.

In November 1952 *Vogue* photographed the blueprint teenager, with ponytail and coke, and from 1953 dedicated a section of their magazine to young fashion. *Harper's Bazaar*, too, began 'The Young Outlook' in January 1958. Teenage girls wore full circular dirndl skirts with numerous petticoats of paper nylon, ideally suited to rock-and-roll dancing, worn with scoop-neck blouses or tight polo-necks and 'flatties' – flat-soled shoes. For casual wear tight trousers, tapering to just above the ankle, and chunky sweaters were adopted throughout the fifties. The bust assumed a new importance, and large, pointed breasts became the new feminine ideal. Pre-formed, conically stitched and often padded bras pushed the bust upwards and outwards, the 'sweater-girl bra', from 1953, exaggerating the bustline in the desired manner. Strapless bras were cleverly constructed for plunging necklines and low-back styles, and 'Lycra' was introduced for underwear, making possible strength and control without stiffening.

In many ways casual fashions were derived partly from the teenage market, with full-skirted shirtwaisters and tight-fitting trousers or slacks and jumpers. The look also owed a great deal to Italian designers, including Pucci and Simonetta, who led the field in casual wear with bright colours – cerise, orange, scarlet and emerald green – and loosely fitting, but nevertheless 'chic', comfortable clothes. Italy also effected a revolution in knitwear, which became smoother and less bulky in the late fifties. Development of machinery and textiles enabled fine, knitted tubular structures, and twelve denier nylon stockings, without seams, could be produced. Fine, knitted sports shirts for men, with turned-down attached collars, short sleeves and tunic-style opening, became popular for general casual wear. Accessories, too, became dominated by this overriding influence: pointed shoes for both sexes and classic stiletto shoes and soft leather handbags for women. Italian fashions in menswear differed from the Edwardian look with extended shoulders and significantly shorter, straight, boxy jackets and narrow trousers. Despite the square silhouette clothes were well-fitted and shapely. Hair was short and tidy, cut in even length all over, in contrast to the more conventional short-back-and-sides.

By the end of the decade life in Britain had changed in many ways. The British people felt optimistic, with outward signs of success in the rebuilding programme and emergence of the affluent society. The average family was beginning to enjoy the luxuries that had previously been accessible only to the middle and upper classes. The fashion industry, likewise, expanded rapidly, the success of styles in ready-to-wear becoming instrumental in establishing fashion. Fashion was never to be the same again after the fifties.

1951

Predominant fashion features

Women

During the fifties women's clothes are generally elegant, well-designed and easily available from ready-to-wear. Two silhouettes prevail throughtout the decade: *narrow*, form-fitting bodices, pencil-slim skirts; or *full*, flaring from the waist to wide hem.

'Skirts are sometimes longer, but nowhere shorter' (*Harper's Bazaar*, 1951) – skirt length at least to mid-calf.

Dior –'princess line': shaped panels fitting the figure, unbelted with waistline outlined rather than specified; worn with blouson jacket gathered into wide belt at hips.

Suits – tailor-made suit essential item of wardrobe. All have narrow skirts, with three types of jacket – very neat and close-fitting, defined waist and peplums; long, belted tunic jackets or loose, casual fingertip jackets.

Coats – main outlines: fitted and often belted, with full skirts which may be three-quarter, seven-eighths or full-length just covering the skirt; tubular; or tremendously big greatcoats, sloping from dropped shoulders into enormous fullness and made in shaggy wools. Pockets are generally large and deep.

General characteristics – shawl or stand-away collars, half-belts above or below natural waistline; swing backs, angled shoulders, three-quarter-length sleeves.

Casual wear – sweaters with 'V' or 'U' necklines with tapered trousers or full dirndl skirts.

Evening – narrow or full skirts. Stem dress flares low from just above the knees. Plunging necklines, between the breasts; strapless or one-shoulder effects. Ground- or cocktail-length, 15.25 – 20.25 cm (6 – 8 in.) from the ankle, just longer than the day dress. Constructed evening clothes with skirt and petticoats sometimes joined, boned bodices and weighted hems.

Fabrics: Day suits – smooth woollens, no nubbly weaves, tweeds are firmer and smoother, occasionally with metallic threads. Flannels and gabardines for sharp, tailored suits. Velvets and velveteens. Surface interest in silks. Long-haired, deep-piled fabrics for coats: mohair, plush, 'teddy bear' fabrics.

Evening – plenty of lace; slipper satin, plain and façonné, faille, silk, jersey.

Colours: Black combined with white. Neutral shades for woollens. Not many strong colours.

Evening – ice pink, lemon, olive, black and white.

Decoration: Fur widely used as trimming: linings, borders, collars, cuffs, hems, muffs, hats, fur necklets on dresses. Much white fur, also persian lamb, mink, beaver, leopard.

Fine pleating. Embroidery, beading, sequins on evening dresses.

Undergarments: 'The hourglass look is out; a new silhouette has come in, narrow and controlled all the way down. The narrow shape must be built on a new sort of foundation, smoothing your hips and behind into a long, slinky line.' (*Harper's Bazaar*, January).

Boned and wired bras with adjustable straps which can be removed for one shoulder, or strapless dresses, wired to separate between the breasts for deep, plunging neckline.

Nylon fabrics revolutionize underwear, making possible lightness and stretch.

Layers of net and paper nylon petticoats emphasize the full silhouette.

Shoes: Fairly clumpy in the early fifties.

Stockings: Fine, seamed nylon stockings – natural shades.

Hats: Always worn – large brim with flat crown (mostly for summer) or small biretta type – perched above the front hairline and worn straight on the head. Chinese coolie hats.

Hair: Worn slightly longer, often swept to one side. Curly or flat and sleek.

Accessories: Take on new importance. Scarves fill in necklines of tightly fitting, tailored suits, blouses not always worn. Long evening gloves, pushed down to the wrist for day.

Evening – embroidered and lace stoles.

Jewellery – black beads; graduated pearls worn high at neckline; pearl earclips; *diamanté* earrings and bracelets.

Make-up: 'Doe eyes' with eyeliner drawn in upward turn at outer corner. Emphasis is on the eyes, heightened with plenty of eye-shadow and mascara.

Lips – 'Cupid bow' line, vivid red.

Faces – fresh-looking, the skin glowing through a filmy foundation; tinted powder.

Men

The lounge suit is worn for all occasions in lighter colours for informal or summer wear, heavier woollens for weekend and country, and dark grey or black for business or formal wear.

Lounge jackets are generally longer, more fitted and with lower waists; the skirt is flared with side or central back vents and three to four buttons. Single-breasted styles popular, and two-piece suits.

Trousers are narrow in the leg, but not peg-top, fitted over the hips and thighs; turn-ups may be present.

Overcoats – chesterfield and raglan styles still worn, loose-hanging with step collars. Flap or patch pockets usual. Duffle coats – see 1948.

Informal wear – lumber jackets, anoraks in leather or cloth, based on army battledress.

Fabrics: Man-made synthetic and mixture fabrics make possible lighter-weight suiting fabrics. Worsted suitings, gabardine, flannel, tweeds. Patterned tweeds, herringbones, cheviots, checks.

Colours: Black and darker greys for business. Lighter greys, blues, fawn, tan for summer wear.

Undergarments: Coloured and boldly patterned shirts. Dark shirts with light-coloured ties and suits.

Shoes: Pull-on boots with elasticated gussets just covering the ankles. Rounded toes, Oxford-style laced shoes. Sandals for summer.

Socks: Short socks with patterned sides, elasticated tops reinforced with nylon.

Hats: Bowler hats for business and with Neo-Edwardian fashions. Pork pies, trilby hats.

Hair: Short-back-and-sides.

Accessories: Driving gloves: unlined leather, or leather palms, with string or fabric tops. Dark ties with light suits. Spotted, striped ties. Cuff links for shirts without buttons at cuffs. Cigarette lighters. Long, tightly furled umbrellas for business.

Details of illustrated patterns

Woman

Lady's top coat which might be described as semi-double-breasted, as it has a narrow front panel, with a pair of fastening buttons at the waist, set very close together laterally. The upper buttons are ornamental and set well back. The back of the coat is panelled, the centre panel being relatively narrow at the waist and hips. The waist is sharply defined by means of shaped panels and underarm dart. The skirt flares over the hips to calf-length.

The roll-collar revers are made to swell out prominently over the bust and to roll softly down to the waistline. The slanting pockets with curved flaps are made in velvet to match the collar facing. Two-piece sleeves fasten with slit and two buttons at the cuff, cut fairly narrow.

Fabrics: Flannel, fine worsted twill.

Colour: French grey, with black velvet trim.

Footwear: Black leather court shoes with all-over punched design, leather bow trim, rounded toes and high, straight heels.

Hat: Small, veiled felt hat with velvet ribbon trim and large bow at the back.

Accessories: Black-and-white check scarf fills in neckline; short grey buckskin gloves; tightly furled umbrella with knotted cane handle; pearl earclips.

Man

Knee-length, loose-hanging chesterfield overcoat with single-breasted, three-button fastening and step collar. Flap pockets at hip-level are set horizontally with an optional slanted welt pocket on left breast. Split set-in sleeves finish with shaped turn-back cuffs.

Top-stitching detail emphasizes front edges and is repeated on sleeve seams, cuffs and pocket edges.

Fabrics: Wool gabardine or Melton cloth for winter wear.

Colours: Camel or grey.

Footwear: Laced, Oxford-style shoes in brown or black.

Hat: Snap-brim hat.

Accessories: Gauntlet-style gloves.

Notes on construction of garments

Woman

Attach tapes inside the coat at the waistline to ensure a close fit. Padding may be required over the hips to give essential roundness. Cut velvet facing for fronts and collar in one piece.

A 1 cm (⅜ in.) seam allowance is provided in the pattern, except at fronts. No hem allowance is included.

Man

Top-stitch front, collar, cuffs and flap pocket 1 cm (⅜ in.) from outer edges, and at centre sleeve seam.

Ease back to front at shoulder seams.

Adapt trouser pattern from 1948.

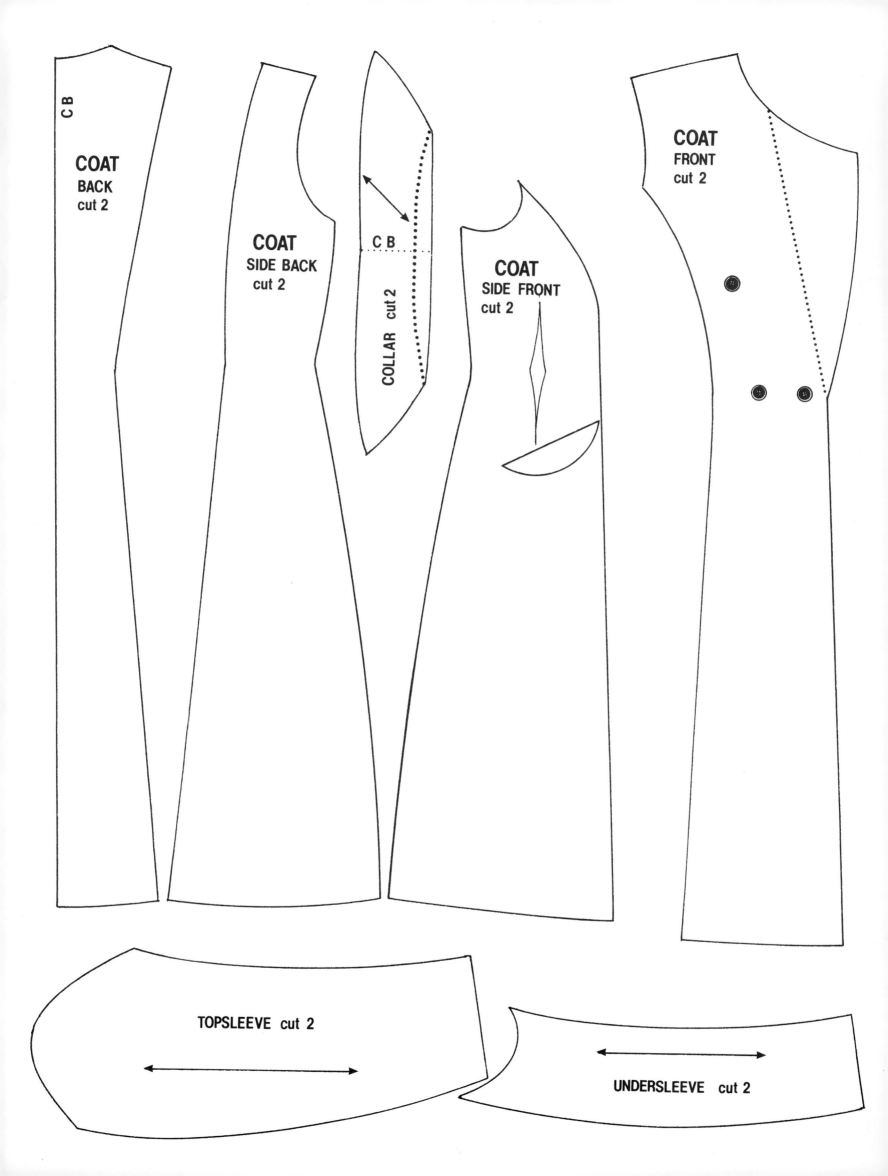

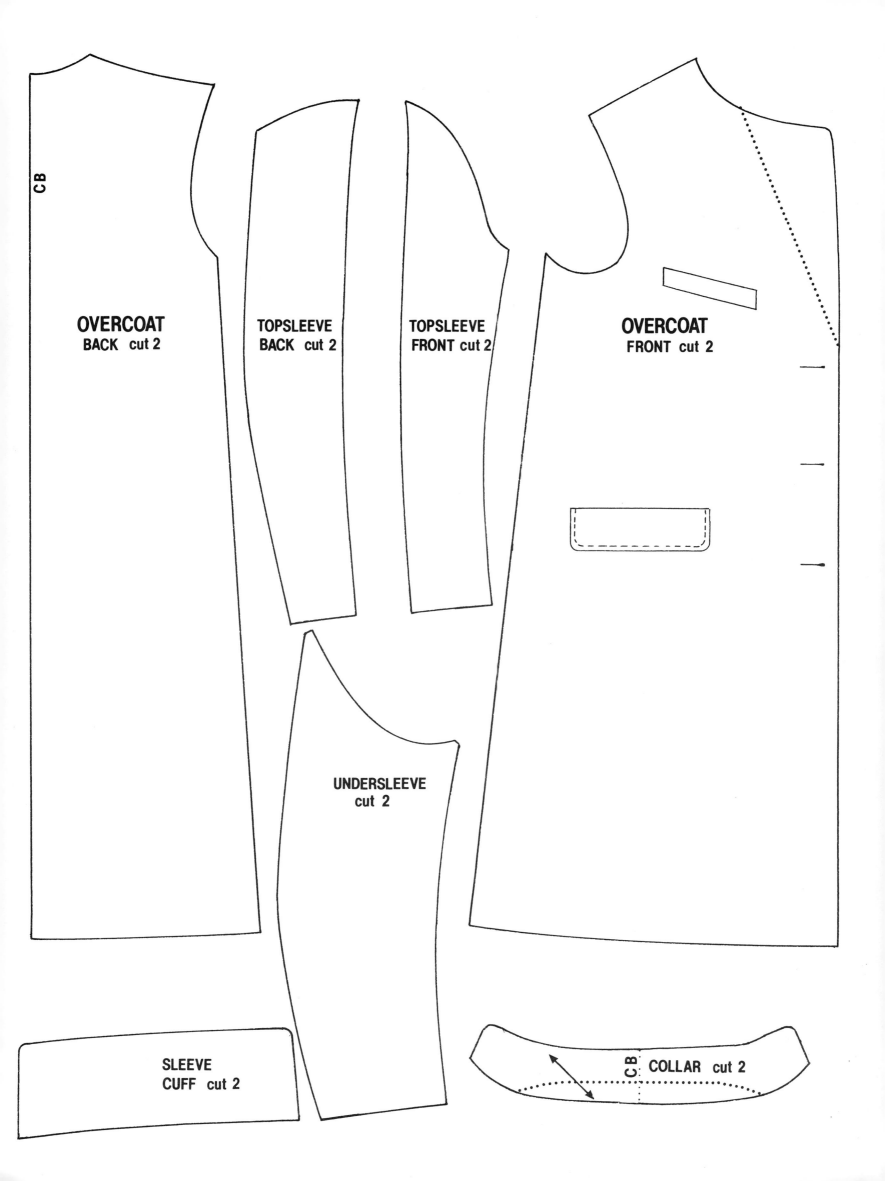

CB

OVERCOAT
BACK cut 2

TOPSLEEVE
BACK cut 2

TOPSLEEVE
FRONT cut 2

OVERCOAT
FRONT cut 2

UNDERSLEEVE
cut 2

SLEEVE
CUFF cut 2

CB COLLAR cut 2

1953

Predominant fashion features

Women
The line is similar to the previous fashion, with the bust assuming greater importance. Suits are padded over the bust. Loose, stand-away necks, dropped armholes.

Dior's 'tulip line' – he adds padding over the bust and shortens the skirt to 40.5 cm (16 in.) from the ground.

Sack or sheath dress – completely straight from the neck down and worn without belt.

Chemise dress – straight and simple, similar to sheath.

Casual wear – 'The sweater has grown in importance and size. Buy it two sizes larger for a casual look.' (*Vogue*, June 1953)

Teenage fashions – chunky sweaters, scoop-neck blouse or tight polo neck with full, circular skirt or drain-pipe pants.

Evening – strapless, full-skirted ball gowns.

Fabrics: Tweeds with neat, definite patterns, herringbones, dogtooth checks, Donegal tweeds; mottled, streaky, two-tone weaves. 'Manufacturers are smoothing the surfaces of their tweed cloths.' (*Tailor and Cutter and Women's Wear*, 2 January 1953) Wool mixed with rayon and nylon. Ribbed jersey fabrics; cotton prints – black and white, small designs, polka dots.

Du Pont introduces Dacron and Orlon.

Evening – lace, satin, organza, chiffon, tulle, paper taffeta.

Colours: Coronation year – heraldic reds and blues, white. Regal glints of gold and purple. Bright colours worn with black and white .

Tweeds – sandy beige, mustard, brown-yellows, mingling with black.

Decoration: Black-and-white prints, small designs, polka dots. Jewels, sequins, beading inspired by coronation.

Undergarments: Lycra introduced for underwear, giving firmer control without stiffening and rolling up.

Sweater-girl bra – two stiffened cones, circular-stitched, tight shoulder straps for uplift – to enlarge size of the breasts and push upwards and outwards.

Padded bust forms of foam rubber to give fuller, pointed bust. Cheap paper nylon petticoats, stiffened nylon net with circular or full skirts.

Shoes: Round toes, sling-back or court shoes with cutaway sides. Flatties or pumps with casual and teenage fashions.

Stockings: Two-way-stretch nylon, seamless stockings.

Hats: Small and neat, similar to previous fashion.

Hair: Hair rollers come into use.

Sleek and waved, or curly swept up at the sides, revealing the ears.

Accessories: Scarves fill in sweater and jacket necklines. Long day gloves in light colours, well above wrist. Evening gloves above the elbow with strapless styles. Jewellery worn in the hair for evening, chokers and earrings. Graduated pearl necklaces for day. Umbrellas, neat handbags – short straps.

Make-up: Liquid rouge on temples and under brows, tinted foundation and powder. Brown, blue-green eye-shadow, eyeliner drawn in upward turn at outer corner, mascara, pencilled eyebrows. Red and pink lipstick. Nylon false eyelashes.

Men
Menswear slims down, more sloping shoulders, less pointed lapels and narrow trousers. Single-breasted styles predominate, and double-breasted styles have same general characteristics. Dark lounge suits for business and formal wear.

Trousers – tapered and more shapely with waistband, permanently pressed creases. Turn-ups die out. Casual tweed sports jacket worn with flannel or corduroy trousers.

Trend of informality in menswear continues – open-neck shirts, slacks, unlined casual jackets for summer, cardigan jackets.

Shirts – no longer considered as an undergarment – jacket-style shirts worn outside the trousers, with long or short sleeves. Plain white shirt re-established with business lounge suits.

Evening – tail coats cut square, narrower and longer. Lapels also narrowed. Tail coat worn less than dinner jacket.

Teenage fashions – leather jackets, T-shirts, blue jeans and leather belts.

Fabrics: Similar to previous fashion. Man-made and cotton mixture fabrics for shirts.

Colours: Bolder variety of colour and patterns for men's shirts – paisley and spot prints.

Undergarments, shoes, socks, hats, hair, accessories: Similar to previous fashion.

Details of illustrated patterns

Woman
Summer dress with low, bias-cut, stand-away neckline. The bodice is close-fitting with high-fitting kimono sleeves and underarm panel cut in one with undersection of short sleeves. The straight skirt fits closely over the hips with front tucks into waist seam.

Fabrics and colours: White-spotted silk shantung or cotton poplin with red or blue background.

Footwear: Silk brocade, barred, toeless court shoes, rounded toes. Seamless stockings.

Hat: White fine straw hat with shallow crown and wide brim. Navy or red ribbon trim and silk-bound brim.

Accessories: White patent-leather belt to emphasize narrow waistline; long cotton gloves worn wrinkled over the arm; navy leather pochette; white clip earrings.

Man
Button-two, show three, double-breasted jacket is characteristic of slimmer line in menswear. Shoulders are less broad and square, giving a more natural line, lapels narrower, and less fullness evident across the chest. Straight welt pockets eliminate bulk, and left breast pocket is set at a slight slant. The jacket is long, fitting fairly closely over the hips. Narrow two-piece set-in sleeves finish with slit cuff and three-button fastening, harmonizing with jacket front. Foreparts are cut square at lower edges.

Trousers are cut narrower in the leg, with turn-ups, pleats into the waistband, and more fitted over the seat.

A plain white or light-coloured shirt with turn-down attached collar completes the outfit.

Fabric: Fine herringbone tweed.

Colours: Black-and-white, grey-and-white mixture.

Footwear: Half-brogues of black box-calf with welted leather toes and heels; rounded toes. Grey or black ribbed socks.

Hat: Snap-brim felt hat, grey or black.

Accessories: Handkerchief in breast pocket; leather gloves, cuff links.

Notes on construction of garments

Woman
Ease bias-cut collar to neckline, overlapping at centre front. Attach belt loops at waistline. Leave opening in centre back above small triangle for zip fastener. Two small pleats on skirt front are caught in at waistline seam.

Man
Trousers: use waistband pattern from 1947-8.

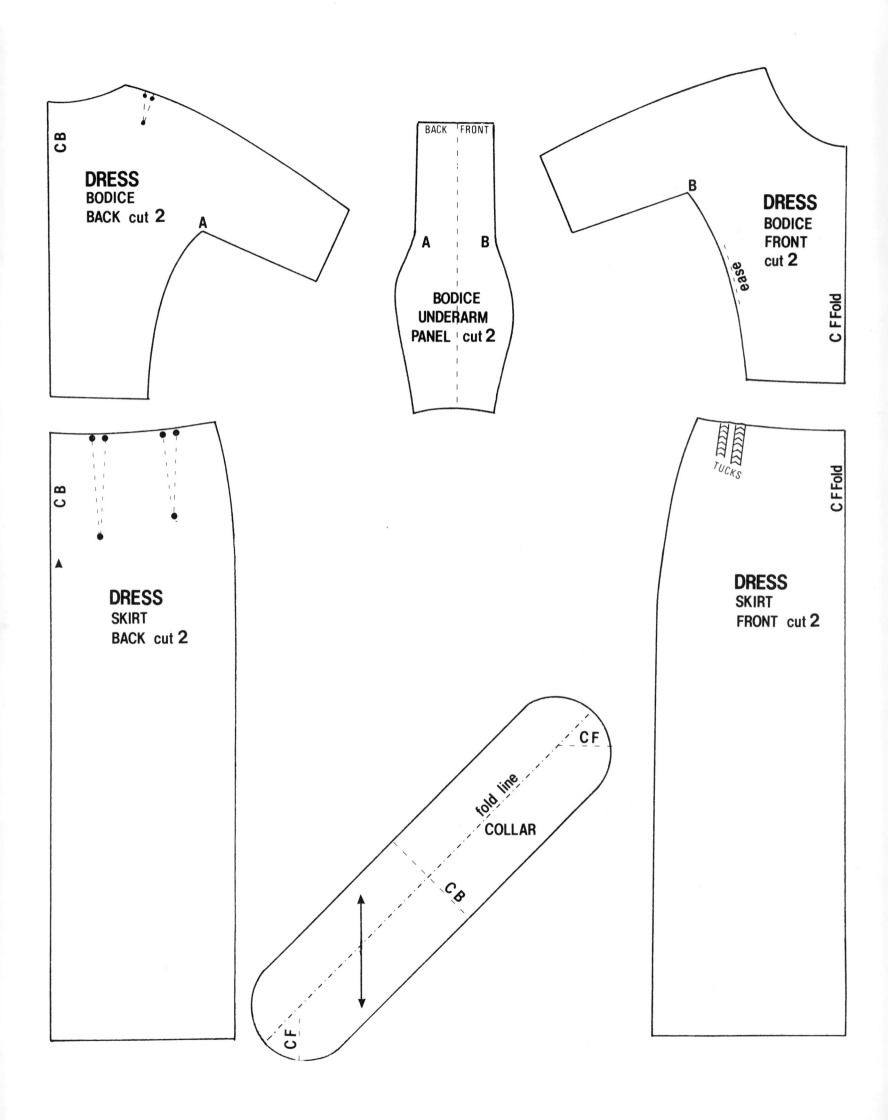

CB

DRESS
BODICE
BACK cut **2**

A

BACK | FRONT

A B

**BODICE
UNDERARM
PANEL cut 2**

B

DRESS
BODICE
FRONT
cut **2**

ease

C F Fold

CB

▲

DRESS
SKIRT
BACK cut **2**

TUCKS

C F Fold

DRESS
SKIRT
FRONT cut **2**

CF

fold line

COLLAR

CB

CF

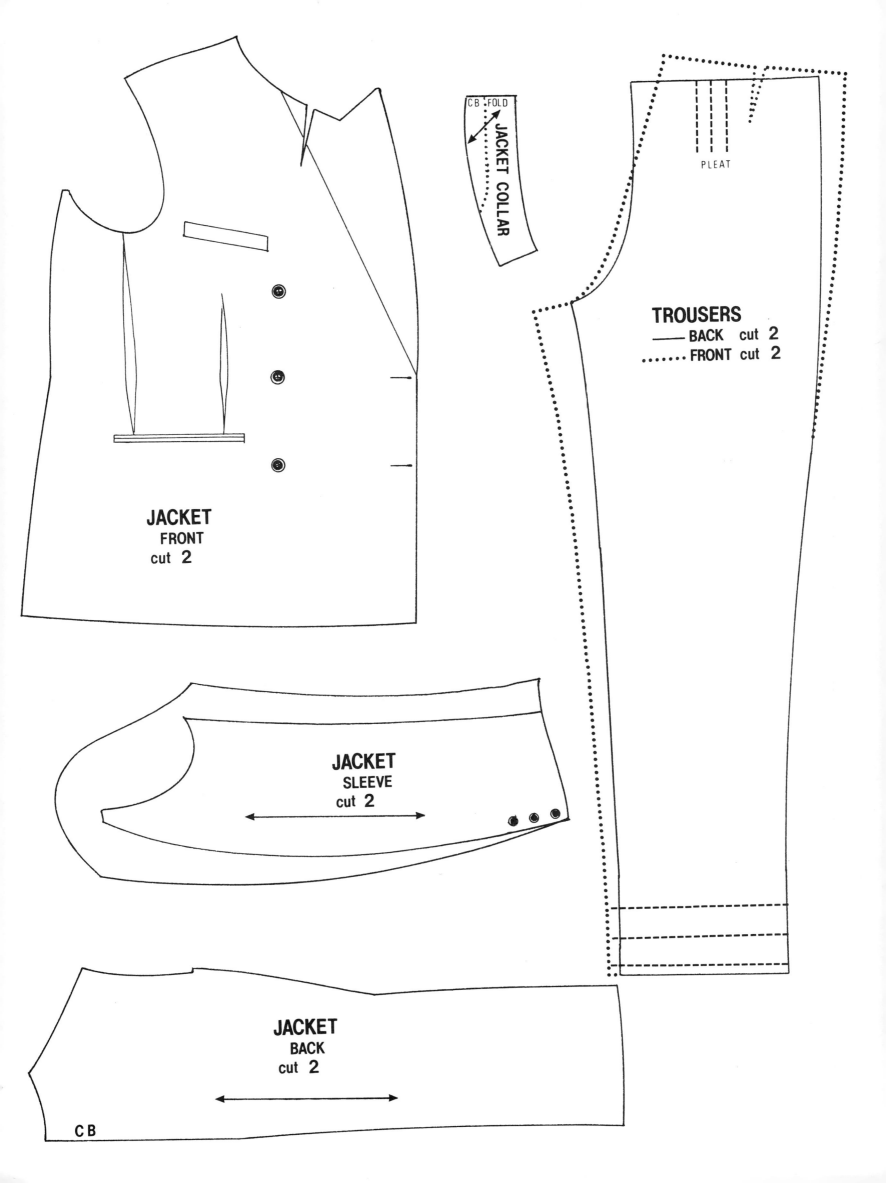

JACKET COLLAR

CB FOLD

TROUSERS
—— BACK cut 2
······ FRONT cut 2

PLEAT

JACKET
FRONT
cut 2

JACKET
SLEEVE
cut 2

JACKET
BACK
cut 2

C B

1955

Predominant fashion features

Women

Main silhouettes continue – narrow or full, the 'waist' fluctuating between Empire-line and hip.

Half-belts popular on suits, coats and dresses, positioned high or low. Semi-fitted suits with shorter jackets. Padding over the bust. Built-in petticoats with full skirts.

Dior's letter shapes.

1954 – Ligne H – pulled-out-telescope silhouette, tunic suits with low-waisted long jackets (sometimes reaching to the knee) over longer, slim skirts.

1955 – Ligne Y – dolman sleeves with longer, tapered skirts. Ligne A – widened from small head and shoulders to full pleated and stiffened hems.

Chanel's collarless jackets and skirts.

Coats – seven-eighths length popular. Trench-style raincoats.

Dresses – 'Suits everywhere tend to be jackets and dresses.' (*Harper's Bazaar*, September 1955) Close-fitting jersey or crêpe dresses with belt interest just above the hips.

Italian influence on casual clothes – bright blouses with tapered corduroy pants. Knitted tops.

Evening – similar to previous fashion.

Fabrics: Black or grey and white tweeds, smoother hopsacks and basketweave. Jerseys, crêpe, cotton and rayon prints.

Evening – brocade, satin, velvet, lace, silk, faille, tulle, chiffon.

Colours: Black predominant for day and evening. For day suits, soft browns, slate and graphite, mauve, bronze, vanilla. Evening – reds, pinks, green, yellow, white, ivory.

Decoration: Bold prints, small floral prints for summer. Bow trimmings.

Jewels, sequins, bead embroidery on evening gowns. Persian lamb trimming, fur collars.

Undergarments: Similar to previous fashion.

Shoes: Less clumpy with more shapely narrow heels. Low-cut court shoes with pointed toes.

Slipsters – slip-ons without heels, usually in suede or satin, for casual evening and day wear.

Stockings: Sheer, seamless, two-way-stretch stockings, one size. Ultra sheer, 12 denier for evening.

Hats: Small and neat, wide brims and shallow crowns for summer – flowerpots, toques, turbans, domed and 'cake-tin' shapes. Bow and ribbon trimming.

Hair: Short bubble-cut with soft curls.

Alice bands – hair bands for younger styles, take the hair away from the face.

Accessories: Short cotton gloves, flared over the wrists. Long evening gloves in kid or fabric. Large handbags, basket-style for summer in straw. Nylon umbrellas. Stoles.

Make-up: Similar to previous fashion.

Men

Lounge suits continue in style of early fifties. Two-piece, single-breasted suits most popular.

Overcoats – chesterfield and raglan styles, loose-hanging, flap or patch pockets usual.

Fabrics: Houndstooth and herringbone tweeds, stripes and checks, worsteds.

Colours: Greys, blues, browns. Summer suits – stone, natural, light tan shades. Slacks – natural, light tan, navy. Shirts – white, light blue, natural, biscuit, grey. Bolder patterns and colours – paisley, spots, checks. Sports shirts – checks of blue, green, fawn, grey.

Undergarments: Cellular brief-style jockey trunks, sleeveless singlets and short-sleeved vests.

Shoes: Toes less rounded, Oxford-style lace shoes in two-tone effects using reverse calf, half-brogues for town. Sandals for summer.

Socks: Made in variety of materials – wool, nylon, cotton lisle, Terylene, plain or fancy in shades of blue, beige, brown, mulberry, yellow or black. Toes and soles of wool socks reinforced with nylon.

Hats: Importance of the hat continues to diminish. Bowler hats for business, small pork pie hats, felt trilby hats.

Hair: Hairstyling for men; short-back-and-sides remains correct for business.

Younger set – Elvis Presley styles longer, combed back and swept up in front to form quiff, greased with long sideboards.

Accessories: Patterned and plain scarves in brushed wool. Leather gloves covering the wrist with centre vents.

Silk or wool, pastel, patterned or regimental stripe ties. Cigarette lighters, wrist watches.

Details of illustrated patterns

Woman

Asymmetrical, full-length evening dress with full skirt consisting of a circular overskirt of double tulle fabric over a semicircular foundation skirt of stiff lining fabric and tulle. The tightly fitting strapless bodice with shaped waist seam is boned to the waistline and draped with tulle, arranged in narrow pleats diagonally. The draping extends into the overskirt, gathered at the left side, front and back. A long piece of tulle is gathered over the left shoulder and may fall freely at the back or be wrapped around the shoulders to form a stole. The dress fastens to the left with zip and hook-and-eye closure at side seam. Bodice and right of skirt are decorated with floral motifs embroidered with silver and green threads and beads.

Fabrics and colours: Sage green tulle and stiff artificial silk lining.

Accessories: Full-length kid gloves, worn wrinkled; pearl choker and drop earrings.

Man

Semi-formal evening dress consisting of dinner jacket, cummerbund and dress trousers. The single-breasted jacket fastens with one button at waistline, with low-rolling shawl collar faced in ribbed black silk or satin fabric. Welt pockets retain slimness over the hips, the skirt cut with little flare and well rounded at lower foreparts. Slanted welt pocket on the breast displays handkerchief with double points. The jacket is cut with shaped centre back seam. Two-piece, set-in sleeves finish with slit cuff and three-button fastening.

Dress trousers are cut on similar lines to day wear trends, with single pleat into waistband at fronts. A single row of silk braid may be present at outer leg seams.

Pleated black silk or satin cummerbund is worn at the waistline. A plain or pleated white shirt with soft front and wing or turn-down collar and black tie completes the outfit.

Fabric and colours: Wool worsted in midnight blue, charcoal grey or white according to occasion. Black silk or satin for cummerbund and collar facing.

Footwear: Black patent leather Oxford-style shoes; plain blue or black silk socks.

Accessories: Black silk tie correct with dinner jacket. White linen handkerchief in top jacket pocket and a second, for use, tucked in sleeve. Gold cuff links, signet ring.

Notes on construction of garments

Woman

Construct bodice of firm silk fabric and double layer of tulle. Position of boning is indicated by solid lines on pattern. Leave open at left side seam.

The semicircular foundation skirt consists of a layer of silk and tulle joined to the skirt and left open above triangle at left side seam, for insertion of 35.5 cm (14 in.) zip fastener.

The overskirt consists of two layers of tulle constructed as one, the upper layer decorated with floral motifs as illustrated on sketch.

Cut two strips of tulle 134 x 122 cm (53 x 48 in.). One long edge of each piece is joined to the overskirt between the hemline and points **A** and **B**. The two strips are then joined together to complete the skirt, for 85 cm (33½ in.) from the lower edge. This enables the two strips to be taken either side of the zip opening in the left side seam. The overskirt is attached to the foundation over the shaped waist seam and each of the attached strips pleated and gathered between points **A** and **C** at front and **B** and **C** on back bodice. The strips will extend above these points and are narrowly pleated across lower front and back, meeting at the right side seam where they are pleated between points **D** and **E**.

The two separate strips of tulle are pleated and attached to the bodice between points **F** and **C**, either side of zip opening at left side seam and draped across front and back bodice. They meet at the right side seam where they are secured between points **G** and **H**. The upper line of draping on the bodice is indicated by dotted lines on pattern.

Narrow pleating of the fabric over the bodice is secured with fine stitching lines to the foundation.

A long strip of tulle 220 x 134 cm (86½ x 53 in.) is gathered on to the left front bodice between points **J** and **K**.

Full length is approximately 103 cm (40½ in.) from natural waistline.

Man

Fold a series of 1cm (⅜ in.) pleats across cummerbund to reduce the width to 13 cm (5 in.). The cummerbund meets at centre back with hook-and-eye closure. Stiffen with firm interfacing.

Trousers: use waistband pattern from 1947-8.

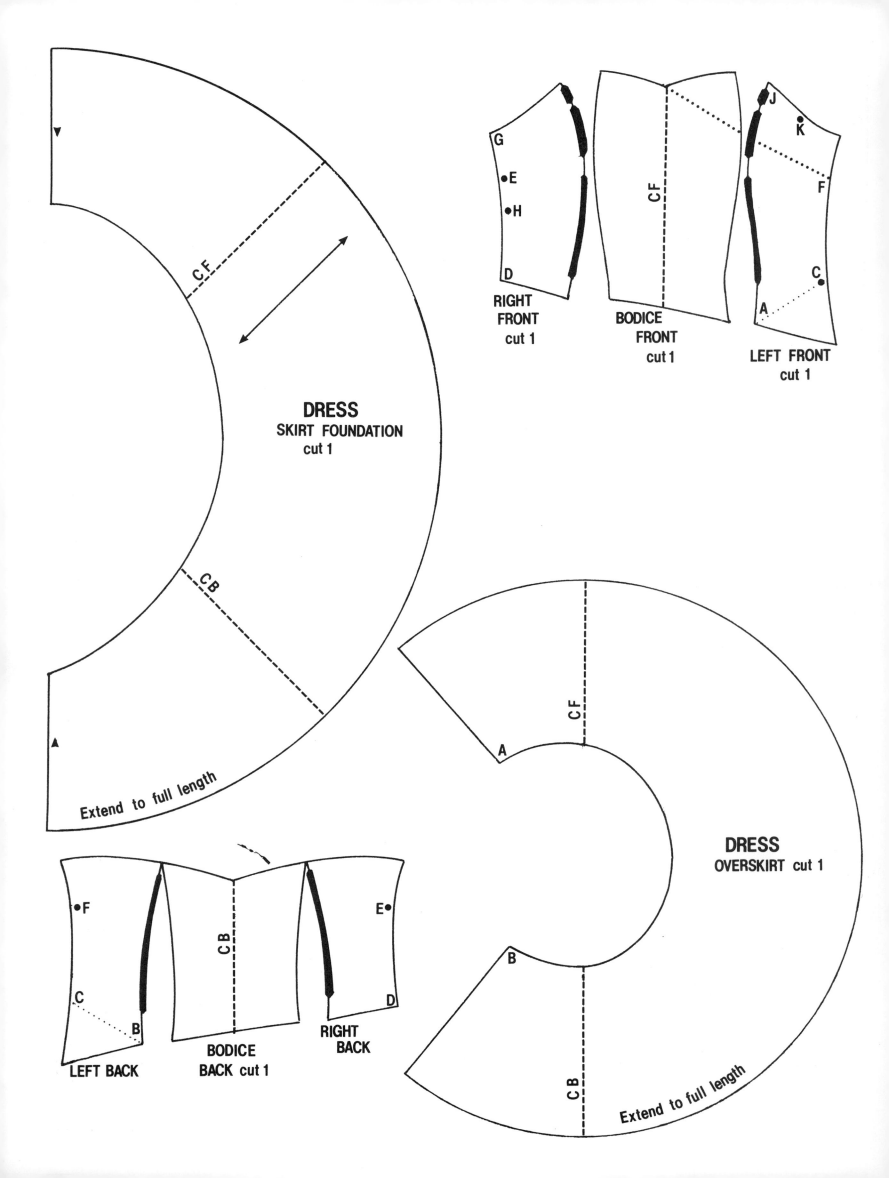

DRESS
SKIRT FOUNDATION
cut 1

CF

CB

Extend to full length

RIGHT
FRONT
cut 1

G

•E

•H

D

BODICE
FRONT
cut 1

CF

J

•K

F

C•

A

LEFT FRONT
cut 1

•F

CB

E•

C

B

D

LEFT BACK

BODICE
BACK cut 1

RIGHT
BACK

DRESS
OVERSKIRT cut 1

CF

A

B

CB

Extend to full length

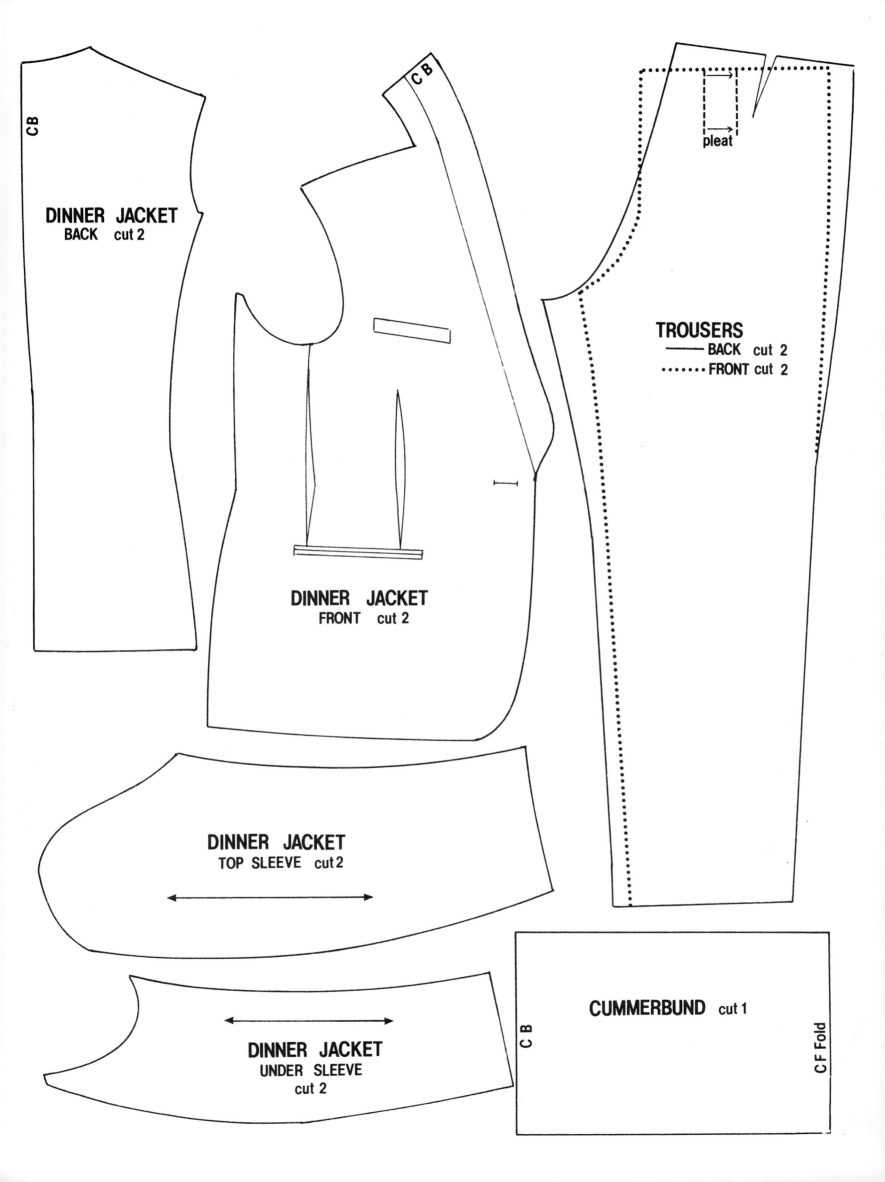

DINNER JACKET
BACK   cut 2

CB

CB

DINNER JACKET
FRONT   cut 2

DINNER JACKET
TOP SLEEVE   cut 2

DINNER JACKET
UNDER SLEEVE
cut 2

pleat

TROUSERS
——— BACK   cut 2
········· FRONT cut 2

CUMMERBUND   cut 1

CB

CF Fold

1956

Predominant fashion features

Women

Narrow and full silhouettes continue.

Longer length skirts, tightened at the hem. Shorter jackets with raised waists. Bulky soft coats. Capes, tapering towards the hem. Chanel's comfortable jersey cardigan suits and wrapover skirts much copied.

Half-belts on suits, coats and dresses. Casual wear - slim pants and chunky sweaters – 'Sloppy joes' – midriff blouses for summer.

Off-the-shoulder tops with skirts, shorts, trousers, jeans. Pin-stripe denim skirts. Knitted twin sets.

Teddy girls – button cardigans, scoop-neck blouse and full skirt over layers of petticoats.

Evening and summer dresses sleeveless, off-the-shoulder bodices more fashionable than strapless.

Fabrics: Fine wools, tweeds, uncrushable cottons for summer dresses. Thick, soft fabrics for coats.

Evening – firm silks, *peau de soie*, brocade, faille, clouds of chiffon, flare-free net, non-tarnishing Lurex.

Colours: Black and white, reds.

Evening – pinks, pale blue, grey.

Decoration: Contrast braiding on suits. Bright cotton prints, spots and stripes, huge coloured checks, larger floral patterns.

Bows in contrast or matching fabric – under the bust, at shoulders, openings, bodices.

Bead and sequin embroidery, flowered jewels.

Undergarments: Brightly coloured underwear in nylon and Terylene. Bra-slips. Stiff felt or paper nylon petticoats, tiered on slim-fitting hip yoke.

Three-quarter and half-cup bras, strapless bandeau bras. Waspie-belt – 10.25 cm (4 in.) wide corset, laced at the back and worn over girdle – boned to exaggerate hips and raise the waist. Corsets and girdles with zip fastenings.

Shoes: High-heeled shoes, narrow foot with pointed toe. Bow decoration popular and cut-out detail. Lower, slim heels for comfort.

Stockings: Sheer skin-tone nylons.

Hats: Breton and turban-style popular. Flowerpot, toque or brimmed styles with black veilings. Veiled cocktail hats.

Hair: Similar to previous fashion.

Accessories: As previous fashion. Larger handbags, clutch bags.

Make-up: Eyes and lips heavily outlined under veils. Pink lipstick and matching nail varnish for evening.

Men

The 'Italian Look' slims down men's fashions further – the cut is skimpy and close-fitting, with short jackets 15–18 cm (6–7 in.) above the usual men's length; the effect is square and straight. Chest width and shoulders are less pronounced and sleeves, collars and lapels are all narrowed. Trousers skimpy and short, without turn-ups.

Two-piece suits are more usual, adding to lighter, slimmer look.

The style remains popular during the latter half of the decade.

Teddy boys (Teds) – thick, draped suit, high-buttoning with long skirt and one or two vents, step collar and drainpipe trousers. White shirts with collar turned up or bootlace tie. Fancy waistcoats of brocade.

Italian knitwear – V-neck sweaters in fine knit and chunky styles with fancy bulked stitches.

Fabrics: Terylene and mixture suiting fabrics promote lighter, slimmer look.

Fine check suiting fabrics.

Linen, cotton and mixture fabrics for shirts.

Colours: Business suits in black or dark grey. Light-coloured suiting fabrics – stone, tan, pale grey. Tweed sports jackets in neutral tones.

White and blue shirts for summer.

Undergarments: Similar to previous fashion.

Shoes: Slim and pointed Italian shoes – 'winklepickers' – extend well beyond natural toeline.

Socks: Made in variety of materials – wool, nylon, cotton, lisle, Terylene; plain-ribbed or patterned. Plain brightly coloured socks with Teddy boy fashions.

Hats: Bowler hat for business. Pork pie, snap-brim-style hats with smaller brims to balance narrow suits.

Hair: 'Italian look' – short and neat, cut an even length all over and styled, in contrast to short-back-and-sides, which still remains popular among older men.

Teddy boys wear their hair longer, greased and swept back at the sides and raised at the front, with long 'sideboards'.

Accessories: Narrow ties with squared ends. Narrow bootlace ties with Teddy boy suits.

Umbrellas, cuff links, scarves.

Details of illustrated patterns

Woman

Teenage 'rock-and-roll' outfit consisting of very full dirndl skirt and scoop-neck top. The skirt is worn over one or more petticoats of taffeta or paper nylon, gathered on to a flat hip yoke. A narrow belt of matching fabric is worn at the waistline. The top, with wide V-neckline at front and back, extends over the natural shoulderline. The V-line is accentuated by seaming in the front bodice ending in small pleats over the bust. Darts at the waistline shape the bodice to the figure and give emphasis to the bustline.

Fabrics and colours: Bold printed check cotton of red, black or blue on white ground; white cotton top.

Footwear: Flat rubber-soled canvas pumps with elasticated front gusset; white ankle socks.

Man

Teddy boy outfit – long drape coat with low-rolling shawl collar and one-button fastening at waistline. The coat is cut with broad shoulders and chest, with moderate waist shaping and only slight flare in the skirt. Flap pockets are set low on the hips and slanted welt pocket on the breast displays white or coloured handkerchief. Set-in sleeves finish with shaped cuff, faced with velvet to match the collar. Many variations of the coat are possible including higher-fastening step collar with velvet facings and pockets.

Drainpipe trousers are cut shorter than conventional trouser styles, and fit the figure closely.

Embroidered or fancy fabric waistcoat, single or double-breasted, white shirt and bootlace tie, complete the outfit.

Fabric and colours: Wool twill tweed or woollen mixture fabric in black, grey or check for coat; lighter weight for trousers, often of a darker cloth than the jacket.

Footwear: Pointed winklepickers or thick crêpe-soled, lace-up casual shoes; brightly coloured socks.

Hair: Worn fairly long, greased and swept back at the sides and raised at the front, with long sideboards.

Notes on construction of garments

Woman

Skirt – front, back and sides are cut to the same pattern. Make an opening of 20 cm (8 in.) at left side. The total length of the skirt at upper edge is gathered into the waistband. For the waistband cut a strip of fabric 68.5 x 5 cm (27 x 2 in.); add seam allowance to all edges.

Cut a second strip of fabric 78 x 5 cm (30¾ x 2 in.) for the belt.

Note: 5 cm = twice finished width of waistband and belt.

Petticoat – pattern is indicated by broken lines. Leave left side of yoke open. The petticoat is fastened with single button and loop at waistline.

Top – allow a 6 mm (¼ in.) seam allowance between point **B** and pleat on top front.

Man

Ease back to front at shoulder seams. Shoulders are well padded to give essential drape to jacket. Collar and sleeve cuffs are faced with velvet; pocket flaps and welt pocket on breast may also be made up in velvet fabric.

Drainpipe trousers should fit the legs closely; adjust the pattern according to individual measurements.

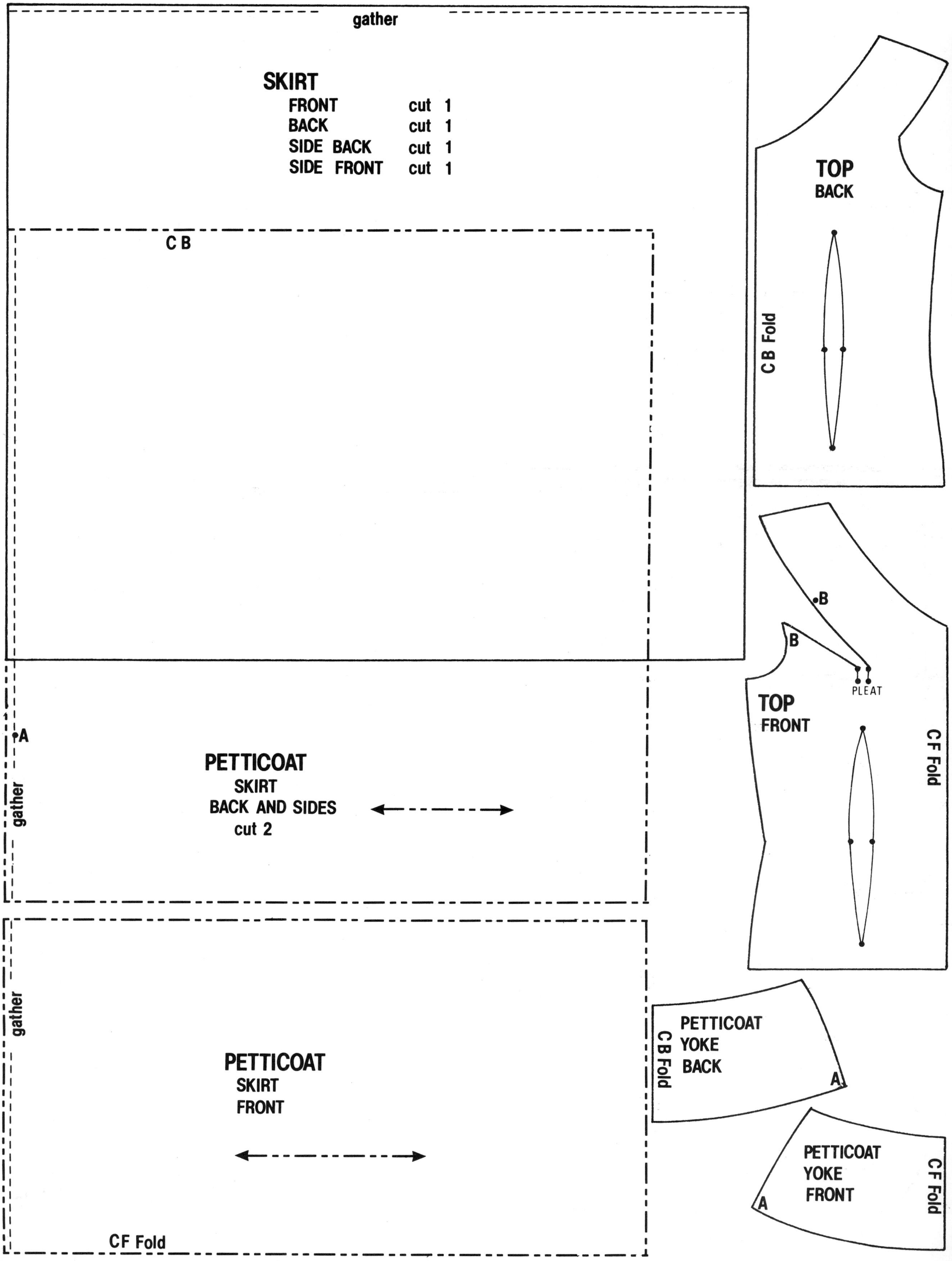

gather

SKIRT

FRONT	cut	1
BACK	cut	1
SIDE BACK	cut	1
SIDE FRONT	cut	1

C B

TOP
BACK

CB Fold

PETTICOAT
SKIRT
BACK AND SIDES
cut 2

A

gather

B

B

PLEAT

TOP
FRONT

CF Fold

PETTICOAT
SKIRT
FRONT

gather

CF Fold

PETTICOAT
YOKE
BACK

C B Fold

A

PETTICOAT
YOKE
FRONT

CF Fold

A

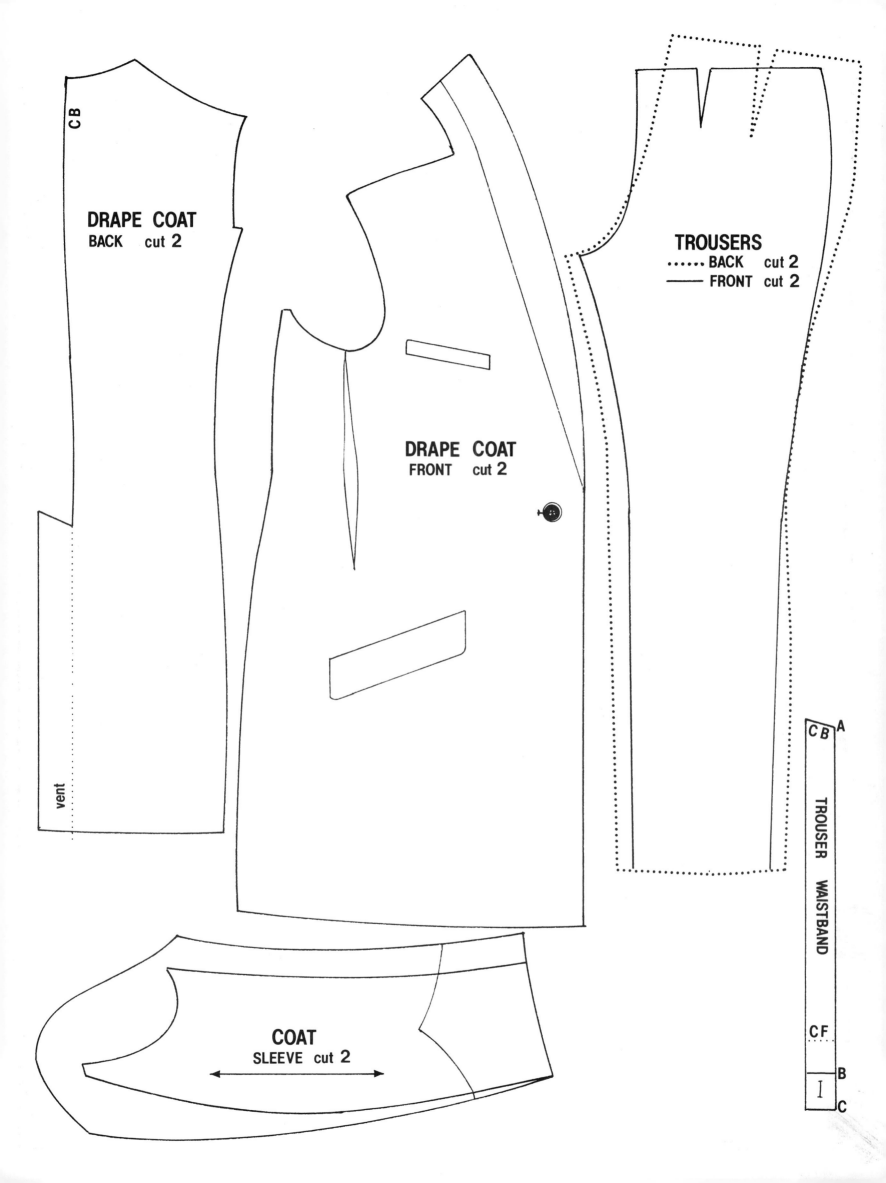

DRAPE COAT
BACK   cut 2

CB

vent

DRAPE COAT
FRONT   cut 2

COAT
SLEEVE cut 2

TROUSERS
······· BACK   cut 2
——— FRONT   cut 2

CB A

TROUSER   WAISTBAND

CF

B

C

1958

Predominant fashion features

Women

General characteristics – skirts barely cover the knee, shoulders less sloped. Half-belts at sides, back, front; high or low; dipping or straight. The waist continues to fluctuate. Rounded 'eased-away' collars, instead of previous stand-away necklines.

Yves St Laurent – 'Trapeze line' – flaring from the shoulders to full, wide hem, giving a cape appearance; three-quarter-length sleeves and the shortest skirts at knee level.

Coats – thick and soft with rounded shoulders. Three-quarter-length coats over slim skirts.

Waistless shift and sack dresses, tapering to the knees. 'Chemise dresses are more popular than ever.' (*Tailor and Cutter*, 13 June 1958) Loose backs sometimes contrast with a front held in with belt, drawstring or darting, giving a curved, concave line.

Button-through, tailored shirtwaisters, full-skirted.

Chanel's jersey suits and blazer jackets continue to be much copied by ready-to-wear.

Brightly coloured blouses to tone with suits, the fabric also used to line the jacket.

Casual wear – tapered jersey trousers with Italian sweaters and blouses. Easy-care Courtelle jumpers in pastel shades – lemon, blue, pink.

Evening – dipping hemlines, raised at the front.

Chanel's tulip line – with fullness billowing out from the waist and caught in at the bottom to a narrow hem.

On similar lines – 'cocoon', 'melon', 'puff-ball', 'barrel' lines used extensively for evening dresses.

Fabrics: 'Wool takes on new textures' (*Harper's Bazaar*, January 1958) – mohair, corded weaves, bouclette – plain, coloured and mottled. Basketweaves, dogtooth checks, herringbones, men's suiting fabrics, slub-weave silks and rayons.

Coats – soft, thick, woollen fabrics: wool velours, Melton cloth. Corduroy, jersey, denim for casual pants, striped denim for skirts. Synthetic and cotton mixture fabrics for easy-care summer dresses. Uncrushable knitted cottons, crease-resistant cotton prints. Check cotton tweeds with knitted look.

Bulked nylons.

Evening – taffeta, satin, brocades, nylon and silk chiffon, tulle.

'Courtelle' first British acrylic fibre, produced commercially by Courtaulds.

Colours: Tweeds – muted colours, mixed with black. Knitted-look tweeds.

Pastels, ice blue, lemon for summer. All shades of green popular. Evening – brighter colours.

'The colour spectrum breaks into five: the blues, the mineral greens, the browns, the marigolds and the sharp reds – all accented by bold black and white.' (*Tailor and Cutter*, 13 June 1958)

Decoration: 'Bows are everywhere.' Floral, paisley and bold, colourful prints, spots of all sizes. Prints resembling leopard skin, herringbone, knitted fabrics. Large and multi-coloured buttons. Mink collars and scarves. Contrast braiding on suits.

Undergarments: Similar to previous fashion.

Shoes: Italian, remaining very narrow with squared-off points and fine stiletto heels. Contrasting toe-caps and cut-out styles popular.

Pumps – low-heeled shoes.

Stockings: Tinted nylon stockings, very sheer, skin-tones. Ankle and knee-high socks for younger set, worn with pumps.

Hats: Small, perched over forehead and worn square on head – veiled flowerpot, cloche, toque, breton styles. Straw for summer, feathered and veiled hats for evening.

The beret is a very popular style 'worn in every size, at every angle.' (*Harper's Bazaar*, January 1957)

Hair: Women brush hair out rather than flatten it; waved, not curly. Fringes popular.

For evening, additional hairpieces swirled around the head.

Accessories: Short, cotton or nylon gloves for day, coloured to match the outfit; washable suede and leather gloves. Over the elbow for evening.

Gigantic bags – clutch, and strap styles.

Make-up: Eyes and lips heavily outlined with veiled hat styles. Emphasis is on the eyes, blue-green eyeshadows, eye-pencil and mascara. Eyebrows softly defined.

Lips outlined with lip-pencil then filled in with lipstick. Red and pink shades.

Men

Similar to previous fashion. Single-breasted suits, narrow lapels, flap and jetted pockets.

Dinner jackets follow day trends, single-breasted with narrower lapels or shawl collar; facings, cuffs, waistcoat lapels and collar trimming of matching satin (usually dark blue) and often lined with contrast fabric, e.g. burgundy.

Fabric and colours: Similar to previous fashion. Wool worsteds, basketweaves.

Fancy checks – blue-and-tan, blue-and-grey combinations popular.

All other details similar to previous fashion.

Details of illustrated patterns

Woman

Slimline shift dress with boat neckline, yoke and sleeves cut in one piece. The dress is gathered in to the yoke at the front and caught on the hips with broad, buttoned tabs, the buttons repeated on short sleeves. The straight skirt narrows to the hemline, shorter than previous fashion.

Fabric and colours: Dogtooth-check rayon, navy blue, red, black and white.

Footwear: High stiletto court shoes in two colours with squared-off toes and cut-out vamp, buckle trim.

Accessories: Very large black leather briefcase-style handbag; above-the-wrist white cotton gloves; choker-length necklace with triple string of pearls; matching clip earrings.

Man

Single breasted two-piece lounge suit with narrow lapels and one-button fastening at waistline. Jetted pockets retain slimness over the hips and welt pocket on left breast displays handkerchief with double points. The jacket is relatively short and close-fitting, with sloping shoulders and narrow, two-piece sleeves finished with slit and single button. The back is cut with centre back seam and no vent.

Trousers are cut closer to the leg and shorter in length than previous styles. They are self-supporting, with straight waistband and adjustable slide fasteners.

The outfit is worn with button-through pastel-coloured shirt with attached collar and narrow, striped tie.

Fabrics and colours: Lightweight linen-look Terylene and wool suiting fabric in grey, fawn or brown.

Footwear: Slim-fitting lightweight laced shoes with squared-off toes and stitched upper. Short wool and nylon socks may be plain or fancy.

Hats: The 'hatless' mode continues. The trilby and snap-brim hat with narrow brim, and bowler worn with business suit, remain popular.

Hair: Cut short and neat, with more emphasis on 'styling'.

Accessories: Jewellery – cuff links, signet ring, tie pin.

Notes on construction of garments

Woman

Gather dress to yoke at front and back as indicated on pattern. Leave opening in left side seam for 33.5 cm (14 in.) zip fastener.

For attached hip belts cut four strips of fabric (top plus facing) 6 cm (2½ in.) wide by 22 cm (8¾ in.); round ends as shown by dotted lines on pattern. Add 1 cm (⅜ in.) seam allowance to all belt edges.

The dress should fit closely over the hips; adjust pattern as necessary to suit individual figures.

Man

Ease back to front at shoulder seams.

For trouser waistband trace off pattern from **A** to **B** for right side with fly extension. Trace off band from **A** to **C** for left side with front button extension. Add 1 cm (⅜ in.) seam allowance to all edges of waistband.

Shirt back pattern is indicated by dotted lines. For pleat at centre back place edge of pleat line on fold of fabric.

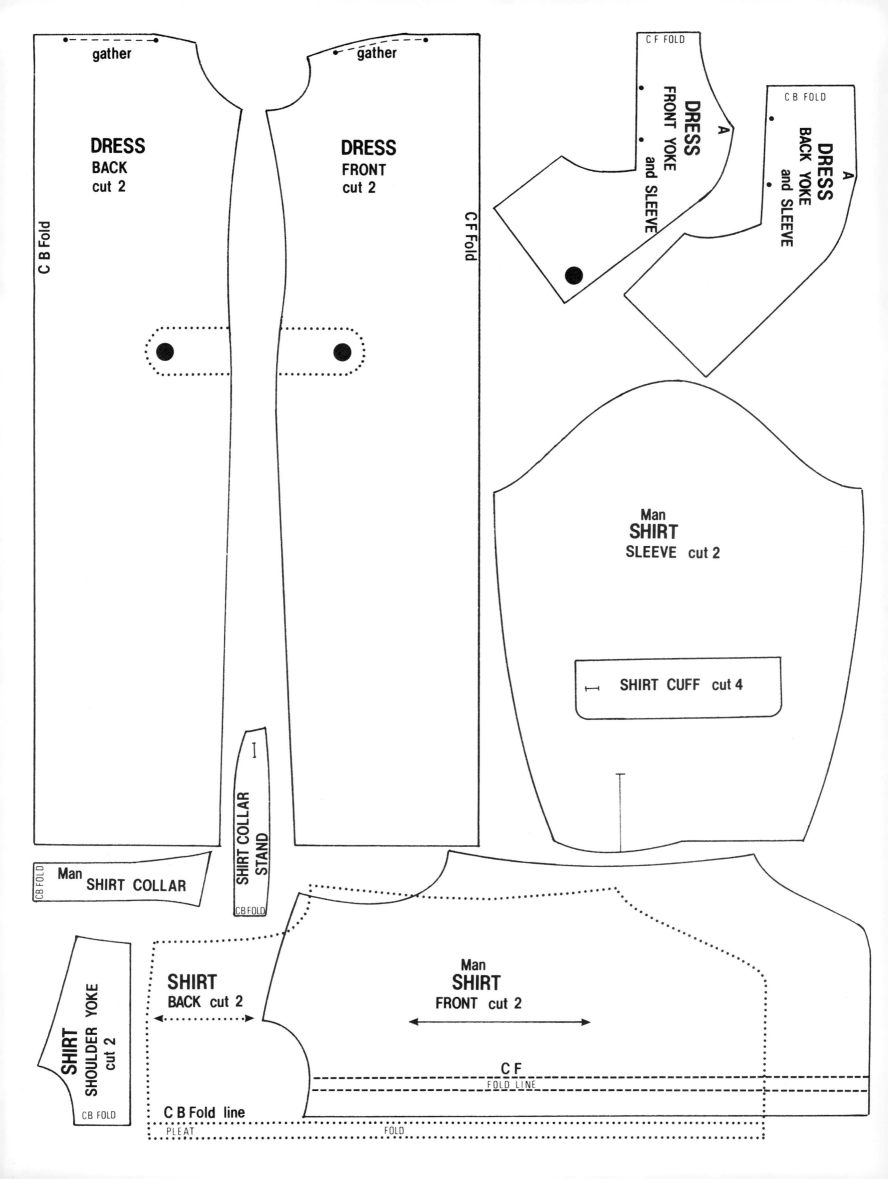

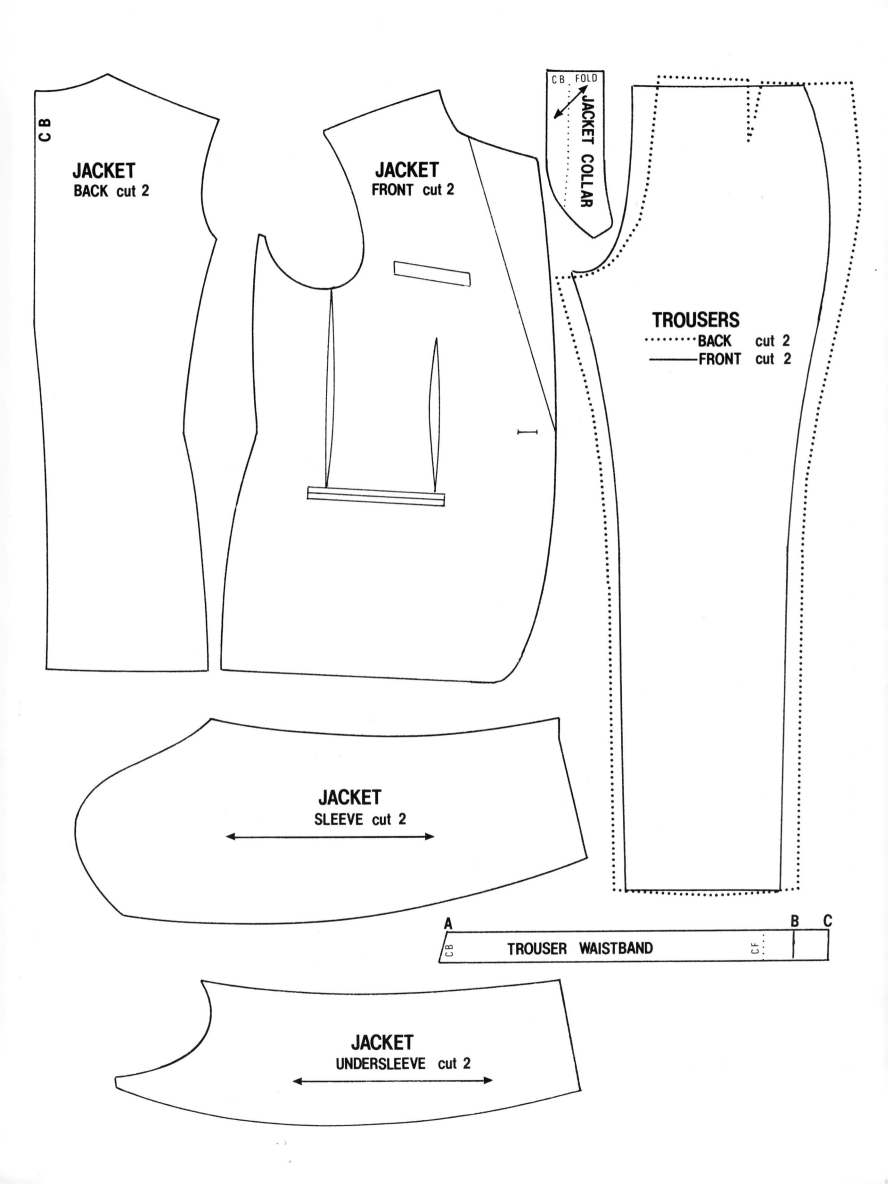

JACKET
BACK cut 2

CB

JACKET
FRONT cut 2

CB FOLD
JACKET COLLAR

TROUSERS
···· BACK   cut 2
—— FRONT   cut 2

JACKET
SLEEVE cut 2

A   B   C
CB   **TROUSER WAISTBAND**   CF

JACKET
UNDERSLEEVE cut 2

1959

Predominant fashion features

Women

'Skirts begin swinging' (*Harper's Bazaar*, October 1959) – shorter, barely covering the knee and wider at the hem.

Shorter jackets, some cropped to waist-length; wide belts, bulky cape collars – wrapover looks, dipping or folding over waist. Round necklines, natural waist.

Jackets button high with neat collars and revers. Coats or jackets with dresses popular combination.

New silhouette – seaming moulds the dress or jacket to the figure under the bust, giving a corselet effect; at the hip-bone the seaming is released into tiny pleats.

Chanel's cardigan suits with weighted jacket hems are universally copied.

Coats – seven-eighths length or shorter. The line may be straight or wide, but always bulky. Heavier sleeves set into rounded shoulders.

Italian influence on casual wear – chunky sweaters with wider armholes, tapered trousers, sweater dresses. Knitted twin-sets and V-neck pullovers specially dyed to match slim, pleated wool skirts.

Knitwear – 'the look still easy and uncluttered, but without the bulky texture of earlier crops'. (*Harper's Bazaar*, November 1959)

Evening – 'cocoon', full skirt caught in at narrow hem, similar to 1958.

Fabrics: Worsted, barathea, jacquards, novelty suitings, jersey, velour, bouclé. Rich lace, firm satins, brocades, velvets for evening.

Rough textures for coats and suits – soft, luxury mohair, loose tweeds, bouclé wool.

Grey flannel for simple winter dresses and suits. Dogtooth checks.

Colours: All shades of green. Pastel summer shades, peach, lemon, pinks, soft blues, white.

Decoration: Paisley prints, spots and bold checks. Large buttons, embroidery and appliqué motifs. Pleats and pockets giving one-sided emphasis. Fabrics with the look of a fine knit. Mink trimming a fashion luxury.

Undergarments: As previous fashion.

Shoes: High stiletto heels, 10.25 cm (4 in.) in height, 1 cm (3/8 in.) in diameter.

Stockings: As previous fashion.

Hats: Taller hats to balance higher hairstyles, line full and rounded covering the whole head and hair, narrow brims. With fuller hairstyles it is permissible to go hatless.

Hair: Back-combed for extra fullness; fringes. Lacquered beehive styles. Wigs and hairpieces – hair built up over wire frames for evening. For young set – short, curly style, pulled back off the face with head bands.

Accessories: Long kid gloves ruched over the wrist for evening; short for day with flared wrists. Large handbags, bags with chain handles. Head bands of metal, or fabric-covered. Wrist watches. Inexpensive costume jewellery.

Make-up: Heavy eyes and paler lips. Eyeliner continues to flick up at outer corners. False eyelashes, shaped and applied to far corner of eyes.

Pastel lip shades and nail varnish – 'frosted pink', 'strawberry vanilla'.

Men

Italian influence on clothes continues.

Knee-length overcoats with 'flared skirt', and belted. Raglan styles popular.

Knitted sports shirt with turned-down attached collar, short sleeves, tunic-style front-button fastening, for casual wear.

Fabrics: Terylene suiting fabrics. Checked tweeds for sports jackets. Trousers in worsted flannel, Acrilan/wool or Terylene/wool.

Colours: Striped fawns and blue. Suits available in light and dark shades, stone, tan, navy, grey.

Undergarments: Underwear in 'Helanca' stretch nylon, easy-care, requiring no ironing. Sleeveless vests, jockey shorts.

Short-sleeved vests and poplin trunks, front-buttoning with elasticated tops.

Shoes and socks: Similar to previous fashion. Slip-on casual shoes with elasticated side-gussets.

Hats and hair: Similar to previous fashion. Beards begin to return to popularity.

Accessories: Similar to previous fashion.

Details of illustrated patterns

Woman

Straight seven-eighths-length coat with wide leopard fur collar. The coat is bulky and loose-fitting throughout with three-quarter-length split sleeves and shaped turn-back cuff. Wide buckle and band trim of self fabric are set well back from front edges which are cut with generous overlap, fastening with four gigantic buttons. Deep pockets are set in at side seams.

The coat is worn over a matching sheath dress with widened scoop neckline, narrow three-quarter-length sleeves, and centre back vent at hemline. The dress fits closely to the figure, shaping achieved by double darts at front and back. The skirt tapers slightly towards the hemline.

Fabrics and colours: Loosely woven, textured tweed fabric in deep brown or tan.

Footwear: Soft leather, high-heeled court shoe with a draped vamp, buttoned down the centre. Sheer, tinted, nylon stockings.

Hat: Leopard fur, flowerpot-style hat with turn-down brim and leather bow decoration

Accessories: Soft leather handbag with metal frame and clasp and semicircular covered handles, to match shoes; over-the-wrist gloves of soft kid with hand-stitching and rolled effect at flared wrists.

Man

Short, double-breasted overcoat with four-button fastening, wide lapels and upper collar of fur. The coat is loose-fitting throughout and cut without shaping. Shoulders are sloped and sleeves plain. Angled welt pockets are set fairly high on foreparts.

Flannel trousers are cut fairly narrow in the leg and short in length. They are self-supporting, with straight waistband and side seam pockets.

Fabrics and colours: Shetland wool dogtooth check top fabric in black and white, lined with tartan.

Footwear: Slim-fitting lightweight laced shoes with squared-off toes and stitched upper. Short wool and nylon socks may be plain or fancy.

Hats: Felt trilby hat with narrower brim, to balance slimmer line in men's fashions.

Accessories: Long, tightly furled umbrella. Jewellery – cuff links, signet ring.

Notes on construction of garments

Woman

Collar facing of leopard fur is cut without seam at neckline.

Make small darts below roll-line of coat collar to ensure stand-away effect at neckline.

Pockets may be set in at side seams.

Man

Cut upper collar of fur 6 mm (1/4 in.) larger all round than the coat collar to allow for extra thickness of fabric. Top-stitch front and lapel edges 1 cm (3/8 in.) from outside edge. Use trouser pattern from 1958.

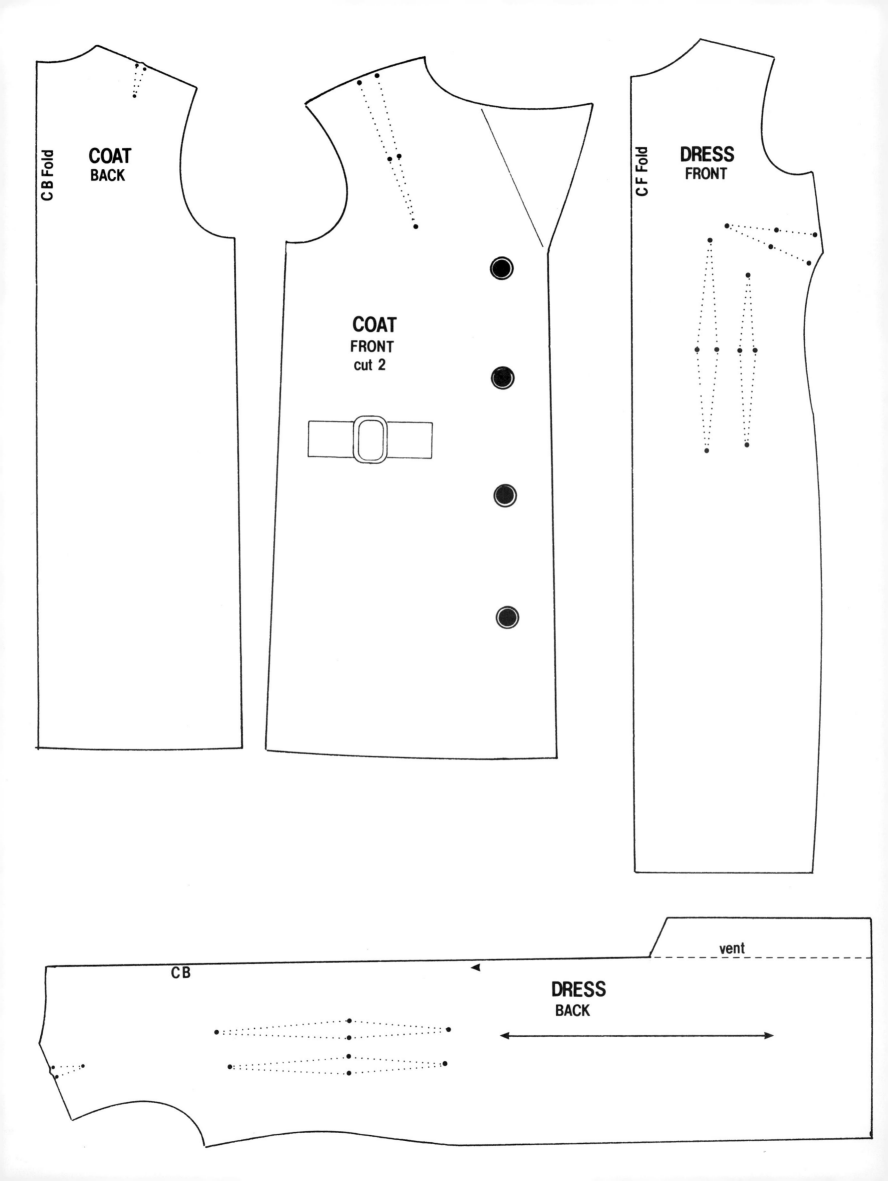

COAT
BACK

CB Fold

COAT
FRONT
cut 2

DRESS
FRONT

CF Fold

CB

vent

DRESS
BACK

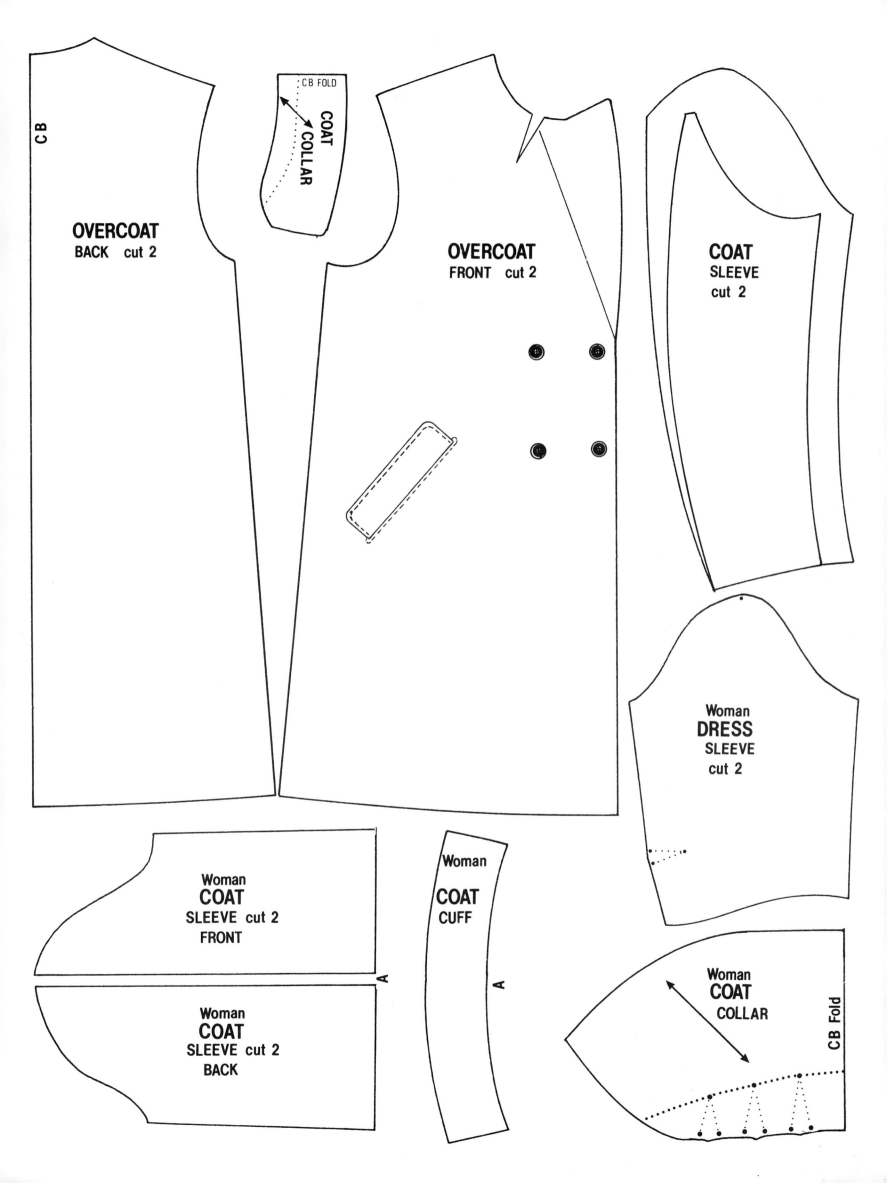

OVERCOAT
BACK cut 2

CB

CB FOLD
COAT
COLLAR

OVERCOAT
FRONT cut 2

COAT
SLEEVE
cut 2

Woman
DRESS
SLEEVE
cut 2

Woman
COAT
SLEEVE cut 2
FRONT

A

Woman
COAT
SLEEVE cut 2
BACK

Woman
COAT
CUFF

A

Woman
COAT
COLLAR

CB Fold

The Sixties

'You've never had it so good' – the words of the Prime Minister, Harold Macmillan, in 1959. The 'Swinging Sixties' came alive as a period of prosperity, a time when anything and everything seemed possible; with full employment, higher wages and a rising standard of living, the people of Britain assumed a way of life they could never have imagined a decade before. An air of optimism prevailed; technological knowledge would advance Britain – a country with a new outlook. The period was not without its similarities to the 'Roaring Twenties': the country favourable to change, initiating new industries, and questioning established values with young ideas, young and daring fashions, new music and ways of life and unprecedented exposure of the legs. Continuing this comparison, the sixties really only 'swung' towards the middle of the decade, in the same way that the characteristics most remembered of the twenties took full effect in the central years.

With her slim, youthful figure and undeveloped torso, the young lady of the twenties led the way in fashion. Fashion was dominated by the younger set, and this was again the case in the sixties, but now the 'Bright Young Things' who led the revolution were no longer made up of the middle and upper classes; the more cosmopolitan 'teenager' was drawn from a far wider section of the population. From the baby boom after the Second World War the sixties youth evolved, sentencing to death the old values. A feeling of battle rose to the surface, of tradition versus change, and of age versus youth – a reaction, perhaps, to the intense boredom of the early fifties, a time still tainted with the austerity and seriousness of war. In addition, fresh influences created an atmosphere in which the youth prospered, and enjoyed a measure of social and economic emancipation. Between 1956 and 1966 the income of the average sixteen-year-old doubled, and without the financial pressures of adult life the prosperous youngster was able to buy records and magazines and take a new interest in fashion. Parents, too, benefited from the economic boom, as car sales doubled and an ever-increasing number of families could afford televisions, fridges and washing machines.

The profiteers of the 'youth explosion' were those best prepared to meet the demands of the new generation. Fashion was the first to exploit the new teenage market, and in doing so established the fashion industry firmly for youth. Mary Quant is the designer who stands out with most conviction at this time, fashion led by the young for the young. 'I always wanted young people to have a fashion of their own, absolutely twentieth century fashion.' She met this challenge by opening her own dress shop, 'Bazaar', in the King's Road, Chelsea, during the mid-fifties. Frustrated with the fashion available commercially, she ventured into the world of designing. In line with the needs of the new society, she presented youthful designs which could be easily adapted to the commercial market; uncluttered grey flannel pinafore dresses and soft blouses met with early success and established her quickly as a major leader in fashion. Evidence of her impact is perhaps denoted by her appearance in 'Long-Life' advertisements in *Vogue* magazine early in 1961, set in her Chelsea workroom. Royal recognition followed with an OBE for her services to fashion. Notably, she arrived at Buckingham Palace in a mini-skirt.

The mini-skirt is the most distinctive trend of the decade. At the extreme of the fashion the thighs became the new erogenous zone, a revolution in that this part of the female body had to date remained covered. Again, a parallel with the twenties is evident, since both periods evinced a desire to shock and challenge and to take the skirt to its extreme.

The shortening of the skirt led inevitably to the replacement of the stocking by tights, which were worn universally from 1965. These might be thick and ribbed in winter or with lacy patterns or even Lurex for evening.

Courrèges is another outstanding sixties designer, remembered chiefly for his space-age fashions from 1964. Incorporating new and exciting materials, plastics, PVC and metallic vinyls, they demonstrated a worldly interest in the space programme and scientific advance. The progress of the first moon landing in 1969 was watched on the television all over the world. The hovercraft early in the decade, Concorde and computers, heralded the sixties as the birth of the technological age.

Fashion became fun, and those unprepared to accept new fashion values fell quickly by the wayside. After the war the age of the fashionable woman had remained somewhere around thirty-five, and many could not readjust fast enough to the younger market. Fashions of the sixties were exclusively for the young, and unsuited to the mature figure. This is not to say that this section of the market was without designers, but their style of clothes became aloof from the frenzy and constant change of the fashion industry. The Chanel suit provided the most adaptable fashion, and with its capacity for successful imitation, kept its place firmly for at least the first half of the decade. Fashion for the young no longer echoed the lines of their parents; conversely, shorter skirts, new fabrics and simpler lines affected all women's wear in a less extreme form. Most women by the mid-sixties accepted a skirt well above the knee without protest.

The desired figure, idealized by models Twiggy and Jean Shrimpton, epitomized the half-starving 'little girl lost' look, a look which demands further comparison with the nineteen-twenties, when the schoolboy figure became the foundation of the mode. The bust and waist were of little importance; 'A' line dresses obliterated the waist, and jeans and chain belts sat at hip-level. The twenties also witnessed the birth of unisex fashion, beginning with the knitted jumper. By 1966 it was often difficult to distinguish between the sexes from the back view; T-shirts, hipster jeans and wide belts with large buckles were worn interchangeably by men and women. The unisex feature was heightened by relaxing the law of fastening, demanded by mass-production, with jeans and skirts for women closing to the right. Skinny-rib jumpers with polo or V-necks also changed hands frequently and suited the skinny boyish male.

Exciting fashion was no longer exclusively the right of women, a trend already established in the 1950s. Men took an active interest in and experimented freely with new fabrics and styles alongside their partners. Trousers were narrow at the turn of the decade and flares and hipsters created an alternative silhouette by the mid-sixties. Men's clothes generally were slimmer-fitting by this time, with darts in shirts, shaped trouser legs and waisted jackets. Neckties widened and the kipper shape evolved, often brightly coloured, patterned or in knitted fabrics, matching or even clashing with the shirt. The car, too, exerted its own influence on fashion; overcoats became shorter, clothes generally lighter and the hatless mode triumphed. Among the young, short casual battledress-style jackets with chunky zips often incorporated the new fabrics; synthetic suedes and leathers, PVC and wet-look; man-made furs decorated collars, cuffs and linings, often brightly coloured for women's wear. With a more relaxed approach in evidence, a decline in the use of evening wear was inevitable. At the same time, however, evening clothes for men became more flamboyant, with coloured silk shirts with frills and jabots. Although it was worn only by the most extrovert, the influence of such clothing was felt, and many adopted turtle and polo neck shirts as well as elaborate lace front bands for dinner jackets. Morning suits remained the correct attire for weddings, most popularly in grey, although some youngsters challenged this convention. At his wedding in 1964 Mick Jagger wore a sweater and corduroy trousers. Patent leather shoes were still correct for formal wear, but plain leather was worn, and by 1964 slip-ons with elastic side gussets became popular. The Chelsea boot, likewise, with cuban heels and fine sole, was universally worn with slim-fitting trousers. 'Corfam', a new plastic, which claimed to breathe like leather, led to inexpensive footwear. For women knee-high boots, or synthetic leather pull-on socks which created the impression of boots when worn with matching shoes, created the total look with the mini skirt.

The extreme of one male fashion was worn by the modernists or 'mods', a culture which exhibited extreme clothes-consciousness. Their major influence came from the cut of Italian suits; always in search of the totally new, they wore clothes not seen before, scouring specialist sports shops for cycling shirts or golf shirts and trousers, and parka anoraks. Some mods wore make-up and were characterized by their regular use of the latest cheap form of transport for youngsters – the scooter.

The major source of mod fashions was Carnaby Street, the hub of the teenage world, full of the new boutique-style shops. John Stevens acquired his first shop in 1963 at the age of twenty, and caught the imagination of the mods with hipsters and high collars. Boutiques sold the latest fashions at reasonable prices, and quickly extended from London to the provinces. The necessary high turnover demanded efficient mass-production, and ready-to-wear steadily replaced couture. Britain emerged as a fashion leader, as *Vogue* tells us in 1965: 'In New York it's the London Look, in Paris it's *Le Style Anglais*', 'Everyone wants to copy the way we look'. Mary Quant responded to the demands of her customers by setting up the Ginger Group in 1963. She extended her influence to America in a whistle-stop tour in 1965, where models in mini-skirts moved rhythmically to popular music, and in 1966 began to manufacture make-up to complete the total look. Another immediate success commercially was the Biba chain of stores from 1964, providing incredibly inexpensive fashion in dark, absolutely sixties-style surroundings.

Fashion became a commodity available to the masses, a distant cry from its exclusive nature at the turn of the century. Commercialization was further advanced by the simultaneous growth of supporting industry, particularly the media and improved communications. Teenage magazines, such as *Honey* from 1966, captured the latest ideas with glossy photographs in exotic surroundings. They provided the essential link with the 'it' world; the fashions were up to the minute and available.

The concept of the boutique spread to other areas. Terence Conran, the 'Mary Quant of the furnishing world', opened 'Habitat' in the Fulham Road, London, in May 1964, reconciling fashion and furnishings. He brought new products to the high street, fresh and fit for the purpose for which they were designed.

Britain led the way in the field of popular music as in fashion, the two interacting, and both entirely to do with being young. The pop scene was filled with British talent, and the Beatles as the centre of popular culture became idols, with the young keen to copy the style of their cheeky and confident Liverpool heroes. Sixty million singles were sold to the affluent teenager in 1963, although the pop record boom had begun in the 1950s with stars such as Elvis Presley and Little Richard (notably American at this stage). The Beatles led the way with collarless jackets and shirts, Chelsea boots and above all the Beatle cut, with hair brushed forward to create a fringe. Men wore their hair generally longer in the sixties.

Out of popular culture came 'pop art' and 'op art', although these never influenced the masses to the same extent as records and fashion. However, bright colours and new ideas epitomized the mood of the sixties and influenced fashion to a degree, with 'op art' fabrics and psychedelic colours. 'Style' was all important, and it became cool for pop stars to appreciate art, encouraging a massive increase in Design and Art Schools, aided by the fact that grants were easy to come by. The art world was creative and forward-looking.

Many were quick to question the morality and behaviour of the teenagers with more leisure time and money, who constantly challenged and seemed keen to destroy the world their parents had fought for. Compulsory National Service was abolished in 1962, adding, in some people's eyes, to the lack of discipline among the young. The attack was launched largely through fashion, as it had been during the twenties, and the scantiness of women's dress was cited as evidence of lack of morality. Nudity appeared to be the keynote, page three of the *Sun* was launched, and 1964 saw the first topless dress. A short-lived summer fashion with few followers, it was however the forerunner of the bare midriff, and of mesh and crochet dresses.

Beneath these flesh-coloured body-stockings and tights heightened the impression of nudity.

The Pill hit the headlines in the 1960s, enabling women to take responsibility for their own fertility. 'Keep taking the tablets' became a national catch-phrase, and married and unmarried women alike obtained supplies from the Family Planning Association, who were responsible for testing the new drug. The FPA had, in fact, been formed before the war, but had struggled to become reputable, since even as late as the mid-fifties the subject of contraceptives was taboo and they were difficult to obtain. The role of women was changing, too; although still tied to the home many women, in particular a growing number of married women, went out to work. The increasing sophistication of labour-saving devices, and the availability of fast convenience foods and easy-care man-made fibres – Orlon, Courtelle, Terylene – took the drudgery out of housework and made this possible. However, women were still expected to perform two jobs equally well, and the conflict of the two roles led to discontent. The permissive society put perhaps even greater pressure on women, who were portrayed and exploited as sex symbols. Men dominated in industry and politics, and even where they did the same job, men's wages were higher. The women's liberation movement, from 1968 onwards, demanded equal pay and equal rights. The seeds of the movement were sown in the sixties, although its influence is more directly associated with the seventies. It is interesting that both the twenties and the sixties were periods of female emancipation.

A new class had arisen without the traditional values. The aristocracy of fashion gave way to the 'popocracy', as a new young class emerged. There seemed to be a tremendous desire to wipe out the old world. 'Modern' and 'big' were beautiful words; reconstruction of bombed-out cities continued with high-rise blocks, clean lines and strong geometric shapes. Sixties planning was conceived in terms of the car, now a mass-produced commodity, and universal mobility. Large, centralized shopping precincts threatened the corner shops, and slum areas were demolished on a massive scale, breaking up the traditional patterns of the neighbourhood and community life. This trend was heightened by the insular effects of the television on family life. Belief in a scientific approach to planning lacked the personal touch, and redevelopment schemes were given further incentive through strong government promotion and subsidy. The sixties saw the wholesale destruction of buildings, homes, shops and churches, and even more disheartening, the

prefabrication systems of building were to prove unsuccessful, causing even greater housing and social problems in later years.

Motorways opened up the country, the M1, from 1959, providing a 'new deal for drivers' – the longest stretch of new road built in Britain since the Romans, 'in keeping with the bold, exciting and scientific age in which we live'. By the early seventies a fairly comprehensive motorway system had been completed across the country, with the M1 and M6 link in 1972. However, the grand plan was delayed, for the money ran out.

'Is it too good to be true, is it too good to last?' Macmillan had asked in 1959. Idealism evaporated at an alarming speed, and with increased competition from abroad Britain failed to capitalize on technological improvement and declined as a world power. Wage freezes and cuts in public spending in 1966, and devaluation of the pound in 1967, set inflation on its upward course. With the economy floundering the people showed less confidence and began to look for the 'alternative' society. The party was over, the year 1968 rife with revolution and rebellion – demonstrations against American involvement in Vietnam, and against nuclear war; violent student riots; revolution versus law, order and establishment. From America came the hippy cult, and with it hard drugs, heroin, LSD and the psychedelic flower-power fantasy world. Long hair and ethnic clothes were evidence of society's drop-outs, and fashion followed the new influence. Clothes became softer and more romantic, and colours faded. Make-up, which had for so long darkened the eyes and paled the lips, looked more natural. Hair was worn loose, plaited or in curly Afro cut, and embroidered afghan coats and long kaftans came on the scene. In 1968, the micro-skirt, the extreme of the mini, made a brief appearance, and in the same year the long, straight midi-skirt. By 1969 the battle of mini-midi-maxi was in full force; the lady with the mini-skirt, high boots and maxi-coat a common sight. The maxi-coat was the longest length seen since 1914, a fashionable expression of the demand for change.

The sixties, then, closed with an air of discontent. It had been almost a freak era of prosperity and growth, an era in which everything had seemed possible. Britain was fashionable and confident, everyone had swung to British records, and British clothes and goods were topping the charts worldwide. The atmosphere of the period was faithfully reflected in fashion, epitomizing the very spirit of the age.

1960

Predominant fashion features

Women

Style of the late fifties continues relatively unchanged, with skirts becoming shorter, especially for younger fashions. Skirt hems, whether full or slim, finish at the knee.

Shirtwaister dresses with full skirts popular.

Chanel's collarless suits in loosely woven tweeds and with contrast braiding much copied by ready-to-wear.

Italian influence continues with casual tapered trousers, boldly printed fabrics for summer, and sweaters.

Knitwear – twin set comprising short-sleeved jumper and matching cardigan essential item of women's wardrobe, and knitted suits – shades of blue popular.

Soft polo-necks.

Increasing interest in young fashions. Mary Quant's slim pinafore dresses of grey flannel are the look of the year, worn with long-sleeved soft blouses or polo-neck sweaters.

Fabrics: 'Grey flannel – the newest, smartest basic for day.' (*Vogue*, 1959) Black- or grey-and-white tweeds, checks, stripes, herringbones. Loose tweeds. Linen, bold cotton prints for summer. Tricel, textured nylon, Bri-Nylon, Orlon, Courtelle, Terylene fibres extensively used.

1961 – ICI introduces 'Crimplene'.

1962 – Courtaulds' first Elastane (highly stretchable fibre), Spanzelle went into production.

Colours: Grey, black and white, in any combination, always fashionable.

Brighter colours for summer and teenage dresses – turquoise, French navy, red, yellow; checks and stripes combining many colours. Chunky sweaters in bright colours – lilac, yellow, gold, red, sometimes combined with metallic Lurex thread.

Decoration: Scarf necks on dresses, suits, coats. Bows remain popular. Striped and checked fabrics in bold, bright colours.

Undergarments: Similar to late fifties. Slim-fitting girdles with diagonal control panels for slim hips and tummy. Bras with pre-formed cups for shape and uplift, circular-stitched and wired.

Shoes: Remaining slim and pointed or with squared-off toes. High, narrow stiletto heels. Low, tapered heels for the young.

Stockings: Matt-finish stretch nylon stockings, seamless. Dark plaid knit stockings for winter.

Hats: Larger hats with tall crowns and wide brims; halo hats.

Hair: Hair remains full, back-combed and waved, with long wispy fringe brushed over forehead, or half-fringe from side-parting.

'A new shorter look is coming in for day'(*Harper's Bazaar*, May 1960) – cut short and close at the nape of the neck, with the side pieces long and curled forward; a smooth sleek fringe comes half-way across forehead. The style retains width and fullness, curled outwards or under at the ends. Hair worn high for evening with false hairpieces swirled on top of the crown. Wigs and hairpieces add fullness and height.

Accessories: Short gloves for day. Handbags with chain handles. Wrist watches – face inset in bracelet strap. Gloves/hats lose importance for young fashion.

Make-up: Eye make-up becomes darker as lips pale. Eyeliner swept upwards at outer corner, beyond natural eyeline. Eyebrows heavily emphasized, straighter, not arched.

Men

Single-breasted jackets and two-piece suits continue in popularity. Jackets fasten higher with three to four buttons instead of usual one or two, are more fitted, waisted and longer.

Trousers remain short and narrow, with or without turn-ups.

Overcoats begin to be replaced by shorter car coats, above the knee, and anoraks. Longer overcoats with business suits. Many styles have detachable, zipped-in warm lining. Unlined casual jackets with zip-up fronts.

Shirts mostly coat-style, i.e. button-through, with attached pointed collars. Single cuffs and button fastening, more usual than double cuffs.

Knitwear – chunky and lightweight sweaters.

Dinner jackets – narrow shawl collars of ribbed silk. Wide silk cummerbunds, worn with plain white shirt, black tie.

Fabrics: Lighter-weight suiting fabrics, wool combined with Terylene and nylon. Less bulky fabrics generally for overcoats, trousers, jackets. Checked tweed for sports jackets.

Colours: Striped fawns and blues – suits available in light and dark shades – stone, tan, navy, grey.

Undergarments: Short-sleeved and sleeveless vests, jockey shorts. Trunks with elasticated tops.

Shoes: Slim Italian shoes continue. Slip-on shoes. Boots with higher heels, rounded toes. Patent leather correct with evening wear.

Hats: Importance of the hat diminishing. Trilby style hats with tapered crowns and narrower brims in tweeds, corduroy. Bowler hat for business wear.

Hair: Remaining short; more emphasis on style.

Accessories: Driving gloves in perforated leather, or leather palms with fabric or string uppers, buttoning or elasticated at wrist. Narrow ties, knitted with squared ends, stripes or subtle patterns. Neatly furled umbrella with business suit. Cuff links with evening dress.

Details of illustrated patterns

Woman

Double-breasted coat-dress with wide neckline, notched collar and detachable over-collar. The dress fastens with six large buttons and wide belt of self fabric, the back bodice gathered into the waistline seam. The straight skirt is shaped to the waistline by means of two small pleats at either side of front opening and darts at back. The two-gore skirt back has a low pleat at centre. Plain, short, set-in sleeves.

Fabric and colours: Grey flannel, with white piqué collar.

Footwear: Slim-fitting pointed leather court shoe with punched design and lower shaped heel; seamless stretch nylon stockings.

Accessories: Short cotton gloves; large leather handbag with metal frame and clasp.

Man

Two-piece lounge suit remains slim-fitting, with high-rolling narrow lapels and three-button fastening. Shoulders are more sloped and there is evidence of less ease across the chest and back. Foreparts are well rounded at lower edges, with flap pockets at hip-level and welt pocket on left breast. Narrow, two-piece sleeves finish with slit cuff and three-button fastening to harmonize with fronts. Trousers are cut on the skimpy side, with narrow leg and short in length.

The suit is worn with light-coloured shirt and narrow knitted tie with squared ends.

Fabrics and colours: Lightweight suiting fabric of Terylene and wool in grey, fawn or brown.

Footwear: Slim-fitting slip-on casual shoes with low heel and elasticated side gussets, rounded toes.

Notes on construction of garments

Woman

Point **S** on collar patterns indicates position of shoulder seam. Make up detachable collar and bind raw neck edges. Hand stitch in position when dress is complete.

Man

Trace off trouser waistband from **A** to **B** for right side, and **A** to **C** for left side, to allow for button extension. Add a 1 cm (³⁄₈ in.) seam allowance to all edges of waistband. Add vent to centre back 24 cm (9½ in.) long and 4 cm (1½ in.) wide.

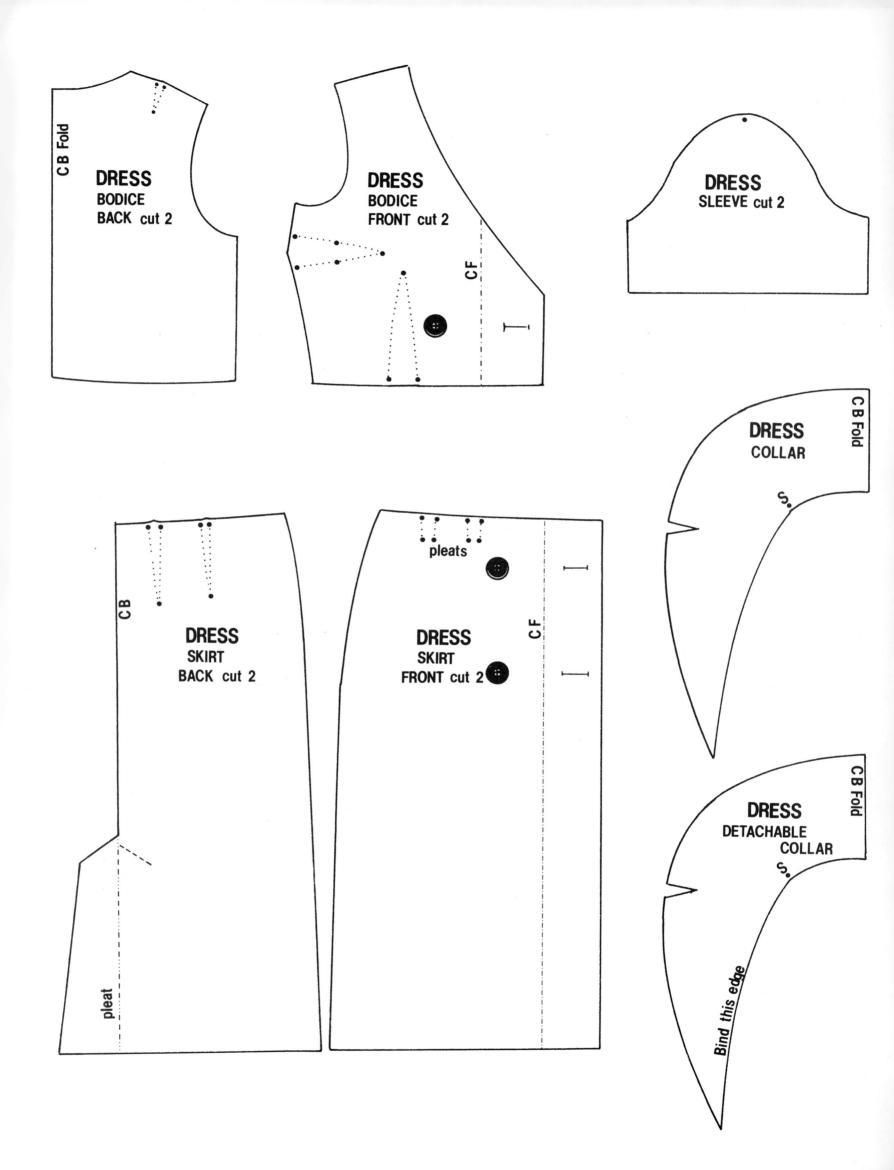

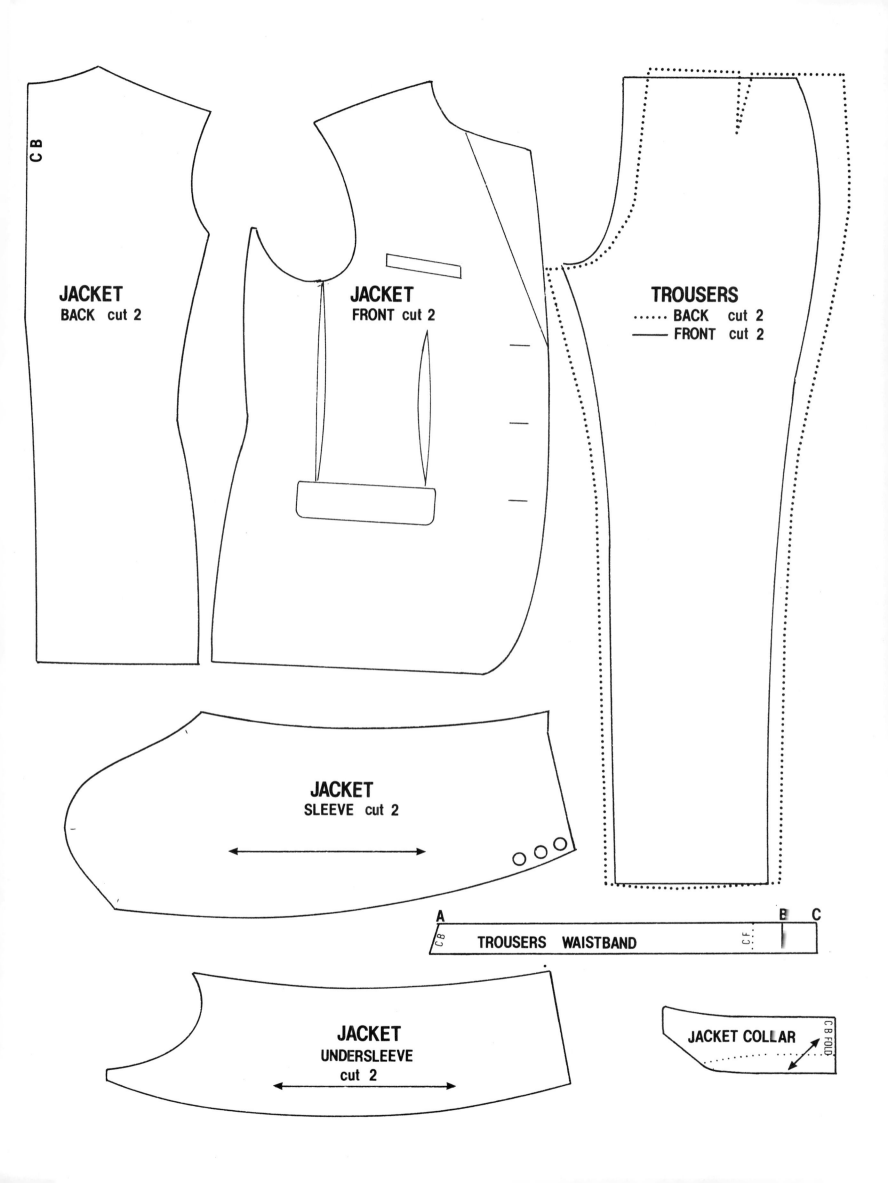

JACKET
BACK cut 2

CB

JACKET
FRONT cut 2

TROUSERS
.... BACK cut 2
———— FRONT cut 2

JACKET
SLEEVE cut 2

A   B C
CB   **TROUSERS WAISTBAND**   C.F.

JACKET
UNDERSLEEVE
cut 2

JACKET COLLAR
CB FOLD

1965~1966

Predominant fashion features

Women

Fashion dominated by the young – the mini evolves as skirts rise steadily, reaching mid-thigh. Simple, uncluttered lines, devoid of pleats, slits and intricate seaming. Sleeves set in, plain or gathered at sleevehead and flared out to wrist. Cut-out sleeveless styles for summer. Collars are pointed or rounded, all large and unstarched, often contrasting with the outfit. White on dark colours.

See-through dresses of crochet net or with net or open midriff.

Trouser suits with tailored or casual jackets. Tabards – sleeveless, hip-length tops tied at the sides, worn with polo-neck jumpers and trousers.

Chunky, zip-fastening casual jackets with synthetic fur trimming or lining. Coats just cover the skirt or finish above it; wide floppy collars.

'Unisex' fashions – denim jeans, close-fitting trousers with no turn-ups made with zip fly front; hipsters; safari jackets – shirt-style with patch pockets; skinny-rib sweaters, polo-necks.

Evening – mini-dresses or trouser-suits dressed up for evening in metallic Lurex fabrics or satins; long kaftans – loose-fitting unbelted robes in bright colours, first ethnic fashion.

Fabrics: Jersey, crêpe. Crocheted or open-work fabrics.

PVC (polyvinyl chloride), synthetic suede and leather fabrics. Vinyl, silver vinyl, plastics.

Fun-fur fabrics – synthetic nylon, Dynel, or Acrilan, dyed in bright colours.

Colours: Grey and black always fashionable; white, shades of mauve – lilac to deep purple. Bright colours – red, orange, purple, combined with black.

Decoration: Paisley prints, op art fabrics, bold geometric prints. Fur trimming, real or fake, in a variety of colours.

Underwear: Becomes briefer with fashion trends; short, tailored bra-slip combines bra and petticoat. Flesh-coloured body stockings give impression of nudity under open-work dresses.

Shoes: Zip-fastening knee-high boots. Black and white predominant. Patent leather and synthetic materials.

Tights: Worn universally, the brief skirt making stockings impractical. Lace, fishnet and patterned tights; Lurex for evening; colourful ribbed tights for warmth in winter. Cream with dark colours.

Hats: Hats are worn less. Helmet styles, peaked Beatle caps – young unisex fashion.

Hair: Sleeker, losing fullness and height of early sixties. Long hair popular, with side or centre-parting and fringe. Some hair cut in very short, boyish style, cropped close to the head, heightening effect of unisex fashions.

Accessories: Increasing use of synthetic materials for gloves, bags, jewellery. PVC gloves, keyhole types. Large drop earrings of coloured plastic, coloured plastic bangles.

Chain belts; wider belts with hipster trousers.

Make-up: Lipsticks continue to pale down as eyes become heavier, achieved with heavy eyeliner, lash-building mascara and false eyelashes shaped and applied to outer corners of eyes.

Men

Age groups dress differently.

'The young class produces most of the experiment, most of the good ideas, almost all the bad ideas, and is the basic pressure for change in appearance.' (*Tailor and Cutter*)

Lounge suits – natural shoulders, minimum padding, slim lapels rounded at notches, slanted flapped pockets, longer vents. When three-button, the jacket is buttoned high above the waist. Four-button jackets increasingly popular, with high, slim lapels, long side vents, centre two buttons only fastened. Double-breasted jackets button high, with little overlap. In multi-button styles the breast pocket is often omitted. Waistcoats remain in the minority.

Trousers add to the long line: straight and slim-fitting, following the shape of the leg, with low rise and vertical pockets. Few turn-ups. Hipster trousers sit well below the waist, flaring from the knees.

Overcoats continue to shorten to well above the knee, almost jacket length. Longer, narrow and close-fitting styles worn by city gentlemen; raglan styles popular.

Zipped anorak styles. Collarless suits and jackets popularized by the Beatles, slim-fitting, high-fastening.

Knitwear – plain polo-neck sweater is the most popular casual accessory.

Young fashion cults. Mods: Italian hairstyles and jackets, suede chukka boots with crêpe soles, narrow trousers. Rockers: long hair, leather jackets, zip-up boots and drainpipe trousers.

Fabrics: Pin- and chalk-stripes, hopsack and twill continue to lead in formal suits. For more casual suits, herringbone tweed and coloured overchecks on dark backgrounds. Floral and op art fabric print for shirts.

Colours: Suit colours remain conservative: blues, greys, brown.

Undergarments: Vests often dispensed with under tighter-fitting shirts. Jockey shorts.

Shoes: A long, flat silhouette with buckles and brass decorations. Leather and crêpe soles. Slip-ons remain popular.

High boots with elasticated sides, higher heels and rounded toes. Chelsea boots popularized by the Beatles.

Squared toes, higher heels with flared trousers. Mods – flat, broad square toes. Man-made materials for footwear.

Socks: As previous fashion.

Hats: Still not showing any signs of returning to popularity. Peaked Beatle caps for the young.

Hair: Short and brushed back, with no parting. Longer hair popular among the young. Beatle cut brushed forward into a fringe.

Accessories: Ties tend to be either very plain, with no pattern or a minimum pattern on self-coloured silks, or very bold indeed. Fancy-knit woollen ties in sober colours. For the more flamboyant, the wide kipper-shape tie 12.75–15.25 cm (5–6 in.) wide. Shirts and ties of matching fabrics. Belts, when worn, are wide, with large buckles. Cuff links with evening wear.

Details of illustrated patterns

Woman

Bold, geometric, 'A' line mini-dress, with long sleeves of small chequerboard pattern complementing large checked fabric at lower edge of dress; length approximately 15 cm (6 in.) above the knee. The uncluttered, simple line of the dress uses contrast to create impact. The dress illustrated is relatively long in comparison with the very short skirts worn during this period. The mini skirt rapidly became briefer and briefer.

Fabric and colours: Crisp printed cotton or rayon crêpe in bold black and white.

Footwear: Black patent T-bar shoes with low square heel and rounded toes, white contrast on toe cap and edges. Shoes are generally low-heeled and clumpy in appearance. Cream ribbed tights.

Accessories: White patent or plastic shoulder bag with optional handles and clasp opening; drop earrings of black and white plastic discs and beads.

Man

Young casual fashion consisting of hipster trousers, black polo-neck sweater and waistcoat. The waistcoat has contrast binding on outside and armhole edges and at upper edge of patch pockets. It fastens with four gilt buttons at centre front.

Hipster trousers, fitting just over the hips and close-fitting throughout, with cross pockets more common than those set in side seams. It is also considered fashionable to tuck the trouser bottoms into the top of calf-length boots.

Fabrics: Cotton gabardine or cotton/polyester mixture fabric for hipsters; loosely woven wool/ Terylene.

Footwear: Calf-length Chelsea boots with elasticated side gussets and pull-on side tabs. Squared toes and heels.

Accessories: Wide leather belt at trouser waistband, signet rings, identity bracelets popular.

Notes on construction of garments

Woman

Alter dress to length of mini required.

Separate dress sections **A**, **B** and **C** at back and front of dress; cut out each in a different fabric. When using check fabric, the hemline is cut straight and not shaped, as on pattern.

For sleeve cuff cut a strip of fabric 21.5 cm (8½ in.) by 5 cm (2 in.), twice finished width. Add seam allowance to all edges.

Man

Bind outside and armhole edges of waistcoat as shown by darker lines on pattern.

Trace off trouser waistband from **A** to **B** for right side and **A** to **C** for left side to allow for button extension. Add a 1 cm (⅜ in.) seam allowance to all edges of waistband. Hipster trousers should fit closely over the seat and legs; adjust as necessary. Construct with cross pockets from lowered waistline as indicated on pattern.

The shirt pattern is provided as an alternative to the polo-neck illustrated. It is close-fitting, shaped into the waistline at the back and has pointed, button-down collar.

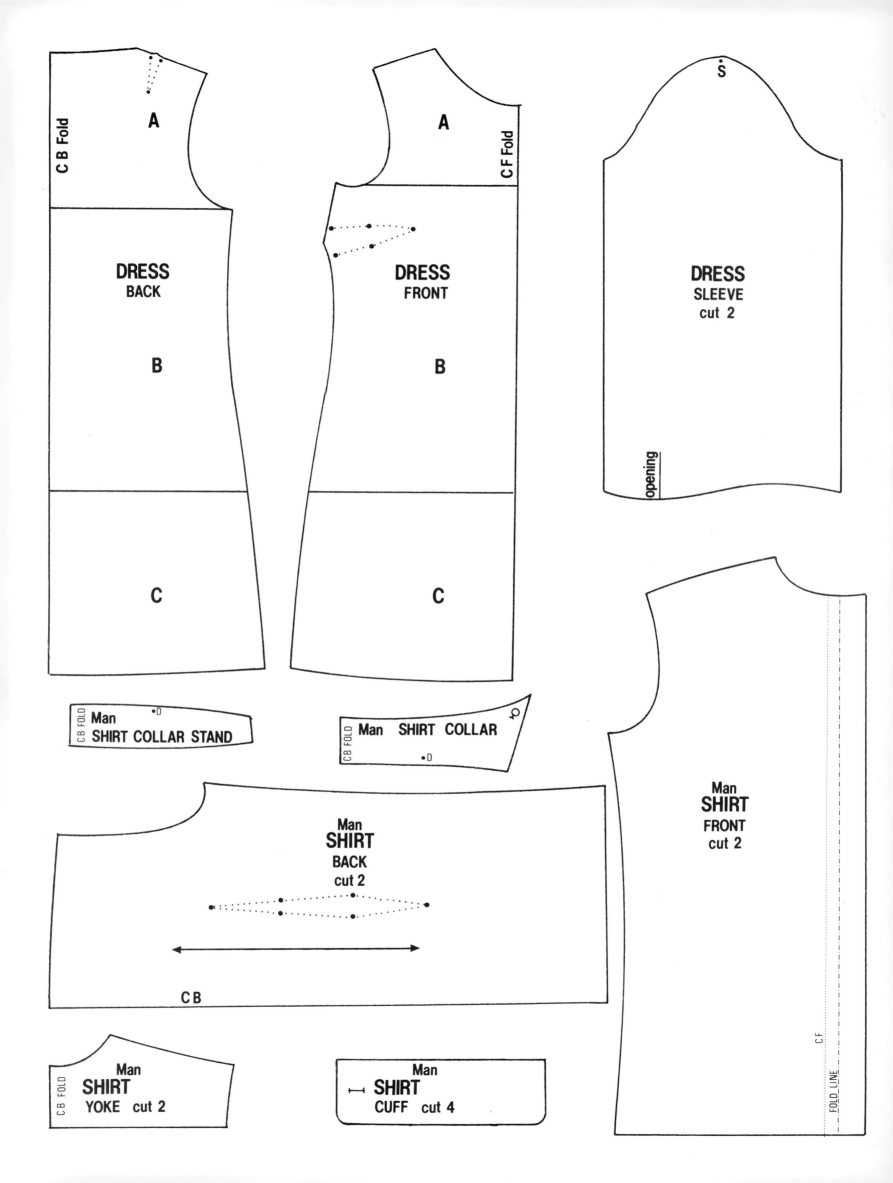

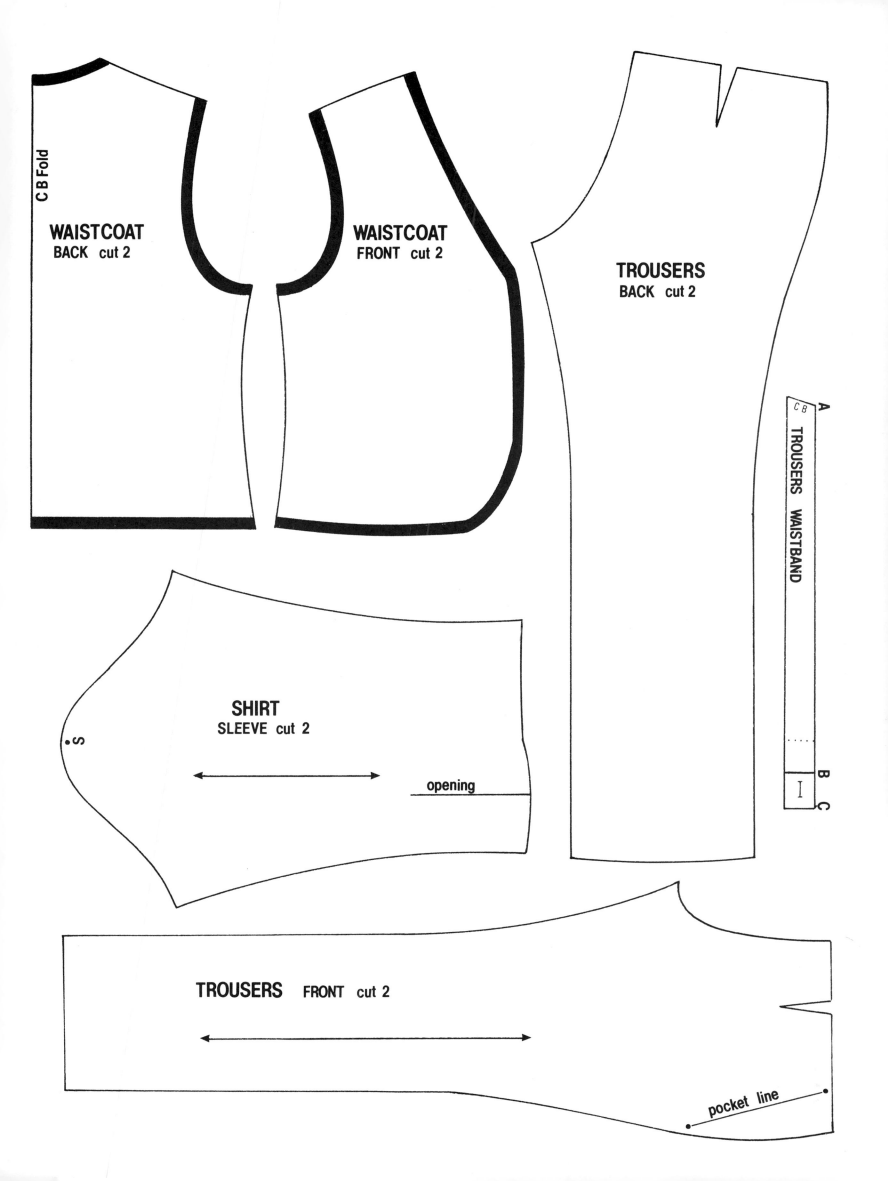

CB Fold

WAISTCOAT
BACK cut 2

WAISTCOAT
FRONT cut 2

TROUSERS
BACK cut 2

TROUSERS WAISTBAND

CB

A

B

C

SHIRT
SLEEVE cut 2

S

opening

TROUSERS FRONT cut 2

pocket line

1968

Predominant fashion features

Women

Extreme of the mini – the micro or 'pelmet' skirt, just covering the upper thigh. The year also witnesses the first signs of change to a more feminine ideal. Mini-dresses, flounced and frilled. Bias-cut skirts give more flare. Simple, uncluttered jersey dresses, long rounded or pointed collars, white to contrast. Tunic dresses worn with or without trousers. Mini-suits – short waist-length jackets, double-breasted, and short pleated or plain skirts. Trouser suits and co-ordinated clothes – matching trousers, jacket, skirts worn with blouses, sweaters, making possible mix-and-match fashions.

Unisex fashions – hipster trousers, jeans, T-shirts. Casual zip-fastening jackets, anoraks.

Evening – dressed-up mini-dresses, velvet trouser suits and mini-skirts worn with more ornate blouses featuring frills and jabots; full-length, loose-fitting kaftans – these diverse styles all equally fashionable.

Flower-power hippy movement – psychedelic, paisley and boldly printed fabrics. Much use of leather and brocade for head bands, belts. Long beads, leather fringing, bells and tinsel. Overall an untidy and 'thrown-together' look. Ethnic fashions – afghan coats (sheepskin with silk and gold embroidery), kaftans.

Fabrics: Softer fabrics: crêpe, jersey, plain and textured velvets, synthetic suedes and leather, synthetic furs. Disposable paper for short-life garments.

Colours: White, black, greys remain fashionable. Softer colours: greys, purples, lilacs. Paisley prints, checks and tartans. Bright psychedelic patterns.

Decoration: Ruffles, lace, ethnic embroidery, fur fabric trimmings, tassels. Large chunky zips in bold colours. Large buttons for coats and mini-suits.

Undergarments: Mini-length bra-slips. Softer bras give more natural bustline. Pantie-briefs. Stretch briefs in nylon and Spandex worn over tights to prevent them slipping down, available in bright colours, since they might be visible under the very brief skirt.

Shoes: Knee-high and over-the-knee boots with zip or front-lace fastening – white popular with the mini-skirt, vinyl and leather. Shoes generally heavier, rounded or square toes, low squared heels. Wide strapped styles, chain and buckle decoration.

Legwear: Coloured and patterned tights, Lurex for evening; cream tights with dark colours. White, patterned knee-high socks.

Hats: Hats worn less by all age groups. Head bands of leather, brocade, beads popular among hippy groups.

Hair: Long, straight hair with centre-parting and fringe. Afro fuzz – very full, tightly permed style, frizzed outwards and following the line of the head.

Accessories: Wide belts with large buckles in PVC and embossed leather, sometimes worn with attached purse pouches. Chunky silver jewellery – large rings, bracelets with semi-precious stones. Enamel pendants and long beads.

Make-up: Similar to previous fashion, with softer eye-shadows – browns, lilacs, mauves with more romantic fashions.

Men

'The silhouette is still a slim line but it is becoming bolder and simpler with more emphasis on shape.' (*Tailor and Cutter*, March)

Coats have a natural shoulderline and fit closely over the chest; waist suppression is very marked and the bottoms of the coats are flared to stand away from the trouser legs.

Style detail follows this same trend towards boldness and simplicity. Lapels are broad. Pockets have deep flaps and clean lines and on some coats there is no outside breast pocket. Buttons are kept to a minimum.

Trousers are generally plain-fronted and slim-fitting, but there is a move away from the 'drainpipe' effect. From the knee down they are cut slightly wider, and there is a trend towards a return of the turn-up for town as well as country wear.

Hipster trousers remain fashionable, and flared velvet trousers and jackets. Increasing fashion for unconnected trousers and jackets, enabling mix-and-match separates. Jerkins and tunics worn with trousers, with or without belts, and polo-neck jumpers – unisex fashion. Casual jackets, knitted cuffs and waistband, chunky zip fastening.

Button-down pointed collars on shirts for men and women. Sports shirts for casual wear.

Greater variety of clothes may be worn for evening – frilled shirts with fuller sleeves and ruffle fronts, pointed, rounded collars, polo-necks often worn with velvet dinner jackets. Shawl-collar dinner jackets with soft dress shirts with tucked or pleated front and frilled centre band which might be separate from the shirt. Classic lounge suits and casual clothes – jerkin outfits or trousers and shirts.

Hippy men wear brightly coloured shirts, leather jerkins, head bands, and beads.

Fabrics: Plain and textured velvets, stretch jersey, suede and leathers and synthetic imitations. Terylene and Crimplene fibres for easy-care clothes.

Colours: Conservative colours for classic suits. Bright floral prints for shirts. Black and white polo-necks most popular.

Undergarments: Similar to previous fashion.

Footwear: Chelsea boots with elasticated sides. Slip-on shoes with squared toes. Higher heels with flared trousers. Buckle decoration popular.

Socks: Similar to previous fashion.

Hats: Hatless mode continues. Bowler hat with curled brim for business.

Hair: Long hair for the young. Very long straight hair for hippies.

Accessories: Scarves and cravats. Wide kipper ties. Shirts and ties often match – flowers and bold stripes. Tightly furled long umbrellas, and white handkerchief visible in breast pocket with business suits. Identity bracelets, wedding rings, neck chains.

Details of illustrated patterns

Woman

Lady's edge-to-edge suit with contrast binding and patent belt at the natural waistline. Flap pockets at hip-level, and two-piece set-in sleeves. 'A' line mini-skirt is cut on the bias.

The outfit is worn with masculine shirt and kipper tie.

Fabrics: Tartan medium-weight woollen fabric.

Footwear: White patent or plastic shoes with squared toes, low square heels and gold chain decoration over flap. Textured cream tights.

Hat: Large felt hat with deep rounded crown and wide, shaped brim with patent band and buckle trim.

Accessories: Black and white patent or plastic box-style handbag with metal clasp fastening; black patent wrist-length gloves.

Man

Close-fitting blazer jacket with moderately wide lapels and two-button fastening; large shaped patch pockets at hip-level and slanted welt pocket on left breast. Foreparts are cut away at lower edges and two-piece sleeves finish with slit and single button.

Hipster trousers fitting just over the hips and close-fitting throughout, with cross pockets more common than those set in side seams.

Boldly striped silk shirt with button-down pointed collar and matching tie and handkerchief.

Fabrics: Wool and Terylene medium-weight flannel suiting fabric for blazer; lighter weight for trousers.

Footwear: Slip-on shoes with leather vamp decoration and flap.

Notes on construction of garments

Woman

Cut skirt on bias of fabric.

Man

Trace off trouser waistband from **A** to **B** for right front, and from **A** to **C** for left front to allow for button extension. Add 1 cm (⅜ in.) seam allowance to all edges of waistband. Trousers should fit closely throughout – if necessary shape leg seams.

Adapt shirt pattern from 1965/1966.

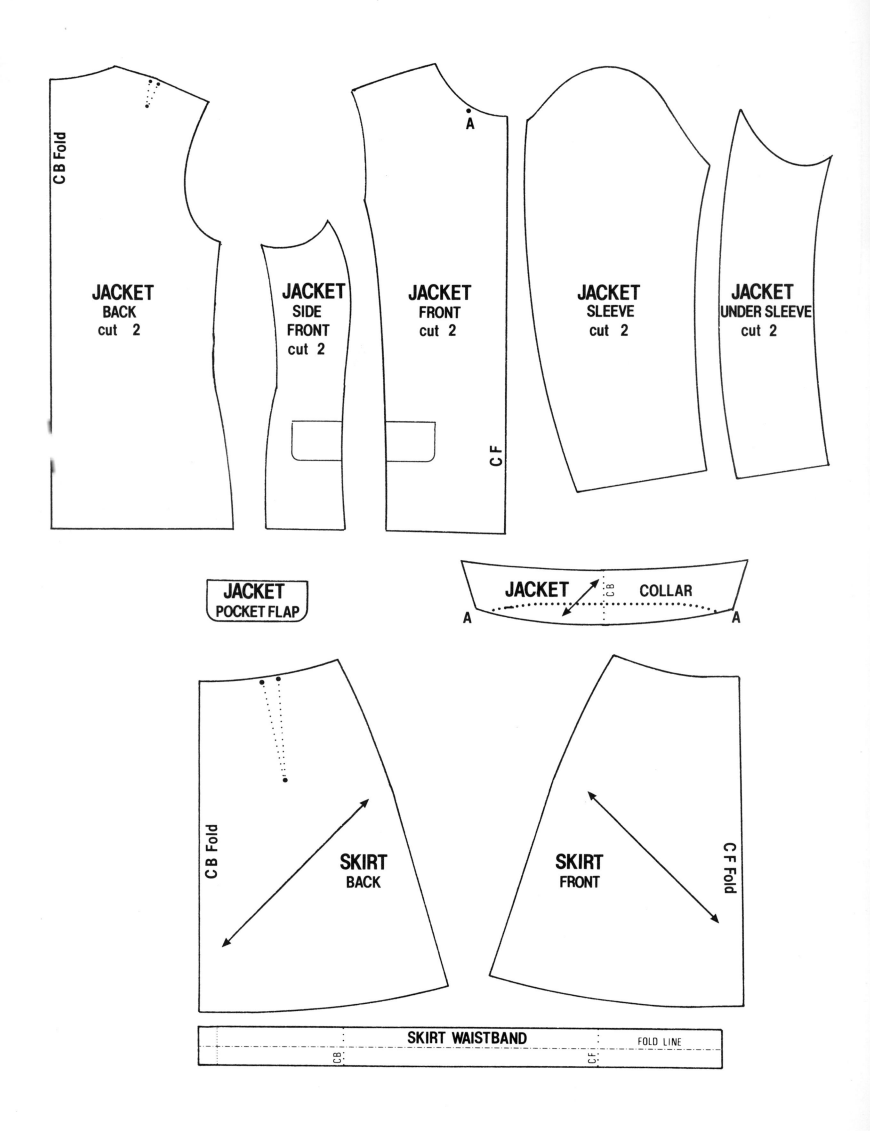

JACKET
BACK
cut 2

C B Fold

JACKET
SIDE
FRONT
cut 2

JACKET
FRONT
cut 2

A

C F

JACKET
SLEEVE
cut 2

JACKET
UNDER SLEEVE
cut 2

JACKET
POCKET FLAP

JACKET C B **COLLAR**

A A

SKIRT
BACK

C B Fold

SKIRT
FRONT

C F Fold

SKIRT WAISTBAND

FOLD LINE

C.B. C.F.

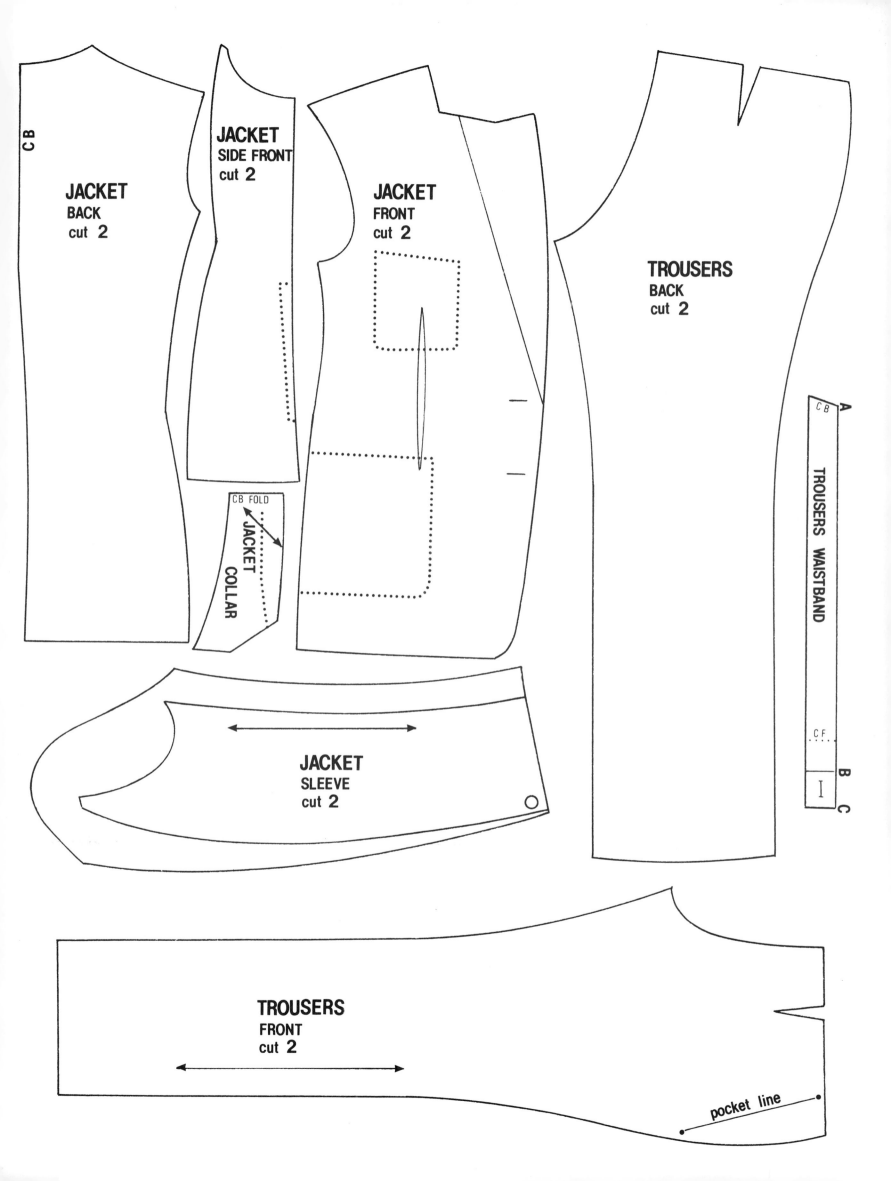

CB

JACKET
BACK
cut **2**

JACKET
SIDE FRONT
cut **2**

JACKET
FRONT
cut **2**

TROUSERS
BACK
cut **2**

CB FOLD

JACKET
COLLAR

A

CB

TROUSERS WAISTBAND

CF

B

C

JACKET
SLEEVE
cut **2**

TROUSERS
FRONT
cut **2**

pocket line

1969~1970

Predominant fashion features

Women

'In fashion the revolution is over. A new quiet reigns.' (*Vogue*, 1969) Mini-skirts are still the predominant fashion, but lose the monopoly retained since the mid-sixties. The battle of mini/midi/maxi lengths begins – a full-length maxi-coat often worn with mini-skirt and knee-high boots. Calf-length midi-skirts are slim-fitting and straight.

Coats, jackets and suits for men and women feature wide, floppy collars and revers. Trouser suits or trousers with tunic tops or jerkins remain popular.

Unisex denim jeans and T-shirts, short-sleeved and collarless.

Beginning of the layered look – long-sleeved shirts with short-sleeved pullovers or sleeveless vests.

Romantic look – blouses with jabots, frills and lace. Long evening dresses and flared mini styles.

Hippy style continues.

Fabrics: Plain and crushed velvet for day and evening. Suede and leather and synthetic imitations. PVC 'wet-look' – crinkled vinyl for coats, jackets and accessories.

Colours: Black, navy and grey for outdoor coats. Softer mauves, browns, greys. Paisley and floral prints remain popular.

Decoration: Buckles, dull metallic snap-fasteners. Jabots, frills and lace.

Underwear: Women's liberation movement stimulates the development of seamless bras, in Helanca stretch lace, and half- and quarter-cup bras, revealing the nipples. 'Don't let them know you wear a bra.' (*Vogue*) Front-fastening styles available. Pantie-briefs.

Shoes: Thigh- or knee-length vinyl boots, white and black. Full-length front lace-fastening for knee-high styles. Stretch vinyl leggings worn with ordinary court shoes to give impression of boots. Shoes retain rounded or squared toes and square heels. Buckle decoration popular. Lace-up shoes, fastening to instep.

Legwear: Similar to previous fashion. Knee-socks worn less frequently. Black tights popular.

Hats: When worn, hats have large, floppy brims or high square crowns and stiffer brim. Pull-on crochet hats.

Hair: For softer, Pre-Raphaelite look, hair is rippled by plaiting when wet and combed out, or is taken back from the face in a chignon, with curled tendrils of hair at the sides.

Accessories: Vinyl and wet-look gloves. Large belts and buckles. Thick plastic bangles, long beads.

Make-up: More natural-looking. Eye-make-up available in many colours – browns, soft lilacs. Lips less pale.

Men

Jackets cut higher, with flared skirts and longer lapels. Suit trousers begin to flare at the knees.

Overcoats – longer-waisted with longer, flared skirt and large collars and lapels. Shorter car coats.

Young unisex fashion – denim suits and separates, hipster jeans and T-shirts.

Hippy styles continue.

Fabrics: Similar to previous fashion.

Colours: Similar to previous fashion.

Decoration: Jacket collars might be faced in velvet.

Undergarments: Similar to previous fashion.

Shoes: Moccasin-style shoes for casual wear; slip-on shoes with squared toes. Ankle boots – buckle fastening or decoration popular.

Socks: Similar to previous fashion.

Hats: Similar to previous fashion.

Hair: Longer hair and 'sideboards'. Very long hair popular among young students.

Accessories: Large belts and buckles. Cravats and scarves. Wrist watches, cuff links with dinner jackets. Chunky jewellery – identity bracelets, rings, neck chains.

Details of illustrated patterns

Woman

Full-length maxi-coat with shaped panels and four-button fastening, pockets set in front panel seams at hip-level. Plain collar and two-piece set-in sleeves. It is worn with simple, two-piece 'A' line mini-skirt and black polo-neck jumper.

Fabric and colours: Heavy wool flannel or similar mixture fabric for coat, in black, grey or navy; imitation suede for mini-skirt in grey or navy.

Legwear: Knee-length stretch vinyl black boots with rounded toes and low squared heels. Black fishnet tights.

Accessories: Grey or purple suede shoulder bag with outside flap pockets and zip fastening; wide patent or plastic belt; plastic clip earrings.

Man

Shirt-style casual jacket with button-through strap front and top-stitching detail; patch pockets with flap and box pleat at centre. Jacket back is cut with straight yoke. Shirt-style sleeves and pointed collar with stand.

Hipster trousers flare from the knees, remaining close-fitting over the seat and upper thighs.

The outfit is worn with open-necked shirt with button-down collar. This is a unisex style, worn by both men and women.

Fabrics: Cotton gabardine, corduroy or denim for jacket and trousers.

Footwear: Casual suede laced Chelsea boot with crêpe sole.

Notes on construction of garments

Woman

Leave opening for pocket in front seam as indicated on pattern.

Man

A 1cm (⅜ in.) seam allowance is given on all edges, including strap and front.

Separate back yoke from jacket pattern along line J–K. Add seam allowance to both cut edges.

Separate back sleeve pattern from sleeve between D–F and E–F. Add seam allowance to cut edges. Construct placket at sleeve opening, indicated by small dot on pattern.

Separate jacket collar from collar stand along line G–H. Add seam allowance to cut edges.

Trace off strap pattern from jacket front to be applied to left side of jacket; right side remains plain.

Trace off trouser waistband from A–B for right side and A–C for left side to allow for button extension. Add a 1cm (⅜ in.) seam allowance to all edges of waistband.

Adapt shirt pattern from 1965/1966.

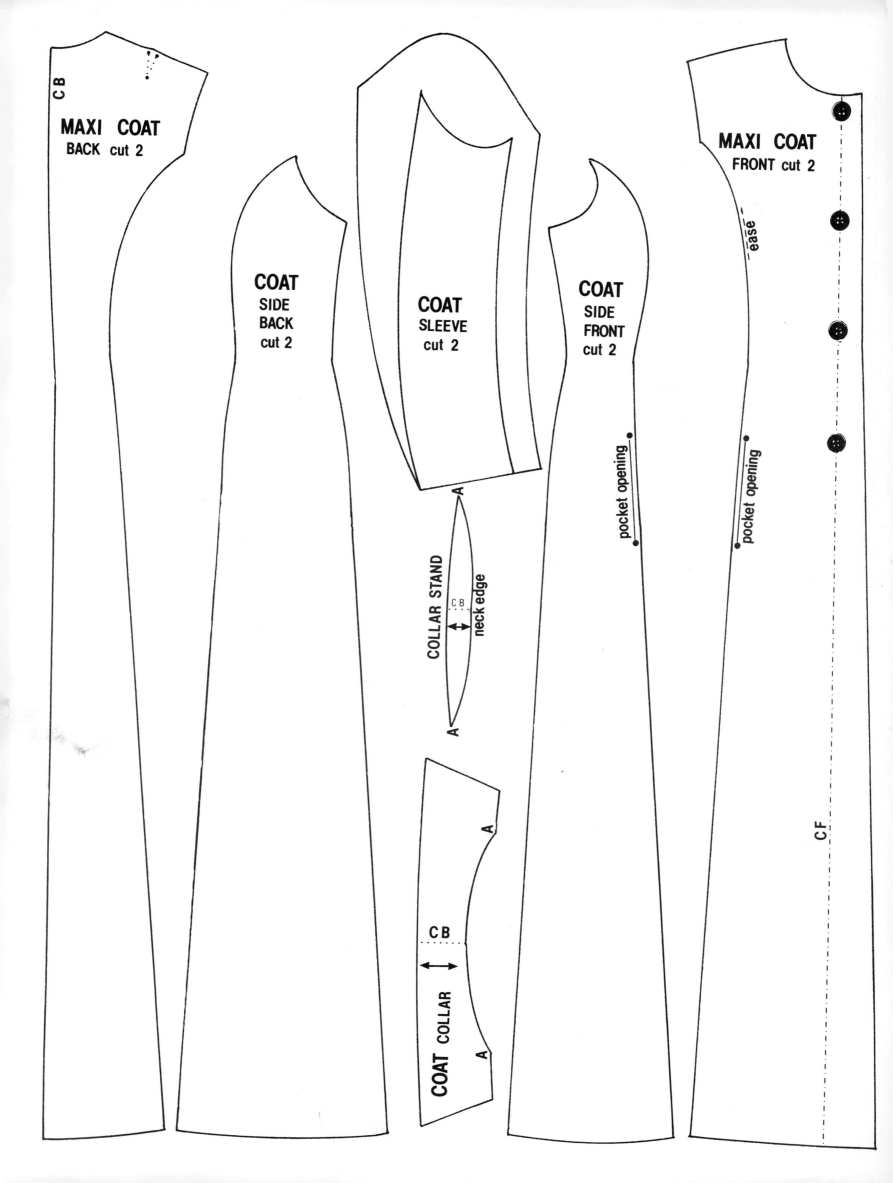

MAXI COAT
BACK cut 2

C B

COAT
SIDE
BACK
cut 2

COAT
SLEEVE
cut 2

A

COLLAR STAND

C B
neck edge

A

COAT COLLAR

C B

A

COAT
SIDE
FRONT
cut 2

pocket opening

MAXI COAT
FRONT cut 2

ease

pocket opening

CF

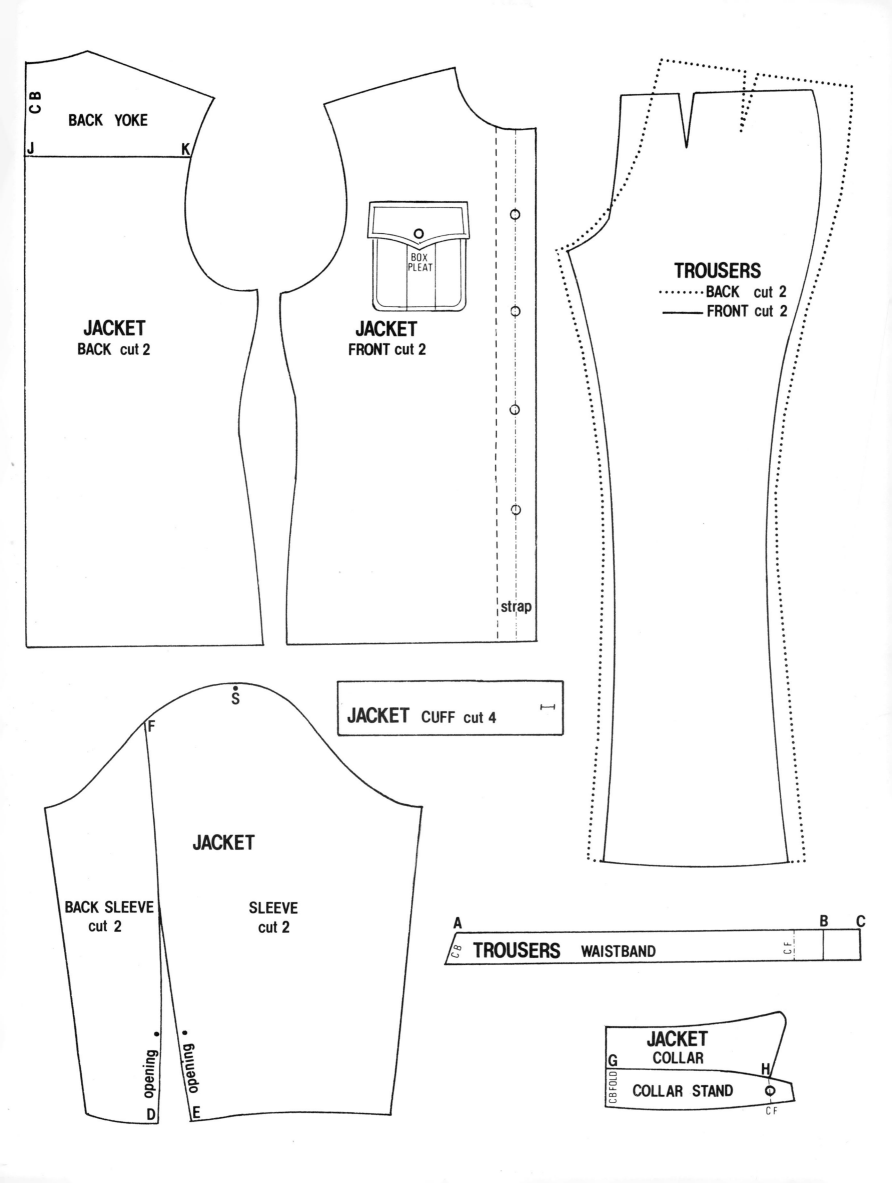

Glossary

accordion pleats   narrow *knife pleats*.

alpaca   fabric made from wool of alpaca animal – usually with black cotton *warp* and alpaca *weft*.

appliqué   fabrics applied to the garment for decoration.

arrowhead   triangular,   hand-worked reinforcement for top of pleats.

Ascot tie   knotted cravat secured with scarf pin.

astrakhan   skin of young Astrakan lamb, or a curled-pile fabric imitating this.

barathea   a soft fabric of fine *worsted* or worsted and silk yarns.

batiste   a soft, fine, plain-woven fabric of flax or cotton.

Bedford cord   fabric with prominent ribbed texture in the *warp* direction; *worsted* yarns used for suiting and woollen yarns for heavier fabrics.

beret   soft hat constructed from a circular piece of fabric gathered on to a band.

bias   fabric cut diagonally across the *warp* and *weft* threads at an angle of 45°. Bias cut fabric has greater elasticity.

biretta   square-shaped hat, similar to that worn by clergy.

boater   straw hat with flat crown and brim.

bolero   short jacket, usually above waist-level.

bouclé   a fabric with a rough texture produced by means of looped yarns.

bowler   man's stiffened felt hat with bowl crown and narrow brim, curled upwards. For city or business wear.

box pleats   composed of two *knife pleats*, the pleats facing each other with folds meeting at the back.

breton   woman's hat with rounded crown and turned-up brim.

Breton net   fine silk or cotton net originating in Brittany.

broadcloth (cotton)   a lightweight fabric similar to *poplin* and suitable for shirtings.

broadcloth (wool)   a smooth cloth made in a *twill weave* from fine, woollen yarns, and given a dress face finish.

brocade   a self-patterned fabric in which the pattern is developed during weaving; a heavy, silky fabric.

buckskin   a soft leather made of deerskin or sheepskin.

bulking   synthetic yarns are naturally smooth and fine. *Bulking* is a process whereby the yarn is heat set, i.e. crimped, giving greater elasticity and softness of handle and appearance – e.g. bulked nylon, Crimplene.

button-two, button-three, etc.   a term used in tailoring to indicate the number of buttons on the garment front.

cambric   a lightweight, closely woven cloth with slight stiffening.

cashmere   fabric made with hair of the cashmere goat.

cavalry twill   a firm, heavyweight fabric with steep, double *twill* lines, and sunken lines between. Originally applied to fabrics for making riding breeches for cavalry.

Celanese   lightweight silky fabric of artificial silk used for lingerie.

chesterfield   gentleman's fitted overcoat.

chiffon   light, sheer open-weave fabric.

chignon   fold or roll of hair worn at the back or nape of the neck.

cloche   a lady's close-fitting hat, bell-shaped, worn well down.

corduroy   a ribbed *pile* fabric, the ribs formed in the *warp* direction.

court shoe   slip-on dress shoe.

cowl neckline   draped neckline where fabric falls in folds.

crêpe   a plain-weave fabric with uneven, crinkled surface texture, made from highly twisted yarns.

crêpe de Chine   a lightweight, plain-weave *crêpe* fabric.

Crimplene   *bulked* polyester *jersey* fabric with a patterned surface.

Cuban heel   a high, straight heel without curves.

cummerbund   a waist belt or sash.

décolletage   low-cut neckline.

denim   a hardwearing, *twill-weave* fabric made from dyed cotton yarn.

diamanté   a sparkling decoration resembling diamonds.

dimity   a fabric, usually of cotton, that is checked or striped by weaving two or more threads as one.

dirndl   full skirt, gathered at the waist.

Donegal   coarse woollen suiting fabric, characterized by brightly coloured flecks.

double-breasted   overlapping closure with double row of buttons.

drill   a *twill* fabric, similar to *denim*, but usually dyed after weaving.

duffle (duffel)   a heavy, low-grade fabric, brushed on both sides, made from woollen yarns – for short coats known as duffle coats.

Empire-line   high-waisted dress, as worn during the first French Empire.

epaulette   shoulder strap for decoration.

facecloth   cloth with finish given to one side of fabric only, e.g. in wool.

façonné   French word for figured, used to describe self-patterned fabrics.

faille   a fine soft fabric, ribbed in the *weft* direction – see *taffeta*.

Fair Isle   geometric designs used in knitwear, named from a Shetland island.

flannel   an all-wool fabric of plain or *twill weave* with soft handle. It may be slightly *milled* or raised.

forepart   front parts of a garment.

foulard   a lightweight silk fabric, frequently printed.

four-in-hand   man's long tie, tied with a flat slip knot at neck.

gabardine (gaberdine)   a firmly woven *twill* fabric, used for outer wear.

gaiters   covering for the ankles, fitting over the shoe tops and secured with strap under the foot.

gauntlet   gloves with wide extensions, covering the wrists.

georgette   a fine, lightweight, open-mesh fabric, made from *crêpe* yarns.

gigot   leg-of-mutton sleeve, tight at the cuff and full above.

gingham   a cotton fabric, woven from coloured yarns into stripes or checks.

godet   a triangular piece of fabric inserted in a skirt to make a flare.

gore   skirt panel, e.g. a four-gore skirt is a skirt with four panels.

grosgrain   a heavy ribbed silk used especially for ribbons and hat bands.

grown-on   cut in one with the garment, e.g. grown-on collar.

harem skirt   divided skirt, similar to Turkish trousers.

herringbone   a *twill-weave* fabric in which the *twill* is reversed to produce stripes resembling herring-bones.

hobble skirt   pre-First-World-War skirt which narrows towards the ankles, restricting the movements of the wearer to a hobble.

Homburg   man's hat, of felt, with narrow brim and dented crown.

hopsack   plain-weave fabric in which two or more *warp* or *weft* threads are used as one.

insertion lace   lace having two straight edges, used for inserting between the edges of two pieces of material.

inverted pleats   two *knife pleats* facing each other, the folds of the fabric meeting at the front – the reverse of *box pleats*.

jabot   a frill of lace worn at front of shirt or blouse.

jap silk (jappe)   a fine, plain-weave silk fabric.

jerkin   a sleeveless jacket, usually collarless.

jersey   a term applied to all knitted fabrics.

jetted pockets   piped or bound with self fabric.

kaftan (caftan)   a long-sleeved oriental garment, full-length.

kimono sleeve   sleeve cut in one with the bodice.

knickerbockers   loose breeches gathered in at the knee.

knife pleat   single fold of fabric, sharply creased.

lamé   a general term for fabrics interwoven with metallic threads.

Lastex   a yarn produced from covered rubber, used extensively for 'stretch' undergarments and swimwear in the thirties and forties.

lawn   originally a type of fine linen fabric, with the term extended to include cotton.

lisle   a highly twisted, good quality cotton hosiery yarn.

longcloth   plain-weave cotton shirting fabric, made in long pieces.

louis heel   high, curved heel.

lustre   a dress material with cotton warp and woollen weft, and highly finished surface.

Lycra   two-way-stretch elastic fibre introduced in early 1950s for underwear, sports garments, etc.

Magyar   short *kimono* sleeves cut in one with the bodice.

marcella   a fancy or figured cotton fabric of *piqué* structure, used for dress shirt fronts.

marocain   a dress material finished with a grain surface like morocco leather.

marquisette   fine, open gauze fabric, usually of silk or cotton.

Medici collar   high-standing collar.

Melton   a strong heavyweight fabric for overcoats, finished by *milling*. The fibres are tightly matted which gives the appearance of a felted material.

merino   a fine dress fabric, originally made from the wool of merino sheep, later mixed with cotton.

milling   the process of smoothing cloth.

moiré   watermarked effect produced on lustrous ribbed or corded cloth, by means of heat and pressure.

monk shoe   plain shoes for men with buckle fastening.

mousseline de soie   a French term describing muslin made from silk.

muslin   a general term for lightweight, open fabric of plain weave.

nainsook   a fine, light, plain-woven cotton cloth with a soft finish.

nap   a brushed appearance produced on a fabric surface.

ninon   a fabric made from very fine highly twisted yarns.

Norfolk jacket   a loose, pleated sports coat with a waistband.

organdie   a plain lightweight transparent cotton fabric, with a permanently stiff finish.

organza   sheer, stiff plain-weave cloth of silk, rayon or nylon, not cotton. Often dyed, printed or embroidered.

ottoman   corded silk fabric.

Oxford bags   man's very wide trousers with turn-up, popular during mid-1920s.

Oxford shirting   a plain-weave shirting fabric made of good quality yarn, usually cotton. Fancy weaves can be incorporated and dyed yarns used to form stripes.

Oxford shoes   a low-heeled shoe, with lace ties.

paisley   a decorative pattern featuring an Indian cone or pine, used on shawls and fabrics.

panama   a hand-plaited straw hat made of plaited strips of the leaves of a South American plant.

panne velvet   velvet fabric with longer *pile* laid in one direction.

paper nylon   a crisp nylon fabric with a papery texture.

paper taffeta   a fine, crisp fabric resembling *taffeta*, with a papery texture.

peau de soie   a French term, literally 'skin of silk', applied to fine, ribbed silk fabric.

peplum   a short, skirt-like section attached to the waistline of a dress, blouse or jacket.

Peter Pan collar   a flat, rounded collar.

petersham ribbon (millinery)   a ribbed cotton ribbon.

petersham ribbon (skirt)   narrow fabric with lateral stiffness, often woven with pockets to insert boning.

pile   a raised surface effect on a fabric formed by tufts or loops of yarn introduced into the fabric during weaving.

pillbox   a small, round, brimless hat.

piping   decorative edging composed of *bias* fabric strips, enclosing narrow cord.

piqué   white cloth in light *Bedford-cord* weave.

placket   form of opening made with additional band of self fabric. It may be visible on the right side of the garment or hidden beneath it.

plissé   a French term meaning pleated fabric, with a puckered or crinkled effect.

plus fours   baggy knickerbockers, the name derived from the four additional inches of cloth required beyond the knee.

polyvinyl chloride (PVC)   a vinyl plastic used to coat dress fabrics.

poplin   plain-weave, medium-weight cotton fabric, with fine *weft*-way ribs.

pork pie   man's hat, similar to *trilby*, with flatter, dented crown.

raglan   man's overcoat with *raglan sleeves*.

raglan sleeve   sleeve is cut in one piece with the shoulder.

raising   brushed effect produced on surface of fabric.

reefer   short jacket, usually double-breasted.

repp   a plain-weave fabric with prominent rib.

rouleau   narrow tubes of fabric cut from bias strips, stitched and turned through (rouleau loops = rouleau used for button loops or decoration).

Russian braid (soutache)   a narrow braid made with two covered cords in a continuous figure-of-eight pattern.

saddle-stitching   hand-sewn running stitches of even length, worked in thicker threads for decoration on outside of garments.

sateen   a glossy fabric of cotton or wool, resembling *satin*.

satin   lustrous fabric with unbroken surface.

scye   armhole.

seersucker   fabric with surface puckered to form stripes or checks.

self fabric   in the same fabric as the garment.

serge   a *twill-weave* wool fabric, traditionally for suitings and outdoor wear.

shantung   a plain-weave silk dress fabric with uneven surface resulting from the use of yarn spun from wild (*tussah*) silk.

shawl collar   smooth roll collar which is often cut in one with the front of the garment. There is only one seam, at the centre back.

single-breasted   fastening with one row of buttons.

snap-brim   hat with brim that turns down.

snood   hair covering of net or fabric.

soutache   see Russian braid.

spats   short ankle *gaiters*.

stetson   broad-brimmed felt hat.

stiletto heels   very narrow, tapered heels of covered steel.

strapping   a narrow strip of fabric or leather applied as a decoration.

taffeta   a plain-weave, closely woven, smooth and crisp fabric with a feint, *weft*-way rib. (*Taffeta, faille,* and *grosgrain* are all weft-way rib cloths, listed in ascending order of prominence of rib.) *Wool taffeta* – plain-woven, lightweight fabric produced from *worsted* yarns.

tam o'shanter   hat with broad, circular flat top.

top-stitching   rows of stitching on the outside of a garment for decoration.

toque   woman's brimless hat.

tricorne   a three-cornered hat.

tricot   plain knitted fabric of silk, cotton or rayon.

trilby   man's soft felt hat with narrow brim and dented crown.

trompe l'oeil (French)   literally something that deceives the eye. Usually applied to sweaters or jumpers popular in the 1920s, with scarves, bows, or collars knitted into the design.

tulle   a fine, lightweight net with hexagonal mesh (woven); a very fine net fabric in plain weave from silk yarns.

tussah   a coarse silk produced by the wild silk worm.

tussore   a fabric woven from coarse, wild silk called *tussah*.

tweed   coarse, rough-textured wool fabric for outer wear.

twill   cloth woven in *twill weave*, giving diagonal lines on surface.

twill weave   *weft* threads are woven in steps across the *warp* threads, creating diagonally ribbed fabric.

ulster   loose-fitting gentleman's overcoat.

unisex   styles of clothes adopted by both men and women.

veiling   plain or ornamental nets used mainly for face veils or hat decoration.

velour   a heavy woollen fabric with surface *raised* to give velvet appearance.

velvet   a soft fabric with close, short *warp* pile – silk, nylon or cotton.

velveteen   cotton fabric with cut *weft* pile resembling velvet.

vicuña   cloth made of wool of vicuña animal.

Viyella   trade name for lightweight fine wool-and-cotton-blend fabric.

warp   lengthwise threads of a woven fabric, interwoven by *weft*.

wedge heels   shoes with continuous sole and heel, and no gap under instep.

weft   crosswise threads of a fabric, woven into and crossing the *warp*.

whipcord   a fabric characterized by bold, steep *warp twill*, used for dresses, suitings and coatings.

winklepickers   shoes with elongated pointed toes.

worsted   twisted yarn of long combed wool; smooth, closely woven fabric made from this.

zephyr   a fine cloth of plain weave used for dresses, blouses and shirtings, and made in various qualities. A typical zephyr has coloured stripes on a white ground and a cord effect made by the introduction of coarse threads at intervals.

Bibliography

FASHION AND TEXTILES

ARNOLD, J., *A Handbook of Costume*, Macmillan, 1973.
— *Patterns of Fashion: Englishwomen's Dresses and their Construction*, vol. 2, 1860–1940, Macmillan, 1973.
BEATON, C., *The Glass of Fashion*, Weidenfeld & Nicolson, 1954.
BELL, Q., *On Human Finery*, Hogarth Press, London, 1976.
BOND, D., *The Guinness Guide to Twentieth Century Fashion*, Guinness Superlatives Ltd, London, 1981.
BROOKE, I., *Dress and Undress*, Methuen, 1958.
— *A History of English Costume*, Methuen, 1974.
BYRDE, P., *The Male Image: Men's Fashion in England 1300–1970*, Batsford, 1979.
CARTER, E., *The Changing World of Fashion*, Weidenfeld & Nicolson, 1977.
CUNNINGTON, C.W., *English Women's Clothing in the Present Century*, Faber & Faber, 1952.
CUNNINGTON, C.W. and P., *The History of Underclothes*, Faber & Faber, 1981.
DORNER, J. *Fashion in the Twenties and Thirties*, Ian Allen, 1973.
EWING, E., *History of Twentieth Century Fashion*, Batsford, 1981.
FLUGEL, J.C., *The Psychology of Clothes*, Hogarth Press, 1930.
GARLAND, M., *Fashion*, Penguin, 1962.
GLYNN, P., and GINSBURG, M., *In Fashion: Dress in the Twentieth Century*, Allen & Unwin, 1978.
HALL, C., *The Twenties in Vogue*, Octopus, 1983.
HEGAN, A.J., LOASBY, G., and URQUHART, R., *The Development of some Man-made Fibres*, The Textile Institute, Manchester, 1952.
HILL, M.H., and BUCKNELL, P.A., *The Evolution of Fashion: Pattern and Cut from 1066 to 1930*, Batsford, 1983.
LAVER, J., *Taste and Fashion*, Harrap, 1937.
— *Taste and Fashion*, 2nd edition, Harrap, 1945.
— *Women's Dress in the Jazz Age*, Hamish Hamilton, 1964.
— *A Concise History of Costume*, Thames & Hudson, 1969.
LEE-POTTER, C., *Sportswear in Vogue since 1910*, Thames & Hudson, 1984.
MANSFIELD, A., and CUNNINGTON, P., *Handbook of English Costume in the Twentieth Century*, Faber, 1973.
SICHEL, M., *Costume Reference 7: The Edwardians*, Batsford, 1978.
— *Costume Reference 8: 1918-1939*, Batsford, 1978.
— *Costume Reference 9: 1939–1950*, Batsford, 1978.
— *Costume Reference 10: 1950 to the Present Day*, Batsford, 1979.
SQUIRE, G., *Dress, Art and Society 1950–1970*, Studio Vista, 1974.
VICTORIA & ALBERT MUSEUM, *Fashion 1900–1939, A Scottish Arts Council Exhibition. An exhibition catalogue*, 1975.
VICTORIA & ALBERT MUSEUM, *Four Hundred Years of Fashion*, Collins, 1984.
WALLBANK, E. and M., *Pattern Making for Dressmaking and Needlework*, Pitman, 1952.
WAUGH, N., *Corsets and Crinolines*, Batsford, 1954.
— *The Cut of Women's Clothes, 1600–1970*, Faber & Faber, 1968.
WILCOX, R. TURNER, *The Mode in Hats and Headdress*, Charles Scribner's Sons, London, 1959.
WRAY, M., *The Women's Outerwear Industry*, Faber, 1957.
YARWOOD, D., *English Costume*, Batsford, 1969.

GENERAL

BANHAM, M., and HILLIER, B. (edited), *A Tonic to the Nation – The Festival of Britain, 1951*, Thames and Hudson, 1976.
BLYTHE, R., *The Age of Illusion: England in the '20's' and '30's', 1919–1940*, Penguin, 1964.
BRANSON, N., *Britain in the Nineteen-Twenties*, Weidenfeld & Nicolson, 1971.
BRANSON, N., and HEINEMANN, M., *Britain in the Nineteen-Thirties*, Weidenfeld & Nicolson, 1972.
BRIGGS, A., *The History of Broadcasting in the United Kingdom*, vol I: *The Birth of Broadcasting*, Oxford University Press, 1961.
— *The History of Broadcasting in the United Kingdom*, vol 2: *The Golden Age of Wireless*, Oxford University Press, 1965.
CASSIN-SCOTT, J., and McBRIDE, A., *Women at War 1939–1945*, Osprey, 1980.
GOLDRING, D., *The Nineteen-Twenties: A General Survey and some Personal Memories*, Nicolson, 1945.
GRAVES, R., and HODGES, A., *The Long Weekend: A Social History of Great Britain 1918–1939*, Faber & Faber, 1940.
HAYWARD GALLERY, *The Thirties, British Art and Design before the War*, Arts Council of Great Britain, an exhibition catalogue, 1975.
INTERNATIONAL COUNCIL OF WOMEN, *Women in a Changing World: The International Council of Women since 1888*, Routledge & Kegan Paul, 1966.
JACKSON, J., *Man and the Automobile – A Twentieth-Century Love Affair*, McGraw-Hill, Maidenhead, 1979.
JEFFERYS, J.B., *Retail Trading in Britain, 1850–1950*, Cambridge University Press, 1964.
MARSH, D., *The Changing Social Structure of England and Wales, 1871–1961*, Routledge & Kegan Paul, 1965.
MARWICK, A., *The Explosion of British Society, 1914–1970*, Macmillan, 1963.
— *The Deluge*, Bodley Head, 1965.
— *Women at War 1914–1918*, Fontana in association with Imperial War Museum, 1977.
MOWAT, C.L., *Great Britain since 1914: The Sources of History*, Hodder & Stoughton, 1970.
NISSEL, M. (edited), *Social Trends: No.5, 1974*, Government Statistical Service, 1974.
PRIESTLEY, J.B., *English Journey*, Heinemann, 1934.
PUGH, M.D., *Woman's Suffrage in Britain 1866–1928*, Historical Association, 1980.
REES, G., *St Michael – A History of Marks and Spencer*, 2nd edition, Pan Books, 1973.
RICHARDSON, R.C., and CHALONER, W., *British Economic and Social History: A Bibliographical Guide*, Manchester University Press, 1976.
STAFFORD, M., and MIDDLEMAS, R.K., *British Furniture through the Ages*, Arthur Barker Ltd, 1966.
TRACEY, H., *The British Press: A Survey, A Newspaper Directory, and a Who's Who in Journalism*, Europe Publications, London, 1929.
WHEEN, F., *The Sixties*, Century Publishing, 1982.
WHITE, C., *Women's Magazines 1693–1966*, Michael Joseph, 1966.

WAR UNIFORMS

MOLLO, A., *The Armed Forces of World War 2*, Orbis, 1973.
— *Army Uniforms of World War 2*, Blandford, 1973.
MOLLO A., and TURNER, P., *Army Uniforms of World War I*, Blandford, 1977.
ROSIGNOLI, G., *Army badges and insignia of World War 2*, Books 1 and 2, Blandford, 1974, 1975.

NEWSPAPERS AND MAGAZINES

Harper's Bazaar from 1929.
Ladies' Home Journal from 1890.
Tailor and Cutter from 1900.
Vogue from 1916.
Woman's Own from 1932.
Women's Wear from 1918–1925.
Woman's World from 1903–1958.
Daily Express from 1900.
Daily Herald from 1912.
Daily Mail from 1896.
Daily Sketch from 1909.